Henry Newland

A practical and exegetical commentary on the Epistle of St. Paul to the Philippians:

In which are exhibited the results of the most learned theological criticisms, from the age of the early Fathers down to the present time

Henry Newland

A practical and exegetical commentary on the Epistle of St. Paul to the Philippians:
In which are exhibited the results of the most learned theological criticisms, from the age of the early Fathers down to the present time

ISBN/EAN: 9783337729974

Printed in Europe, USA, Canada, Australia, Japan

Cover: Foto ©ninafisch / pixelio.de

More available books at **www.hansebooks.com**

A new Catena on St. Paul's Epistles.

A

PRACTICAL AND EXEGETICAL

Commentary

ON

THE EPISTLE OF ST. PAUL

TO THE

PHILIPPIANS:

IN WHICH ARE EXHIBITED THE RESULTS OF THE MOST LEARNED
THEOLOGICAL CRITICISMS, FROM THE AGE OF THE EARLY
FATHERS DOWN TO THE PRESENT TIME.

EDITED BY THE LATE

REV. HENRY NEWLAND, M.A.,

VICAR OF ST. MARY-CHURCH, DEVON, AND CHAPLAIN TO THE BISHOP OF EXETER;

"Erudite Lector, in hoc libro si aliquid tibi supervacaneum visum fuerit, id
minus eruditis relinque."

Oxford and London:
J. H. AND JAS. PARKER.
1860.

TO

THE MEMORY OF

HENRY NEWLAND,

PRIEST OF THE ENGLISH CHURCH,

This Volume

IS GRATEFULLY DEDICATED, IN REMEMBRANCE OF

A HAPPY FRIENDSHIP,

BY HIS AFFECTIONATE BROTHER IN CHRIST,

THE AUTHOR.

AUTHOR'S PREFACE.

THE practical and exegetical Commentary on the Epistle of St. Paul to the Ephesians, lately published, was intended, as the title denotes, to be the first link of a new Catena on St. Paul's Epistles. The Commentary on the Epistle to the Philippians, now published, was written before the Commentary on the Ephesians; both were submitted to my late dear and valued friend the Rev. H. Newland; the whole of both passed under his hand, and it was by his advice, and under his editorship, that the Commentary on the Ephesians was published first.

His lamented, and to me, as well as to others, irreparable loss, renders it necessary for me to speak in my own person, and to announce myself as the author of the works which I was but too happy to see introduced to the public under the authority of his honoured name.

His character and writings have long been well known and appreciated, and will only cease to be so when unswerving rectitude of purpose and valour for the truth are no longer considered qualities to be admired in an author. When I say that he was a sound and honest theologian, one who never sacrificed even the smallest principle to "content the

INTRODUCTORY OBSERVATIONS ON ST. PAUL'S EPISTLE TO THE PHILIPPIANS.

PHILIPPI was a city of Macedonia, on the borders of Thrace, and not far from the coast. It was originally called Datos, and in still earlier times was known as Crenides, from the springs of water which abounded in the hill on which the city was built. Philip of Macedon fortified it, and called it after his own name, and in his hands it became an important military post. In after times the city acquired a world-wide reputation from the victory gained in its immediate neighbourhood by Anthony and Octavius over Brutus and Cassius, the murderers of Julius Cæsar. Mention is made of it in Acts xvi. 12, where it is called " the chief (or first) city of that part of Macedonia, [the word 'first' referring either to its *position* relative to one crossing the Strymon, or to its military and mercantile *importance*,] and a colony." St. Paul, was the first to preach the Gospel there, having crossed over to Europe in obedience to a heavenly vision [a]; and so successful were his labours, that many of the inhabitants believed. It was here, as St. Chrysostom remarks, that the seller of purple was converted, a woman of rare piety and earnestness; it was here that the keeper of the prison believed. Here St. Paul was scourged with St. Silas. Here the magistrates requested them to depart, and were afraid of them. Here the preaching of the Gospel had a most glorious commencement. It may be truly said that this city shewed great readiness for the faith, inasmuch as the very jailor (a class of persons not usually susceptible of religious impressions) at once, upon seeing one miracle, ran to the Apostles, and received Baptism with all his house. Even the magistrates who scourged

---
[a] Acts xvi. 9, 10.

them seem to have done this rather from a sudden impulse than malice, as may be concluded both from their sending at once to let them go, and their afterwards being afraid, when they learnt that they were Romans.

This Epistle arose out of the following circumstances. The Philippians, hearing of St. Paul's imprisonment at Rome, sent Epaphroditus, their Bishop, (according to St. Pacian, Theodoret, Baronius, and others,) to carry him money, and make enquiries about his state, which was causing them much anxiety. While with the Apostle he fell sick, almost to death; but having at length recovered, St. Paul lost no time in sending him back to his diocese with a letter to his flock, in which, while praising them for their liberality and affectionate care, he exhorts them to stand fast in the faith, and not be troubled about his bonds; and, above all, that they should be of one mind, shewing that unanimity comes of humility. No doubt Epaphroditus would have told him of certain painful dissensions which, it appears, existed among some private members of the Church, and also of the danger which was imminent to the whole body from the insidious advances of false teachers; and so we find, as might have been expected, special reference made to each of these, accompanied by earnest cautions and exhortations.

The Philippians seem to have been very much attached to St. Paul personally; and he, in turn, bears them many and high testimonies, shewing them special honour, calling them his 'crown,' and saying that they had suffered much for the Gospel. It may be truly said that no Epistle is so full of tenderness and fatherly affection as this, and it is the highest proof of the virtue and excellence of the Philippian converts that they gave no occasion to their teacher to speak sharply to them, but only in the way of exhortation and encouragement.

Respecting the authorship of this Epistle there has happily been but little difference of opinion, and it has been all but universally ascribed to St. Paul. It is satisfactory to know that it is quoted largely by the early Fathers. Some modern German critics (who, for obvious reasons, are interested in undermining the authority of certain passages in this Epistle) have found difficulties in believing that St. Paul was its author. No one, however, can read their criticisms (especially those of Schrader and Baur) without concluding, with Dean Alford, that they deserve to take rank with Abp. Whately's " Historic Doubts Respecting Napoleon Buonaparte."

Various dates have been assigned to this Epistle; but there seems sufficient internal evidence to shew that it was written from Rome towards the conclusion of St. Paul's first imprisonment, that is to say, the end of A.D. 62 or beginning of 63. The grounds which Conybeare and Howson give for fixing the date appear to be satisfactory and conclusive. They say:—

" I. It was written during *an imprisonment at Rome*, because (A) the Prætorium was at Rome[b]; (B) so was the Emperor's household[c]; (C) he expects the immediate decision of his cause[d], which could only have been given at Rome.

" II. It was written during the *first* imprisonment at Rome, because (A) the mention of the Prætorium agrees with the fact that during his first imprisonment he was in the custody of the Prætorian Prefect; (B) his situation described[e] agrees with his situation in the first two years of his imprisonment[f].

" III. It was written *towards the conclusion* of this first imprisonment, because (A) he expects the immediate decision of his cause; (B) enough time had elapsed for the Philippians to hear of his imprisonment, send Epaphroditus to him, hear of Epaphroditus' arrival and sickness, and send back word to Rome of their distress[g].

IV. It was written *after* Colossians and Philemon; both for the preceding reason, and because St. Luke was no longer at Rome, as he was when those were written; otherwise he would have *saluted* a Church in which he had laboured, and would have cared in earnest for their concerns[h]."

---

[b] c. i. 13. [c] c. iv. 22. [d] c. i. 19, ii. 27, and possibly ii. 23.
[e] c. i. 12—14. [f] Acts xxviii. 30, 31. [g] c. ii. 26. [h] c. ii. 20.

This Epistle, so suggestive of comforting thought to every devout Christian, becomes doubly precious when we view it as St. Paul's parting address to the Church *as a body*. The Second Epistle to St. Timothy is of later date, though written under similar circumstances, and shews the feelings of the Apostle in the prospect of death which was now close at hand; but that Epistle, though it is now the property of all the Church, was written to an individual, and so far differs from the present one wherein the Apostle pours out his soul towards *all* believers.

This Epistle has not always received full justice from commentators. It has been thought to be deficient in interest, and to afford little scope for exegetical labours. It is difficult to say how such an opinion could ever have got abroad. It is true that this particular portion of St. Paul's writings may not have the *depth* of others of his Epistles, as, for example, that to the Ephesians, but it has at least a *beauty* all its own. There is a rich tone of colouring about it which the light of the Eternal Day, even then breaking through the bars of the Apostle's prison-house, alone could give.

COMMENTARY ON

ST. PAUL'S EPISTLE TO THE PHILIPPIANS.

SUMMARY OF CHAPTER I.

Having given thanks to God for the constancy of the Philippians in the faith, and having shewn his exceeding earnestness for their salvation, the Apostle proceeds to explain that his imprisonment at Rome has turned out for the furtherance of the Gospel; and then, having expressed a good hope of his speedy restoration to them, he exhorts them to a course of life conformable to the doctrine of Christ.

This chapter may be divided into five chief parts:—
(1.) The epigraphe, or inscription, containing the names of the writer and of those to whom it is written: ver. 1.
(2.) The salutation: ver. 2.
(3.) Thanksgiving for the faith of the Philippians, and a prayer for their perseverance: ver. 3—11.
(4.) An account of the spread of the faith at Rome, and how his bonds have greatly assisted it: ver. 12—26.
(5.) Exhortation to a life worthy of the Gospel: ver. 27—30.

CHAP. I.

VER. 1. Paul and Timotheus,

St. Timothy is associated with St. Paul, as joining in his salutation to the Christians at Philippi, to whom he must have been well known, having accompanied the Apostle in both his journeys to that city. See Acts xvi., xx. It is not to be supposed, however, that he had any share in the composition of the present Epistle, any more than 'all the brethren' whom St. Paul joins with himself in his salutation to the

Galatians, chap. i. 2. That this Epistle was the work of St. Paul *alone* appears from verse 3, where he proceeds in the first person singular; but it is quite possible that Timothy may have written it at his dictation. So Zanchius. Caietan says, "He was unwilling to keep the salutation of Timothy for the end of the Epistle with the rest, but gave him a pre-eminence, that the Philippians might the better understand how highly he valued him." Haymo thinks that the name of St. Timothy was added to give greater weight and authority to the Epistle, according to our Lord's words, "In the mouth of two or three witnesses every word shall be established^a." Menochius has something similar; but probably this mode of interpretation is more ingenious than true; for the simplest reason appears to be that St. Paul associated the name of Timothy with his own for the sake of humility; intending thereby to show that he did not despise him, as inferior to himself in spiritual gifts, but that he honoured him as a brother. A most illustrious example for Christ's ministers to follow.

the servants of Jesus Christ,

St. Paul does not here insist upon his rank as teacher, as at 1 Cor. i. 1, but claims for himself another and a higher title, (see Matt. xx. 26, 27,) calling himself a 'servant,' and not an 'apostle;' "for great truly is this rank, and the sum of all good things, *to be* a servant of Christ, and not merely to be called so^b." In one sense, indeed, all faithful Christians are the 'servants' of Christ; but SS. Paul and Timothy were so in a higher degree, having been called to serve Him publicly in preaching the Gospel. Compare James i. 1; 2 Pet. i. 1. It is well known that the bishops of Rome subscribe themselves "Servant of the Servants of God," following the example of St. Gregory, who was the first to adopt this style.

It is probable that St. Paul does not prefix his title of 'Apostle' to this Epistle lest he should seem to have received as a matter of right, and not of liberality, the contribu-

---

^a Matt. xviii. 16.   ^b S. Chrysos., in loc.

tions which the Philippians had sent by the hand of Epaphroditus. Another reason for the omission of this title may be found in the fact that this is the least *official* of all the Epistles. "The Philippians did not doubt that he was an Apostle and teacher of the Gentiles, and therefore in writing to them it was not needful that he should style himself Apostle[c]." Caietan accounts for the omission on the ground that as St. Paul wished to join Timothy with himself as a colleague, he used a title which would suit them both. See remarks on Eph. i. 1.

to all the saints

'All,' see also vers. 4, 7, 8, &c.; he repeats the word to shew that he loves them all alike, and to excite in them a corresponding love one for the other.

In the term 'saints' are included "all who have been sanctified in Baptism, and continue in that sanctification[d]." "Sanctos vocat fideles, quorum congregatio sancta est, licet non singuli sancti, id est, a peccatis mundi[e]." The sense of ἅγιοι in the New Testament is nearly equivalent to modern 'Christians;' but it would be an anachronism so to translate it, since in the time of St. Paul the word 'Christian' was only used as a term of reproach. The objection to translating it 'saints' is that the idea now conveyed by that term is quite different from the meaning of οἱ ἅγιοι as used by St. Paul[f]. Compare Eph. i. 1, and iii. 8.

in Christ Jesus which are at Philippi,

The use of the word 'in' is to be observed; implying that the baptized are actually *part of Christ*, as living members of His Body. See remarks on Eph. v. 30. He calls them 'saints in Christ Jesus' to distinguish them from the Jews, who would be likely to claim this title exclusively for themselves. See Exod. xix. 6; Deut. vii. 6.

with the bishops and deacons:

St. Chrysostom thinks that this Epistle was written only to the *clergy* of Philippi, and reads συνεπισκόποις as one

---
[c] Haymo. [d] Ibid. [e] Estius.
[f] Conybeare and Howson, Life and Epistles of St. Paul, vol. ii. p. 26, note.

word—*coepiscopis*, 'fellow-bishops.' This reading, however, cannot be maintained. St. Ambrose [g] distinctly asserts that the Epistle was written to the people at large, but, curiously enough, makes the words 'bishops and deacons' refer to those at Rome, who joined with St. Paul in his salutation to the Church at Philippi. He accounts for the plural (bishops) being used, by supposing that bishops flocked together to Rome from all parts during the imprisonment of St. Paul, for the purpose of performing kind offices. This, however, is simply an assumption, resting on no known foundation; not to mention that the solitary condition which the Apostle complains of, chap. ii. 20, would be inconsistent with the presence of numerous provincial 'bishops' and 'deacons' at Rome.

Theodoret also says that the Epistle was addressed to the laity as well as the clergy of Philippi; a conclusion which, in the absence of other evidence, might safely be arrived at from its structure; "for the praises, exhortations, consolations, doctrine, and precepts which are read in it are common to all people alike. Moreover, the liberality of the Philippians towards St. Paul was not merely on the part of the clergy, but of the whole Church [h]." It was quite natural that, having previously mentioned 'all the saints,' he should then make a separate notice of the 'bishops' and 'deacons;' for it is by no means uncommon, even among ourselves, that the chief person should be mentioned last.

A learned writer (Hammond [i]) supposes that under the general term Philippians must be included more than the inhabitants of that single city, and that the word refers either to all the Christians throughout Macedonia, or at least to all that were under that metropolis; for that Philippi was such, he says, is the distinct affirmation of St. Luke [k]. Hence it appears that there might have been at Philippi more bishops than one; indeed, as many as were in all Macedonia, at least in the cities under that metropolis. For more on this subject, see Thorndike, "Of the Laws of the Church,"

---

[g] In loc. [h] Estius. [i] Paraphrase, fol. ed., p. 636. (London, 1675.)
[k] Acts xvi. 12.

c. xvii. 10. The objection to this interpretation is that St. Chrysostom, Theodoret, and St. Jerome all affirm that 'bishops' in this place must signify 'presbyters' or priests; and that Thessalonica, and not Philippi, was at that time the metropolis of Macedonia. St. Chrysostom, *in loc.*, enquires, " Were there several bishops of one city ? Certainly not; but he (St. Paul) called the *presbyters* so. For then they still interchanged the titles, and the bishop was called a deacon." It is common enough in the Greek Fathers to find the bishops called presbyters, and *vice versâ*. And this, says Theodoret, is manifest in this place, because he here adds 'deacons' to the 'bishops,' making no mention of their presbyters. Assuming, then, (as there is good reason for doing,) that Epaphroditus, who was now at Rome with St. Paul, was the Bishop of the Church at Philippi, it was natural that in sending a letter by his hands he should address it, not to the Bishop, but to the presbyters (priests) and deacons.

'Deacons' in this place must be understood in the same sense as in the Epistle to St. Timothy, i. e. the ministers of the altar, next to the presbyters. See Acts vi. It is important to observe that there is no authority for the introduction of the *article* before 'bishops and deacons,' the Greek being σὺν ἐπισκόποις καὶ διακόνοις, 'with presbyters and deacons,' where the absence of the article seems to distinguish the true Church, *having threefold orders*, from Gnostics, or any unepiscopal sectarians, such as St. Ignatius hints at when he says, χωρὶς τοῦ ἐπισκόπου μηδὲν ποιεῖτε, (ἐπίσκοπος in St. Ignatius having the sense of 'bishop'). This seems to make the threefold orders a note of the Church.

2. Grace be unto you, and peace,

For the connexion between 'grace' and 'peace,' see remarks on Eph. i. 2.

from God our Father, and from the Lord Jesus Christ.

Compare Rom. i. 7; 2 Cor. i. 2; Gal. i. 3; Eph. i. 2,

He brings out the notion of adoption by using the word 'our,' as in the Lord's Prayer. So true is it that all 'peace' which does not flow from the sense of our adoption, and of God's love and favour obtained thereby, is unsound and uncertain. For further remarks see Eph. i. 2.

3. *I thank my God upon every remembrance of you,*

ἐπὶ πάσῃ τῇ μνείᾳ ὑμῶν: i. e. as often as I remember you; or it may mean, "on the whole of my remembrance of you," intimating that the whole of his recollections were those of joy. Compare Rom. i. 8; 1 Cor. i. 4; Eph. i. 16. "Latum erat cor Pauli[1]." And no wonder that he was so thankful, for these were the Macedonians of whom he makes such honourable mention[m], who "first gave their own selves unto the Lord," and then contributed to the relief of the necessities of the saints.

It is to be observed that he says 'my God,' (with an evident emphasis on the pronoun,) as he says in another place, "Whose I am, and Whom I serve[n]." The reason of this is to shew that it is he *alone* who writes the Epistle, although the name of St. Timothy is united with his in the salutation, see verse 1; and then that God, as He is the common possession of all the saints, so is He in a special manner the property of each. Compare ch. iv. 19, "But *my* God shall supply all your need."

The Apostle here, as elsewhere, commences with thanksgiving, which is not merely a sign of affectionate regard, but a powerful incentive to perseverance, "Virtus enim laudata crescit[o]." This verse, then, furnishes us with a fitting example to follow in our devotions, where the grateful recollection of past mercies and blessings should stimulate us to seek for fresh ones. "Prayer, or invocation, consists of confession and petition; confession is divided into *confessionem fraudis*, which the Greeks call ἐξομολόγησις, that is, the confession of sins, whereunto they add supplication to God for pardon, like that of the Publican[p], 'God be mer-

---

[1] Bengel.   [m] 2 Cor. viii. 5.   [n] Acts xxvii. 23.
[o] Hemmingius.   [p] Luke xviii. 13.

ciful to me a sinner.' The other kind of confession is *confessio laudis*, that is, thanksgiving to God for His goodness in pardoning our sins, and bestowing His benefits upon us; which kind of confession is called αὐτομολόγησις. This also is a part of prayer, and ought to go with it, as appears when the Apostle doth 'thank God always' for the Churches in his prayer q."

4. This verse is evidently parenthetical, since St. Paul εὐχαριστεῖ for the κοινωνία, verse 5.

Always in every prayer of mine for you all

See Ps. xxxiv. 1. For observations on the duty of perpetual thanksgiving, see Commentary on the Ephesians, pp. 28, 78, 300, 330, 394, 395.

'In every prayer.' Here we have the overflowings of a full heart. Surely it is the sign of great affection that in *all* his prayers he mingled petitions for them.

'For you all.' Compare ver. 8, "How I long after *you all*." "Omnes complectitur suo affectu, respiciens saniorem partem, nam indubiè erant in eo cœtu etiam improbi, hypocritæ et similes, sed eorum non offensus numero totam Ecclesiam piorum titulo complectitur r."

making request

τὴν δέησιν ποιούμενος. It is to be observed that δέησις is used *twice* in this verse. It means *petition*. Prayer *generally* (including confession, petition, oblation, intercession, and thanksgiving) is προσευχή, which Polus renders 'preces ad bona impetranda,' while he translates δέησις 'deprecatio arcendis malis quæ metuimus,' for, as he remarks, this last word is derived ἀπὸ τοῦ δέους, 'from fear.' See observations on chap. iv. 6, and compare Eph. vi. 18.

with joy,

i. e. with spiritual joy, derived from the comforting accounts which he received of their state. This is the sum and substance of the whole Epistle. It is natural that in a com-

---

q Bp. Andrewes, Sermon vi., "On Preparation to Prayer."   r Aretius.

position like this, where *love* predominates, there should be a constant mention of 'joy.' See ch. i. 18; ii. 2, 19, 28; for love and joy are both fruits of the same Spirit.

It will be the easier for us to understand why St. Paul makes special mention of 'joy' in this place, when we find from 2 Cor. ii. 4 that it is quite possible for a pastor's recollection of his flock to be one of *grief*.

5. **For your fellowship in the Gospel**

ἐπὶ τῇ κοινωνίᾳ ὑμῶν εἰς τὸ εὐαγγέλιον, 'for your communication *unto* the preaching;' or, 'with reference to your liberality towards the Gospel;' i.e. for the share you have had in promoting the preaching of the Gospel; εἰς τὸ εὐαγγέλιον meaning "in usum Evangelii." This verse contains the reason why St. Paul gives thanks for the Philippians. They had zealously entered into his Apostolical labours, and had become sharers in them, specially by contributing largely of their worldly substance. While others proved faithless, and deserted him in the hour of peril[s], they remained stedfast, and "although absent, took part in his tribulations, both sending men to him and ministering to him according to their ability, and leaving out nothing by any means[t]." In chap. iv. 15—18 he thanks the Philippians for the pecuniary assistance he had received of them. Κοινωνία occurs in this sense Heb. xiii. 16.

St. Ambrose, Aquinas, Caietan, and others explain this verse differently. According to their interpretation, the Apostle's meaning is, 'I rejoice and give thanks to God that ye have been made partakers of the Gospel of Christ; that is to say, by believing and shewing your faith by your works; and that ye have been stedfastly pursuing the same course from the day in which ye began to believe until now." For this use of the word 'fellowship' see 1 Cor. i. 9, and Gal. ii. 9. There can be no doubt, however, that the former interpretation (which has the authority of St. Chrysostom) is the best, being more in accordance with the Greek and the general bearing of the Apostle's language,

---

[s] 2 Tim. i. 15; iv. 10, 16.   [t] S. Chrysos., in loc.

for in other places also he calls assistance of the kind rendered by the Philippians 'fellowship.' See Rom. xii. 13, xv. 26; 2 Cor. viii. 4, and ix. 13; Gal. vi. 6.

from the first day until now;

i. e. from the time of their conversion to the time when he wrote the Epistle. Their religion had stood the test of time.

We gather from this verse that giving assistance to those who are ministering in Christ's Name and by His authority, (of whatever kind this assistance may be, as prayers, money, sympathy, &c.), is actually 'a fellowship of the Gospel,' and entitles the givers to the highest rewards. It was the appreciation of this that caused the early Christians, "as many as were possessors of lands or houses," to sell them, and to bring the "prices of the things that were sold" and "lay them down at the Apostles' feet [u]." And surely it is a sweet and comforting thought for those who have not been called in the course of God's providence to teach and preach in His Name, that by making His priests partakers of their worldly substance they are becoming fellow-heirs with them in their reward. See Matt. x. 41. "He that receiveth a prophet in the name of a prophet shall receive a prophet's reward; and he that receiveth a righteous man in the name of a righteous man, shall receive a righteous man's reward."

St. Gregory, commenting on this passage, remarks, with great beauty and force:—" Qui recipit prophetam in nomine prophetæ mercedem prophetæ accipiet. In quibus verbis notandum est quia non ait mercedem *de prophetá*, sed *mercedem prophetæ.*"

6. In this verse the Apostle incidentally teaches a lesson of *humility*. He does not say, 'Being confident that as ye have begun, so ye will finish,' but, "that *He which hath begun* a good work in you will *perform* it," plainly shewing that the 'good work' of which he is speaking is wrought from beginning to end by God working in us. See chap. ii. 13, and Eph. ii. 8, 9. St. Paul affirms this, not out of any

---

[u] Acts iv. 34, 35.

opinion of the election of *all* the Philippians to eternal life, or of the certainty of their perseverance to the end[x], but he speaks from a judgment of charity, which in doubtful matters ever inclines to the more favourable side[y], conjecturing, as Theophylact says, from what was *past*, what they would be for the *future*.

Being confident

πεποιθώς, 'persuasum habens,' see Eph. iii. 12. "Hæc fiducia nervus est gratiarum actionis[z]."

of this very thing,

viz., that God will not forsake His work.

that He which hath begun a good work in you

ὅτι ὁ ἐναρξάμενος ἐν ὑμῖν ἔργον ἀγαθόν. The repetition of the preposition ἐν makes this expression very emphatic. It is as if he had said, 'He who hath *inbegun* a good work in you'—for the work is wholly *inward* and spiritual. See 2 Cor. vi. 16.

'A good work;' i.e. the preaching of the Gospel among them, and their consequent conversion.

will perform it

ἐπιτελέσει, 'absolvet,' 'ad finem perducet,' so that by daily growing in grace, ye may at length attain to everlasting life. This verse teaches us that the smallest indications of grace are to be lovingly cherished, since God will not desert His work. As Bengel truly says, "Initium est pignus consummationis." And yet because it is *His* work it must not be thought that our co-operation is excluded. God's indwelling and inworking are not indiscriminate, but belong to those who make a right use of the grace vouchsafed to them. This verse tells strongly against the Semipelagians, who thought that the *beginning* of good actions was to be ascribed to man's free-will, while the *completion* of them belonged to Divine grace.

---

[x] See chap. ii. 12, 16; iv. 1.   [y] 1 Cor. xiii. 7.   [z] Bengel.

It must not, however, be inferred from this place that grace is indefectible, and that all who have once been made partakers of the Divine Nature will necessarily attain to everlasting glory; but this passage contains, for the comfort of all believers, the confident assurance of the Apostle, (abundantly confirmed by other parts of Holy Scripture,) that God, Who is the Author of grace in the soul, will continue that grace to the end, in the case of those who are desirous of retaining it. There is no promise, however, here or elsewhere, that the operations of that grace will not be suspended, and finally withdrawn, from those who neglect or misuse them. The distinction between justifying grace and the gift of perseverance must be carefully marked, or sad consequences will ensue; for many heretics have rashly concluded that God always grants perseverance to those who have once been made partakers of spiritual life. But to suppose that God continues His grace irrespective of the way in which it is used, would be to say that He deals with us as with logs and stones. See Commentary on Ephesians, p. 31.

St. Augustine says [a], "Being sanctified, the faithful make progress in holiness and become more holy; not without the aid of the grace of God, but by His sanctifying their advancement Who sanctified their beginning." And the Council of Trent declares [b], "Deus enim, nisi ipsi homines illius gratiæ defuerint, sicut cœpit opus bonum, ita perficiet operans velle et perficere."

until the day of Jesus Christ:

i. e. The day of judgment; or, as it is called, "the times of restitution of all things [c]." Bengel says, "Diem Christi potius quam suam mortem sibi pro metâ proponebant credentes." The meaning of the Apostle is, The Holy Spirit of God will not desert you even in death, but will continue with you up to that day when time shall be swallowed up in eternity. For ἡμέρα in the sense of *judgment*, see 1 Cor. iv. 3, ὑπὸ ἀνθρωπίνης ἡμέρας. The good work of God will go on and

---

[a] Hom. cviii. 2, in John.   [b] Sess. vi. c. 13.   [c] Acts iii. 21.

prosper *up to* the judgment of Christ, in which, of course, it must stand and be approved, since God will not condemn His own work. The wicked will *not* stand. "Therefore the ungodly shall not be able to stand in the judgment ᵈ."

Bp. Andrewes remarks ᵉ, "The day of the Lord" (equivalent to "day of Jesus Christ" used here); "the prophet calls it *dies Domini*, as it were opposing it to *dies servi*, to our days here. As if he said, These are your days, and you use them, indeed, as if they were your own. You pour out yourselves into all riot, and know no other pouring out but that. . . . These are your days. But know this, when yours are done God hath His day too, and His day will come at last, and it will come terribly when it comes."

There is something very grand in the expression, 'day of Christ.' It is true that *all* days are His; yet there is one day of such overwhelming interest and importance, that in a special sense it is His above all others. In another place St. Paul calls it 'that day' ᶠ, (though he had previously mentioned no particular day), plainly indicating where all his thoughts were fixed, and how they were centred in the glory that should then be revealed.

7. Even as it is meet

Καθώς ἐστι δίκαιον, 'Par est enim.' See Acts iv. 19. "Piorum est semper de bene cœptis optime sperare ᵍ." He here gives the reason why he speaks of the Philippians in terms of such affectionate regard. Wetstein certainly does not go far enough when he explains this place, "justum est vos omnes et singulos à me amari, quia omnes communi consensu contulistis ad inopiam meam sublevandam."

for me to think this of you all,

The word 'think' (φρονεῖν) may very properly be viewed as a kind of qualification of the 'being confident' (πεποιθώς) in verse 6; shewing that though he believed them to be sincere Christians, yet, as he could not read their hearts, it

---

ᵈ Ps. i. 6.   ᵉ Serm. xi., "Of the Sending of the Holy Ghost."
ᶠ 2 Tim. iv. 8.   ᵍ Hemmingius.

was out of his power to pronounce a positive judgment upon their state.

because I have you in my heart;

q. d. 'I bear you in my mind, or recollection, *as a beloved object.*' See 2 Cor. iii. 2, "Ye are our epistle, *written in our hearts.*" And again, vii. 3, "Ye are in our hearts to die and live with you." It is to be observed that the sentence might be rendered 'because *you* hold *me* in *your* hearts.' This would be quite in accordance with the Greek text, and would give a very good sense, though probably the usual rendering is more consistent with the general scope of the Apostle's meaning.

inasmuch as both in my bonds,

" Vincula non constringunt amorem [h]."

and in the defence

i. e. '*My* defence.' He means either his public speeches when brought before the Roman magistrates, or his private conferences with those who came to him. See Acts xxviii. 17, 30. The word 'defence' is well used, since he was compelled to plead his cause as a prisoner.

and confirmation of the Gospel,

St. Paul *defended* his doctrine by words, and *confirmed* it by deeds. See ver. 17. There can be little doubt that he is here alluding to his bonds, for in the truest sense they were a 'confirmation' of his preaching. If he had shrunk from imprisonment, or borne it impatiently, endeavouring to procure his release by any of those unworthy means that were then so common, he might have been thought to be a deceiver; but now, by patiently submitting to bonds and affliction, he shewed that he was suffering for no human cause, but for God, Who would reward his sufferings with a crown. No one surely would have chosen of his own free will to come into collision with such an emperor as Nero,

---

[h] Bengel.

unless he had looked to another and a greater King. But while accepting this interpretation, (sanctioned as it is by the most venerable names,) it must be observed that the structure of the Greek seems rather to point to another: βεβαιώσει τοῦ εὐαγγελίου are the Apostle's words, there being *no article* before βεβαιώσει, and the meaning would be the general work of *settling* the Gospel *by organizing the Church*. Now the Church at Philippi had been fully organized, as is shewn by the opening address to the priests and deacons. See observations on verse 1. The sense of the passage will then be this, 'It is but fair that I should think this of you, because ye retain me in your affections, being all of you severally (πάντας, not ἅπαντας,) my helpers, (1) in my imprisonment, (2) in my public trial, (3) in Church work generally.'

ye are all partakers of my grace.

The pronoun 'my' being highly emphatic; and the 'grace' being that referred to in verse 29, ὅτι ὑμῖν ἐχαρίσθη, κ.τ.λ. involving *belief* in Christ, and *suffering* for His sake. For this use of the personal pronoun see 1 Cor. iii. 10; Eph. iii. 8. This sentence is sometimes translated 'partakers with me of grace,' but wrongly, since this would require συγκοινωνούς μοι χάριτος. It is evident that the Apostle here applies the term 'grace' to his sufferings; for indeed it is a great 'grace,' a distinguished mark of God's favour and love, to be permitted to suffer for the cause of Christ. This is brought out very forcibly in the last two verses of this chapter. Although no persecution of the Church at Philippi is recorded in the Acts of the Apostles, yet it is only natural to suppose that the violence of unbelievers soon spread from St. Paul to those who were converted by him.

It has been thought by some that the χάρις here referred to was the *Apostolic office* (see Rom. xii. 3), of which the Philippians became συγκοινωνοί, by assisting in, and rejoicing at, the preaching of the Gospel. There is another reading of χαρᾶς ('joy'), for χάριτος, 'partakers of my joy,' but the commonly received one gives the deepest sense.

8. For God is my record,

The Apostle having declared that he has the Philippian Christians 'in his heart,' now calls God to witness to the truth of what he has said. And this he does, not from any fear that his sincerity would be called in question, but because God alone searches the heart, and would therefore know the depth of his affection. Compare Rom. i. 9; 2 Cor. i. 23; 1 Thess. ii. 5, 10. See also Gen. xxxi. 50; Job xvi. 19.

The word 'for' (γάρ), with which the sentence is introduced, must be noticed. It means 'yea,' and is used by way of preface to the explanation of verse 4, which follows.

how greatly

" I am unable in words to represent unto you my longing; wherefore I leave it to God, whose range is in the heart, to know this [i]."

I long after

ἐπιποθῶ; this word denotes great ardour of affection. It occurs again, chap. ii. 26. See also Ps. xlii. 1 (LXX), ὃν τρόπον ἐπιποθεῖ ἡ ἔλαφος ἐπὶ τὰς πηγὰς τῶν ὑδάτων, οὕτως ἐπιποθεῖ ἡ ψυχή μου πρός σε ὁ Θεός. It may, therefore, be taken to mean "desiderium quod non patitur dilationem aliquam."

you all

'All' is emphatic, shewing the expansiveness of the Apostle's love, and is added in case the less advanced Christians among them should think themselves excluded. And then, lest it should be thought that his fervent longing towards them was merely the effect of the contributions which they had sent by the hand of Epaphroditus, he hastens to say

in the bowels of Jesus Christ.

The word σπλάγχα ('viscera,' 'bowels'), denotes the 'inward parts,' especially the heart, lungs, liver, &c., and then comes to mean metaphorically (like our 'heart') the *affections*, especially pity. In this place it means 'omnis affectus.'

---

[i] St. Chrysostom.

See 2 Cor. vi. 12; Eph. iv. 32; Col. iii. 12; Philem. 7, 12, 20; 1 John iii. 17.

The words 'of Jesus Christ' very much intensify the force of the expression. It is as if he had said, 'with that wondrous depth of love wherewith Christ loves you and all Christians.'

Wetstein says, "Eo affectu qui in ipso Christo fuit erga nos omnes," and Gagneius, "Amicitiâ quæ est in Christo."

Bengel admirably remarks here, "In Paulo non Paulus vivit, sed Jesus Christus; quare Paulus non *in Pauli* sed in *Jesu Christi* movetur visceribus." He has here very happily expressed the meaning of the Apostle; for all real love among Christians is but a fragment of the great love wherewith Christ loves us, and which lives and yearns in all who are in union with Him.

For reconciling this adjuration of St. Paul with our Lord's command, "Swear not at all," see St. Augustine, *de Mendacio*, xv.: "It is also written, 'But I say unto you, Swear not at all.' But the Apostle himself has used oaths in his Epistles[j]. And so he shews how that is to be taken which is said, 'I say unto you, Swear not at all;' that is, lest by swearing one come to a facility in swearing, from facility to a custom, and so from a custom there be a downfal into perjury. And therefore he is not found to have sworn except in writing, when there is more wary forethought, and no precipitate tongue withal. And this indeed came of evil, as it is said, 'Whatever is more than these is of evil[k];' not, however, from evil of his own, but from the evil of infirmity which was in them, in whom he even in this way endeavoured to work faith. For that he used an oath in speaking, while not in writing, I know not that any Scripture has related concerning him. And yet the Lord says, 'Swear not at all;' for He hath not granted license thereof to persons writing. Howbeit, because to pronounce Paul guilty of violating the commandment, especially in Epistles written and sent forth for the spiritual life and salvation of the nations, were an impiety, we must understand the word that

---

[j] Rom. ix. 1; Phil. i. 8; Gal. i. 20.   [k] Matt. v. 34, 37.

is set down, 'at all,' to be set down for this purpose, that as much as in thee lies, thou affect not, love not, nor as though it were for a good thing, with any delight desire, an oath."

For further remarks on this subject, see Trench's "Exposition of the Sermon on the Mount," 2nd ed., pp. 217—222.

9. From verse 3 he has been declaring that he prays for them; he now proceeds to shew what is the special subject of his prayers.

And this I pray, that your love

i. e. towards God and man. See whither those desires which are according to 'the bowels of Jesus Christ' tend! The Apostle does not pray on behalf of the Philippians for riches, or power, or praise, or anything that is usually esteemed among men, but for 'love;' the 'more excellent way,' which he points out to the Corinthians in 1 Ep. xiii.

may abound yet more and more

"Ignis in Apostolo nunquam dicit, sufficit [1]."

By the use of the expression, 'yet more,' he recognises the existence of love among the Philippians; but his prayer is that it may increase and develope itself. And this with good reason, for "Love," says St. Chrysostom, "is a good of which there is no satiety; see how, when loved, he would be loved still more of them; for he who thus loves the object of his love will stay at no point of love, for it is impossible there should be a measure of so noble a thing, whence Paul desires that the debt of love should always be owing, in that he says, 'Owe no man anything, but to love one another.' The measure of love is to stop nowhere."

With the expression "more and more," compare Eph. iii. 20, "exceeding abundantly above all," &c., and see remarks there.

in knowledge and in all judgment;

ἐν ἐπιγνώσει καὶ πάσῃ αἰσθήσει. The word γνῶσις having been perverted by those called γνωστικοὶ (Gnostics) to an

---

[1] Bengel.

evil sense, (ψευδώνυμος γνῶσις, 1 Tim. vi. 20,) St. Paul prefers to use ἐπίγνωσις for *true* knowledge. It is here (and in other parts of his writings) equivalent to the Aristotelian φρόνησις, and perhaps the Platonic σοφία, being that practical wisdom which enables us to apply the best means, morally and intellectually, to compass a virtuous end. Αἴσθησις is moral sense, the intuitive perception of right and wrong. St. Paul here prays that the Philippians may be guided, both in their deliberations and intuitions, by the great ruling principle of love.

10. That ye may approve

This is the fruit of ἐπίγνωσις and αἴσθησις, that ye "may be able to comprehend with all saints what is the breadth, and length, and depth, and height; and to know the love of Christ, which passeth knowledge, that ye might be filled with all the fulness of God [m]."

This word (δοκιμάζειν) is properly used of metals which are tested in the fire, so that their quality may be ascertained. See Prov. viii. 10 (LXX); xvii. 3. It occurs in this sense in 1 Pet. i. 7, χρυσίου διὰ πυρὸς δοκιμαζομένου. It then comes to mean 'to examine, prove, or try,' 'probare.' (See Luke xiv. 19; Rom. xii. 2; 2 Cor. viii. 8, xiii. 5; Gal. vi. 4; Eph. v. 10,) and then 'to *discriminate*,' Luke xii. 56; Rom. ii. 18; 1 Cor. iii. 13. Bengel renders it here, "explorare et amplecti."

things that are excellent;

τα διαφέροντα=τα συμφέροντα, 'ut probetis quæ sunt utilia.' Sedulius says 'altiora mysteria.' "Non modo præ malis bona, sed in bonis optima, quorum præstantiam non nisi provectiores cernunt. Sane in rebus externis eligimus accurate, cur minus in spiritualibus? Theologia comparativa magni est [n]." "Pertinet ad rectum mentis judicium in actionibus probare, id est eligere meliora [o]."

The object of the Apostle is evidently to guard them against receiving false doctrine under the specious pretence of love. Aretius says, "διαφέροντα, I understand simply

---

[m] Eph. iii. 18, 19.   [n] Bengel.   [o] Estius.

'pro rerum discrimine;' as if he said, Charity must be tutored by discretion, that ye may be able to discern what makes for your salvation, and what falls short of this end, so that ye may exercise love with good effect."

that ye may be sincere and without offence

εἰλικρινεῖς καὶ ἀπρόσκοποι, that is, εἰλικρινεῖς πρὸς τὸν Θεόν, ἀπρόσκοποι κατ' ἄνθρωπον. εἰλικρινεῖς literally means examined by the light of the sun, and so found genuine. The meaning will then be not merely (as St. Chrysostom, Œcumenius, Theophylact,) that your faith may be so free from alloy of heresy that it may be able to bear the all-penetrating light of "the day of Christ," but that your *morals* also may be able to stand the test of that day. The same word occurs in 2 Pet. iii. 1, τὴν εἰλικρινῆ διάνοιαν, which the English version translates 'pure mind.'

ἀπρόσκοποι. This is a word of somewhat doubtful signification, and may be taken *actively* or *passively*, either, that you cause scandal to none, see 1 Cor. x. 32; or, that you yourselves stumble not at any of the difficulties of the Christian path, Acts xxiv. 16; the metaphor is borrowed from Grecian games. This last is probably the best sense in this place. The Apostle might very fitly caution them not to stumble at anything they might hear or see. All sorts of evil rumours might be carried to them from his prison, and evil teachers might make them believe that he was deserted by God, and that the preaching had come to an end.

till the day of Christ :

i. e. not merely for a season, but continuously till the day of judgment. See verse 6. It is they who endure *to the end* that will be saved. See Rev. ii. 10.

11. Being filled with the fruit ('fruits' E. V.) of righteousness,

πεπληρωμένοι καρπὸν δικαιοσύνης. We meet with the same construction in Col. i. 9, ἵνα πληρωθῆτε τὴν ἐπίγνωσιν τοῦ θελήματος αὐτοῦ, the preposition κατὰ being understood. The English Version, 'fruits,' in the plural, misses the delicate sense of the text, and is at variance with most of the best MSS. The Apostle is not speaking of *many* fruits of righteousness, but of *one*, viz. *love*, as manifested in works of mercy, with a special reference to the contributions sent to him by the Philippians. That this is called 'righteousness' in Holy Scripture may be seen from 2 Cor. ix. 9 : "He hath dispersed abroad ; he hath given to the poor : his righteousness remaineth for ever." And it is well worthy of remark that it is only to the *merciful* that our Lord awards the crown of righteousness, Matt. xxv. 35, and foll. See also Dan. iv. 27.

We meet with the phrase 'fruit of righteousness,' in the singular, Heb. xii. 11, ὕστερον δὲ καρπὸν εἰρηνικὸν τοῖς δι' αὐτῆς γεγυμνασμένοις ἀποδίδωσι δικαιοσύνης. See also James iii. 18, and Rom. vi. 22.

St. Anselm understands by 'the fruit of righteousness' the reward which is laid up for the faithful in a *future* state; but the meaning of the Apostle evidently requires the words to be explained in reference to the *present life*.

which are by Jesus Christ,

Since there is a kind of righteousness apart from Christ, to which heathen philosophers attained, but which does not avail to eternal life.

The Christian's righteousness is derived to him through sacramental union with the Humanity of Christ. See John xv. 5, 6.

unto the glory and praise of God.

See 1 Cor. i. 31. By this 'the fruit of righteousness' will be distinguished from all counterfeits, as not being a matter of self-gratulation, or furnishing ground for boasting, but redounding to the glory of God. Compare 1 Cor. xv. 10. The meaning of the Apostle is, "I wish you to abound in works of love and mercy; not indeed that ye may glory *in yourselves*, or *I in you*, but that through them *God* may be praised and glorified." See Matt. v. 16.

12. But I would ye should understand, brethren,

It was a great matter that they should be thoroughly

persuaded of this, since probably their minds had been preoccupied by conflicting rumours as to his condition. Sedulius remarks, "For three reasons he says this; that he might magnify the power of God; that he might set an example to others; that he might console the Philippians, who were sorrowful about his bonds and tribulation at Rome."

that the things which happened unto me

Τὰ κατ' ἐμέ, 'ea quæ me circa sunt,' 'my affairs;' i.e. my imprisonment and bonds. Compare Eph. vi. 21.

have fallen out rather unto the furtherance of the Gospel;

Προκοπή ('furtherance') = αὔξησις, so that the Church *grows* in persecutions and afflictions, just as of old it was with the Israelites, "the more" the Egyptians "afflicted them, the more they multiplied and grew [p]." Compare Ps. lxxvi. 10, 'The fierceness of man shall turn to Thy praise.'

Tertullian [q] calls "the blood of martyrs the seed of the Church." And St. Hilary [r] says, "while it is persecuted, it flourishes; while it is oppressed, it grows." St. Augustine [s] shews that the efforts of the wicked pass away like winter torrents:—"Be not terrified, brethren, by certain streams which are called torrents: with winter waters they are filled up; do not fear; after a little it passeth by, that water runneth down; for a time it roareth; soon it will subside: they cannot hold long. Many heresies now are utterly dead; they have run in their channels as much as they were able, have run down, dried are the channels, scarce of them the memory is found, or that they have been."

13. He points out three ways in which his bonds and affliction have furthered the spread of the Gospel, (1) by the constancy with which he has endured them, (2) by the spread of the rumour concerning them, not only in the palace, but

---

[p] Exod. i. 12.   [q] Apol., cap. ult.   [r] Lib. vii. de Trinit.
   [s] In Ps. lviii. 16.

throughout the city, (3) by the confirmation of weak brethren, which resulted from them.

So that my bonds in Christ are manifest

"Ὥστε τοὺς δεσμούς μου φανεροὺς ἐν Χριστῷ γενέσθαι. It is to be observed that ἐν Χριστῷ may be connected either (1) with δεσμούς, 'so that my bonds in Christ,' i.e. which I suffer for the sake of Christ, (which agrees very well with what he says of himself, Eph. iv. 1, παρακαλῶ οὖν ὑμᾶς ὁ δέσμιος ἐν Κυρίῳ, which, however, the English version renders 'the prisoner *of* the Lord;') or, (2) with φανεροὺς γενέσθαι, and then the meaning will be, 'so that my bonds have become manifest in Christ;' i.e. they have become generally known (since God wills not that His faithful witnesses should lie concealed[t]) not merely as a matter of notoriety, but of notoriety *in Christ;* as being in connexion with Christ's cause, and as being endured for His sake, and not for any fault of my own. This probably is the better sense, and is more in harmony with the Greek. Bengel says, "Paulus cum aliis captivis traditus par eis visus erat ; deinde innotuit aliam esse Pauli causam, et sic invaluit Evangelium." St. Anselm says, " Ut manifestum fieret quod propter Christum vinctus sim, non propter debita aut scelera ; sicque per vincula mea Christi nomen ubique clarescit."

There is a force about the word 'manifest' (φανεροὺς) which must not be overlooked in its practical application to our own case. The Cross which Christians bear is a μαρτύριον to the world, because it is a testimony to the doctrine of Christ, and is, as it were, a sealing of the truth of the Gospel. "Nam cum homines vident sanctos non propter crucem abjicere confessionem, cogitant eos certis niti fundamentis [u]."

in all the palace,

The Prætorium. It seems most probable that this was the barrack of the Prætorian Guards attached to the palace of Nero[x]. Estius says, "The Apostle calls the palace of Cæsar *Prætorium*, (ἐν ὅλῳ τῷ πραιτωρίῳ) using a Latin word, be-

[t] Gagneius. [u] Hemmingius. [x] Comp. iv. 22.

cause it was commonly so called, even by the Greeks. And so also in Matthew, Mark, and John, we read of the *prætorium* of Pilate; and in Luke of the *prætorium* of Herod." "When the blessed Apostle came to Rome, bound for the Name of Christ, and when he had been committed to prison in the palace of the Emperor, and had begun to teach, to heal the sick, and to work many miracles, many believed; to such an extent, indeed, that as St. Jerome says, he made the palace of the persecutor Nero a Church of the Redeemer[y]."

and in all other places;

Καὶ τοῖς λοιποῖς πᾶσι: this might also be rendered 'to all the rest;' i.e. to all persons throughout the whole city. "Amplam et extensam notitiam suorum in Christo vinculorum etiam extra Prætorium significat, dicendo 'et cæteris omnibus[z].'" The story of the prisoner would rapidly be carried through the city by the soldiers, and others whose business led them to the Prætorium; and so opportunity would be furnished for persons at a distance to come from curiosity, if from no better motive, to hear what sort of Gospel it was that he preached. Without drawing upon our imagination, we may well conclude that the doctrines taught by the Apostle were so strange, considering the licentiousness of the time and place, that multitudes must have been attracted to him merely from the desire of hearing something new.

St. Chrysostom[a] says of this passage, that it is "an instance of the wise contrivance of God, that by these things which are opposite He brings in the preaching." So true is it that He makes persecution the means of spreading the faith. See Acts viii. 4, and the remarks on verse 12.

There is a very interesting passage in St. Athanasius Histor. Tract., viii. 34, illustrative of the benefits accruing to the Church from persecution. Speaking of the second Arian persecution under Constantius, and relating how the Emperor had drawn his sword upon certain Catholic Bishops, he continues, "The holy men therefore shaking off the dust, and looking up to God, neither feared the threats

[y] Haymo.   [z] Caietan.   [a] Hom. xii. in 2 Cor. vi. 8.

of the Emperor nor betrayed their cause before his drawn sword, but received their banishment as a service pertaining to their ministry. And as they passed along, they preached the Gospel in every place and city, although they were in bonds, proclaiming the Orthodox faith, anathematizing the Arian heresy, and stigmatizing the recantation of Ursacius and Valens. But this was contrary to the intention of their enemies; for the greater was the distance of their place of banishment, so much the more was the hatred against them increased, while the wanderings of these men were but the heralding of their impiety. For who that saw them as they passed along did not greatly admire them as Confessors, and renounce and abominate the others, calling them not only impious men, but executioners and murderers, and everything rather than Christians?"

14. And many of the brethren in the Lord, waxing confident by my bonds,

Τοὺς πλείονας τῶν ἀδελφῶν, not 'many,' as English version, but 'most of.' He calls Christians 'brethren in the Lord,' such as are saluted by the Apostle [b], and who are called 'brethren in the Lord' to distinguish them from the Jews, who were St. Paul's brethren 'according to the flesh [c].' St. Chrysostom, Œcumenius, Theophylact, Anselm, and others, connect 'in the Lord' with what follows; thus, 'being confident in the Lord.' The former reading is, however, the more natural, and therefore the best, as if he had said, 'my brethren in the faith and religion of Christ.'

are much more bold

They had begun indeed to preach before, but timidly. St. Paul's bonds add confidence, and encourage them in their preaching. A marvellous illustration of the words, 'When I am *weak*, then am I strong [d].' "See the grace of Paul's bonds as far as others are concerned [e]." If, therefore, so much benefit was derived to the Church from the contemplation of the sufferings of St. Paul in the cause of Christ, who shall say but that much of the timidity and want of zeal

---

[b] Rom. xvi.   [c] Rom. ix. 3.   [d] 2 Cor. xii. 10.   [e] Caietan.

which now overspread us may not arise from the fact that the lives and sufferings of God's saints are not studied and reverenced as they ought to be?

speak the word without fear.

i.e. the Gospel, which is 'the word,' κατ' ἐξοχήν.

15. Some indeed preach Christ even of envy and strife;

St. Paul here divides the preachers of Christ into two classes; the one acting from an impure, the other from a pure, motive. It has been well said that envy is the companion of virtue. So it was with the Apostle; for certain of the Church seeing how great a reputation he had acquired through preaching, were desirous of setting themselves up as rivals; not, indeed, preaching from love of souls and zeal for God, but to acquire popularity and influence for themselves. It has been well remarked (Blunt's "Lectures on the Early Fathers," p. 291,) that "the terms κηρύσσω (in this verse) and καταγγέλλω (in verse 16) are not used in any *technical* sense, or as having here the meaning of *preach*, as usually understood, but simply conveying the idea that St. Paul's imprisonment had excited a strong sensation (as we say in these days) and led to the discussion of the merits of the cause for which he suffered; one party assailing and vilifying it and him, and another party warmly defending both; and thus both parties, whether actuated by spite or by charity, still serving by their disputes to spread the knowledge of Christ, and to proclaim Him; a good result at all events, in which St. Paul rejoices. The passage thus explained holds out no sanction for heretical preaching, as it is often made to do.

The 'envy and strife' would mean, 'envy' at the reputation of St. Paul, and 'strife,' those endeavours whereby they were seeking to push forward their *own reputation* at the expense of that of the Apostle. Caietan supposes the words 'envy and strife,' as well as 'contention,' in the next verse, to refer to some variation *in doctrine* on the part of these teachers. He thinks that they had corrupted the

Catholic faith, probably by the introduction of Jewish observances. This opinion, however, is entirely inconsistent with the *joy* expressed by the Apostle in verse 18. If their teaching had been erroneous, he would rather have mourned over them.

St. Chrysostom thinks, that since St. Paul was now under restraint, many unbelievers, wishing to stir up the Emperor to a fiercer persecution, themselves also preached Christ, in order that his wrath might be increased at the spread of the Gospel, and all his anger fall on the head of St. Paul. But this would have been a perilous experiment, to say the least; and the former interpretation seems to be the best.

and some also of good will:

i.e. out of love, and singleness of purpose, being bent only on the salvation of souls.

16. The Apostle here repeats somewhat more strongly the two divisions of verse 15. Some old versions transpose verses 16 and 17; but the sense is not affected.

The one preach Christ of contention,

'Ἐξ ἐριθείας. This word means more than ἔρις in the preceding verse, which simply implies contention, while ἐριθεία means contention accompanied with the idea of venal partizanship. The word occurs also in Rom. ii. 8; 2 Cor. xii. 20; Phil. ii. 3; James iii. 14, 16.

not sincerely,

Οὐχ ἁγνῶς, ' non simpliciter [f],' i.e. not from a pure love of truth. St. Augustine [g] calls these men "false brethren, driven on by the devilish stings of envy." Haymo rightly says that it was for temporal advantages, and not merely for vainglory, that these men preached. "They gave themselves," he says, "to preaching on account of the interests of this present life and temporal gains, so that they might receive from their converts food and clothing." And he concludes by saying that they wished St. Paul to be put to

---

[f] Ambrose.   [g] De Fide et Oper. ii.

death in order that they might spoil the Church with the greater ease.

So also St. Augustine [h], who says, "For many preach the truth impurely; for they sell it for the bribe of the advantages of this life. Of such the Apostle says, that they declared Christ not purely." And again [i], "Doth not the Apostle say of these men, that *not chastely* they were proclaiming the Gospel, but desiring earthly things they were preaching the kingdom of heaven, their own things they were seeking, and Christ they were proclaiming."

supposing to add affliction to my bonds:

He says 'supposing,' with an evident desire to shew that the cruel designs of these men did not turn out according to their expectation.

'Affliction,' more especially that sort which is received at the hands of false friends, such as David and Job so often complain of. In the case of the Apostle, it would either be the increased wrath of Nero, excited by the preaching of these men, and manifested either in the withdrawal of the liberty which was permitted to him even in his confinement [k], or in torture and other kinds of cruelty; or it may mean the grief of mind that he would feel when he heard of their insincerity; and the more so, from not being able on account of his bonds to do anything to counteract their evil influences. St. Chrysostom exclaims, "O cruelty! O devilish instigation! They saw him in bonds, and cast into prison, and still they envied him." St. Paul might well have exclaimed with Socrates, "Non Nero, non Romani, sed sola, quæ tot viros præstantissimos, me quoque occidit invidia."

This verse drew from Luther the following wholesome counsel to ministers, that they should take care that those three dogs did not follow them into the pulpit,—pride, covetousness, and envy.

Speaking of the danger of *pride*, Bishop Andrewes remarks [l], "St. Bernard in the midst of a sermon was solicited

---

[h] In Ps. xii. 8. [i] In Ps. lii. 4. [k] Acts xxviii. 16, 30, 31.
[l] Sermon on Temptation of Christ.

to vainglory because he thought he pleased his auditors, and thereupon broke off his speech and turned it to the devil, saying, 'Non propter te hoc opus cœptum est; nec propter te nec in te finitur.'"

17. **But the other of love,**

The same as 'good will' in verse 15. They were actuated solely by the desire of bringing souls to Christ, and so advancing His glory. He does not say 'love of *me*;' but absolutely 'of love,' meaning of course, as Caietan says, the love of Christ.

knowing

In contrast with 'supposing' in the former verse.

that I am set

Κεῖμαι = τέθειμαι. The word is so used, Luke ii. 34, 1 Thess. iii. 3, and the meaning is, Knowing that I have not *taken upon myself* the work of preaching the Gospel, but that I am ordained thereto by God, see 1 Cor. ix. 16; or it may mean 'jaceo in vinculis,' i. e. 'knowing that I am in prison on account of Christ and the Gospel, and so am unable to preach throughout the city, they, out of a feeling of love, whereby they desire the salvation of souls, make up for my inability by their preaching. The first, however, is much the best interpretation, and more in accordance with the English version, "am set," which is equivalent to "am appointed," that is to say, appointed by God.

for the defence of the Gospel.

Knowing that I am a champion of the Catholic Faith, especially in having been called to maintain it before Nero.

18. **What then ?**

Τί γάρ; Scil. διαφέρει, an elliptical form of speech. But what does this matter to me? he would say. I do not discuss the *intention* wherewith they preach Christ, my only care being that Christ should be preached. "He passed over the evil for the sake of the good that followed [m]."

---

[m] Estius.

notwithstanding, every way,

"Sive modo simulato sive sincero [n]." "The Apostle speaks cautiously, not giving a command, but simply saying how the matter stood. For if it had been in his power he would have changed their designs; but since he could not, he passes over the evil reasons which moved them, and likewise the perverse end that they had in view. God was bringing *good* out of it; and for that he rejoices [o]." See, then, the wisdom of the Apostle! He did not vehemently accuse them; for this would only have excited them to greater bitterness; he simply mentioned the *result* with thankfulness. He did not lay it down as a rule, 'Let Christ be so preached,' but he was reporting the event; for, as St. Augustine well remarks [p], "In no wise could he say, in order that Christ may afterwards be preached, let Him first be denied."

whether in pretence,

Πρόφασις signifies not only a *pretext* and so is opposed to αἰτία, a *true cause*, but also an *occasion;* and so it seems to be taken here; thus, by all means, whether by *occasion* only, i. e. accidentally, and not by a designed causality; or, whether by *truth*, i. e. by a direct, real way of effecting the end in view; in either case I rejoice.

or in truth,

Εἴτε ἀληθείᾳ: this expression must be understood to mean 'sincerity, honesty of purpose,' as at 1 Cor. v. 8, where εἰλικρίνεια and ἀλήθεια are joined together.

Christ is preached;

The one object that was ever near to the Apostle's heart.

St. Augustine says [q], " It was truth which they preached, though they preached not with truth, that is, with a true heart. These now speak what they believe not, and are therefore reprobate; although they may be profitable unto those whom the Lord teacheth, saying, "Whatsoever they

---

[n] Zanchius. [o] Aretius. [p] Contra Mendacium, 16. [q] In Ps. cxvi. 1.

bid you observe, that observe and do; but do not ye after their works, for they say, and do not [r]."

and I therein do rejoice,

viz. that Christ is preached; i.e. I rejoice in the *fact*, and not in the *way* in which it is done. Estius says, "It is better to have a hireling for a shepherd than none at all." And so St. Augustine, who, borrowing an illustration from agriculture, says that the evil disposition of husbandmen does not affect the crop.

yea, and will rejoice.

The ground of his joy is twofold; first, that a certain portion of the brethren preach the Gospel with such fidelity, and, secondly, that the efforts of his adversaries are overruled by God for the advancement of the Faith. Hence the repetition of these words.

Note here, (I.) how when a person is bent, as St. Paul was, solely on promoting God's honour and glory, he rises above all the attacks of envy. By the grace of God he is enabled to turn the most venomous shafts of malice and rancour into instruments of good.

And (II.), that "if we envy another person who does anything for Christ, our envy passes on to Christ. We pretend to wish the benefit to come not from others but from ourselves. But this cannot be for Christ's sake, but for our own; otherwise it would be a matter of indifference whether the good were done by others or ourselves; we should say as St. Paul said, 'whether in pretence,' &c. In the same spirit Moses answered when some would have excited his displeasure against Eldad and Medad, because they prophesied." Numb. xi. 29 [s].

St. Augustine [t], referring to this verse, says, "For they proclaimed Christ; through 'envy' indeed, but still Christ. Regard not the inducement whereof, but the person whom they preach. Is Christ preached to thee of envy? Look at Christ, eschew the envy. Do not copy the bad preacher, but copy the good Christ who is preached to thee."

---

[r] Matt. xxiii. 3.   [s] St. Chrys. in 1 Tim. i. 14.   [t] Hom. v. 10, in Joh.

Nothing can fairly be drawn from this verse to support the unauthorized teaching of dissenters, since even admitting that the word 'preach' is here used in its modern sense, it is perfectly clear that St. Paul is not speaking of such as are *out* of the pale of the Church, but of those who are within its Communion. They were *brethren* of whom he was speaking, though undoubtedly *false brethren*. He would have held far different language towards schismatics or heretics. Thus, Rom. xvi. 17, "Now I beseech you, brethren, mark them which cause divisions and offences contrary to the doctrine which ye have learned, and avoid them."

St. Cyprian[u], remarking on this verse, says plainly that St. Paul "was not speaking of heretics, or of their baptism, whence it could be shewn that he had laid down anything thereto relating. He was speaking of brethren, whether of such as walked disorderly and contrary to ecclesiastical discipline, or such as kept the truth of the Gospel in the fear of God. And he alleged that some of these spoke the word of the Lord stedfastly and fearlessly; others were acting in envy and strife; that some had maintained benevolent affection towards himself, others had cherished malevolent strife."

19. This verse contains further cause for joy.

For I know

Either by direct revelation, or from the earnest contemplation of God's dealings, which teach that all things work together for good to those who love Him; or, most probably, by the assurance of hope. See next verse.

that this

i. e. The greater spread of the preaching of Christ, and the consequent increase of believers. It may perhaps refer to the 'affliction,' of verse 16; but the former interpretation is best.

shall turn to

ἀποβήσεται. Compare Luke xxi. 13. ἀποβήσεται δὲ ὑμῖν

---

[u] Ep. lxxiii. 12, ad Jubaianum.

εἰς μαρτύριον. "Quod mihi nocere putant in salutem provenict; quia non solum per verbum et passionem meam, sed etiam per odium Christi Ecclesia augmentatur ˣ."

my salvation

It not only will not "add affliction to my bonds ʸ," as they intend, but will turn out 'to my salvation' (εἰς σωτηρίαν); this word meaning either present deliverance from the power of Nero, or, better, eternal life and glory. How beautifully does the Apostle here shew that the enmity and jealousy of his adversaries will be overruled by God for the furtherance of the Gospel, and so be the means of increasing his own individual happiness! But it is to be observed that as the pronoun 'my' does not occur in the Greek, the word 'salvation' need not necessarily be referred to St. Paul, but may mean the salvation of mankind in general. This is one of the texts in which it is impossible to determine which of two perfectly legitimate meanings was in the mind of the Apostle at the time when he was writing the passage. Alford says decisively that σωτηρία, *from the context*, must refer to his own spiritual advantage, and this certainly seems the most probable idea; still it must be said that herein he differs from St. Chrysostom, Theodoret, Michaelis, and other good authorities.

This verse furnishes a striking proof of the marvellous way in which God makes all things work together for the good of the faithful; just as the skilful apothecary compounds wholesome medicines out of the most poisonous drugs. "Eventus est in manu Domini positus, non invidorum arbitrio, ut eliciant id quod ipsi cupiunt. Magna est consolatio eventum scire Dei judicio gubernari, et non hominum libidini permissum esse ᶻ."

through your prayer,

He incidentally seeks the prayers of the Philippians, and points out the way in which his afflictions will turn to 'salvation.' "He takes the prayers as the cause, and the supply of the Spirit as the effect ᵃ." "By a delicate touch

---

ˣ Sedulius.   ʸ ver. 16.   ᶻ Aretius.   ᵃ Vorstius.

at the same time of personal humility, and loving appreciation of their spiritual eminence and value to him, he rests the advancement of his own salvation, on the supply of the Holy Spirit won for him by their prayers [b]." We may gather from this verse how much ministers need the prayers of their people. If St. Paul, who had done and suffered so much for the Name of the Lord Jesus, and for whom 'a crown of righteousness' was already 'laid up [c],' could speak of his 'salvation' as being *advanced* by the prayers of the faithful, how earnestly should Christ's ministers, in a day of trial and rebuke, invite their people to remember them and their special needs, more particularly in the presence of the blessed Sacrament!

and the supply of the Spirit of Jesus Christ,

'Supply,' ἐπιχορηγία, 'subministratio;' see remarks on Eph. iv. 16. " Ideo ' subministratio' dicitur, quia non quod adversarii volunt, sed aliud in occulto Spiritus subministrat [d]." It is called "the Spirit of Jesus Christ as well because He proceeds from Christ according to His Divine Nature, as because He leads to Christ [e]."

Observe how closely St. Paul connects the prayers of the faithful with "the supply of the Spirit of Jesus Christ," i.e. with the help of God, and that he mentions 'prayer' *first*, not, indeed, as being the worthier of the two, but because it is by this that 'the supply, &c.,' is obtained. Rom. xv. 30, 31; compare 2 Cor. i. 11; Philem. 22.

For reasons why ministers are specially entitled to the prayers of their people, see Commentary on Ephesians, p. 395.

20. According to my earnest expectation and my hope,

St. Chrysostom [f] explains the word ἀποκαραδοκία ('expectation') to mean ἡ μεγάλη καὶ ἐπιτεταμένη προσδοκία. Alford, however, objects to the translation 'earnest expectation,' and says that ἀπό never has this meaning in composition; still less is ἀπό superfluous, but καραδοκεῖν signifies ' to at-

---

[b] Alford. [c] 2 Tim. iv. 8. [d] Sedulius.
[e] Caietan. [f] In Rom. viii. 19.

tend,' 'look out,' and ἀπό adds the signification 'from a particular position;' or, better still, that of exhaustion, 'look out until it be fulfilled,' as in the Latin word *exspectare*. This explanation gives a very good sense. The whole phrase, 'my expectation and hope,' is a hendiadys, and means 'my hopeful waiting for the result.' "Quod vehementer expecto et spero futurum [g]." See Ps. xxxiv. 22.

Observe what stress the Apostle lays on trust in God! So mighty a thing is a well-grounded confidence, a hope that maketh not ashamed! We must also notice from this place that everything is not to be left to the prayers of *others*. We must not be unmindful of ourselves, but must wait diligently upon God in prayer, with a hopeful expectation for the result.

that in nothing I shall be ashamed,

Some refer these words to what immediately precedes, as if he said, 'I hope that in nothing I shall be ashamed.' But this sense is weak, and it is better to understand them in connexion with, 'I know that this shall turn to my salvation,' &c.; q. d. 'I am persuaded that this malice and envy now exhibited by my adversaries will turn out to my happiness and glory; because whatever happens, prosperous or adverse, I shall not be put to shame.' It is to be observed that he expresses no hope that he will be exempt from afflictions or persecutions. His confident expectation is, that come what may, no *shame* or confusion will attach to him. Zanchius explains the words "Novi et spero Deum non permissurum ut ego Christum aut abnegem, aut dissimulem," &c.

but that with all boldness,

ἐν πάσῃ παρρησίᾳ. Παρρησία means, in the first instance, liberty of speech, and then it comes to signify confidence in general. "Significat agendi loquendique ingenuam et imperterritam libertatem [h]." He says not merely 'with boldness,' but 'with *all* boldness,' of course in direct contrast with αἰσχυνθήσομαι. "Seest thou then, he says,

---

[g] Vorstius.   [h] Estius.

how entirely I am freed from shame? For if the fear of death had cut short his boldness, death would have been worthy of shame; but if death at its approach casts no terror on me, no shame is here; but whether I live, through life I will not be ashamed, for I still preach the Gospel; or whether I die, through death I will not be ashamed, for death hath not disgraced me, since I still exhibit the same boldness. Do not, when I mention my bonds, think shame of the matter; so manifold good hath it caused to me, that it hath given confidence to others. For that we should be bound for Christ is no shame; but for fear of bonds to betray aught that is Christ's, this is shame. When there is no such thing, bonds are even a cause of boldness [i]."

as always,

i.e. from the time when I became an Apostle of Christ. " Ex præteritis sumens fiduciam futurorum [k]."

so now also

i. e. now that I am in prison.

Christ shall be magnified

μεγαλυνθήσεται : for this word see Luke i. 46, 58; Acts x. 46, xix. 17. His humility prevents him from saying 'I shall magnify,' &c., but he says, ' Christ shall be magnified.' Whichever way his imprisonment turns out, he says it will be well. "If I endure torments, they who hear of it will say, 'That God is great for Whose Name His servants fear not to die [l].'"

in my body,

The word 'body' is here highly emphatic. Christ was to be glorified not by his soul or spirit only, (as some would have it,) but actually in his 'body.' His life or death in the *body* would be a glorifying of Christ. Such is the result of the Incarnation. (Compare Rom. viii. 11, "But if the Spirit of him that raised up Jesus from the dead dwell

---

[i] St. Chrysostom, in loc.   [k] Caietan.   [l] Haymo.

in you, He that raised up Christ from the dead *shall also quicken your mortal bodies* by His Spirit that dwelleth in you." See also chap. iii. 21, and the remarks made there.) It is worthy of notice that the carnal are not said to glory in the 'body,' (ἐν τῷ σώματι,) but in the 'flesh,' (ἐν τῇ σαρκί [m]) : a most important distinction. The martyrs are said δοξάζειν τὸν Θεόν by their *death*. See John xxi. 19.

whether it be by life, or by death.

Compare Rom. xiv. 8; i. e. "whether my adversaries compass my death, then Christ shall be magnified in my body by the constancy with which I suffer it; or whether I shall escape from their malice, Christ shall be magnified in the same body, which He has so often delivered from their snares [n]." In the occurrence, therefore, of either life or death the Apostle would not be ashamed; the one bringing active service for Christ in the world; the other, union with Him in heaven. Sedulius well remarks "that St. Paul here triumphs over his enemies, because they are not able to harm him. For if they kill him he will be crowned with martyrdom; if they keep him alive, he will by preaching Christ procure more abundant fruit."

It is not probable that St. Paul had any supernatural means of knowing what the issue of his imprisonment would be. Bengel well says, "Paulus ipse nesciebat quo evasurum esset; neque enim Apostoli erant omniscii, sed potius in rebus ad sese pertinentibus per fidem et patientiam exercebantur."

21. For to me to live is Christ,

He here supplies a reason for what he had said in ver. 19, shewing that he is fully prepared for any turn of fortune." "Let matters fall out as they will," he would say, "one object is immovably fixed before me, viz. Christ. All my life, the powers of my soul and body, are His; *I live Christ;* my present and my future life are alike in Him." (See John i. 4.) What St. Paul intends to convey is, "If I live it is to act Christ; that is to say, to do what Christ did

---

[m] Gal. vi. 13.   [n] Gagnæus.

in suffering and teaching in order to bring men to salvation, and this is (as Caietan calls it) *life* to me." "For the sake of this life he delivers up his mortal body that he may receive it again for eternity; and in this way he counts it gain to die for Christ[o]." In Col. iii. 4, Christ is called "our life." Caietan remarks, "As those who are given to the pleasure of hunting say that this pursuit is life to them, and as those who are addicted to the luxuries of the table say that meat and drink is life to them, and so in the same way of others; thus St. Paul says that Christ is life to him, because he has consecrated all his desires and all his pursuits to Christ."

and to die is gain.

Because death to a good man is the day-break of eternal brightness; 'janua vitæ,' as St. Bernard calls it, a valley of Achor, a door of hope[p] to give entrance into paradise. "Accounting it," says St. Cyprian[q], "the greatest gain to be no longer holden of the claims of this life; no more exposed to all sins and vices of the flesh; redeemed from poignant tribulations, and delivered from the poisoned jaws of the devil, to pass at the call of Christ into the joy of everlasting salvation." Haymo explains the verse thus: "If I shall die under punishment, it is the greatest gain to me, and Christ will be more and more preached. Or, it is gain to me simply to die, because if I die, I shall receive the greatest gain, that is, eternal life."

See, then, the wonderful effect of divine grace! "He who accounted it great gain to him to slay Christ in His disciples, now holds Christ to be his life, and death gain[r]."

How fully it may be permitted to the faithful to realize the truth that 'to die is gain,' is shewn by the glorious death of the Venerable Bede, attesting to all that even the valley of the shadow of death may smile like the green pastures, and be tranquil as the waters of comfort, to one who descends into it sustained by the staff, and defended by the rod of the Good Shepherd, Whose guidance he has followed

---

[o] St. Ambrose.   [p] Hosea ii. 15.   [q] De Mort., 4.
[r] St. Greg., Moral., xi. 16.

all his life through. His death is thus described by the author of *Justorum Semita*, who quotes probably from St. Cuthbert's Life of the Saint: "About the hour of none he said to Cuthbert, 'I have a few trifles in a box, run and fetch them, and call the brethren of the monastery that I may distribute these among them.' When they were come he gave each of them a little memorial of his love, and besought them all to be mindful of his soul in their prayers, and especially when they offered the adorable sacrifice. The brethren wept abundantly; but he comforted them and said, 'The time of my freedom is at hand. I long to be dissolved and be with Christ; for my soul desires to see Christ my King in His glory.'"

The following beautiful passage from St. Ignatius, Ep. ad Rom., is quoted by Wordsworth in his Greek Testament: "Suffer me to be the food of wild beasts, that I may attain unto God. I do not *command* you as Peter and Paul did; they were Apostles, I am condemned. They were freemen, I am only a slave. Suffer me to die. Pardon me in this; I know what is best for me. Now I begin to be a disciple. Let nothing that is seen or unseen envy me the joy of being Christ's. Fire and the Cross, the assaults of wild beasts, lacerations, distractions, and dispersions of my bones, the crushing of my joints, the grinding of my whole body—welcome, welcome to them all—so that I may gain Him! I covet not kingdoms of earth. I long to *die into Christ Jesus*, rather than to be king of the world. Him I seek Who died for me; Him I long for Who rose again for me. Now my *birth* is near. Forgive me, brethren; do not hinder me from being *born;* do not desire that I should *die*—I who desire to be God's. Allow me to emerge into the pure light; when I shall arrive there I shall be a man of God. Suffer me to be an imitator of the Passion of my God."

St. Chrysostom uses this verse as ground for consolation on the death of friends. "Let us," he says, "lament for them, let us assist them according to our power, let us think of some assistance for them, small though it be, yet still able to help them. How, and in what way? By praying ourselves for them, by entreating others to make prayers for them, by continually giving to the poor on their behalf. This deed hath some consolation; for hear the words of God Himself when He says, 'I will defend this city for Mine own sake, and for My servant David's sake.' If the remembrance only of a just man has so great power, how, when deeds are done for one, will it not have power? Not in vain did the Apostles order that remembrance should be made of the dead in the dreadful mysteries. They know that great gain resulteth to them, and great assistance; for when the whole people stands with uplifted hands, a priestly assembly, and that awful Sacrifice lies displayed, how shall we not prevail with God by our entreaties for them?"

There is another reading here of χρηστόν for Χριστός,—'to me life is good, though death is gain;' but this is a very inferior reading; for the whole force of the passage is to contrast the Apostle's death with his life; q. d. Christ shall be glorified in me whether I live or die. If I live, it is Christ to me; i. e. I become by suffering more and more like Christ. If I die, it is gain to me, for then I depart to Christ.

22. But if I live

The Apostle here begins to treat of the first member of the alternative; the second is in ch. ii. 17. Lest any one should think that reproach is cast upon life, lest any one should say, if we gain no advantage here, wherefore do we not make away with ourselves? He answers, By no means. It is open to us to profit even here; if we live not *this*, but *another* life [s]. Εἰ, 'if,' in this verse does not imply doubt; the meaning is, *since* to live in the flesh, &c.

in the flesh,

i. e. in this perishable body. Compare Gal. ii. 20. "Limitat; nam etiam morientes vivunt [t]."

this

i. e. life in the body. It seems best to connect τοῦτο in this verse with τὸ ζῆν, and to construe 'this life in the flesh.'

---

[s] St. Chrysostom, in loc.   [t] Bengel.

There is no reason that this should not be done, and it is preferable to making τοῦτο redundant, as some do. The full meaning will then be, "If then this life in the flesh is καρπὸς ἔργου, worth the trouble, which it assuredly is if it makes me like Christ, καὶ, *then*, I cannot tell which I shall choose." He would naturally prefer to die, and be with Christ; still, if his living glorified God, and was Christ to himself, he would consent to it.

is the fruit of my labour:

"For the edification of others[u]." "Mihi maximus laborum atque operum meorum fructus est[x]:" i. e. the occasion of my bringing forth much fruit by winning souls to Christ. Compare Rom. i. 13. The expression καρπὸς ἔργου would appear to be a Latinism *operæ pretium*, and to signify 'worth my labour,' 'worth doing,' or, as we should say, 'a desirable thing.'

Observe here the total want of selfishness displayed by the Apostle. Another person would be discouraged if he did not receive some fruit from his toils, more especially when they had been very irksome and severe; but not so St. Paul; with him toil and fruit were identical. Cicero well says, "Ego mihi fructum amicitiæ propono ipsam amicitiam, quâ nihil est uberius."

yet what I shall choose I wot not.

καὶ τί αἱρήσομαι : for the meaning of καὶ in this place see above. He had declared death to be gain, yet life is needful, not indeed for himself, but for his spiritual children. As Fulgentius says, he had "mortem in desiderio, vitam in patientiâ."

'what,' i. e. of these two things ; either that by dying I may be with Christ; or living, may bring forth fruit for the Church. St. Paul professes himself unable to choose. On both sides were weighty reasons, "To remove to the assembly of the saints was for the good of the Apostle, but, on the other hand, he sees that the Churches stand in need of his help[y]."

---

[u] Sedulius. [x] Wetstein. [y] Aretius.

How great must have been his love for souls, that he could postpone his own happiness to the welfare of his converts! It is only by considering what his life was, its toils, anxieties and distresses, (see 2 Cor. xi. 23, and following,) the fightings from without and the fears within, that we shall be able at all to estimate the nature of the sacrifice which he made in choosing life for the sake of his spiritual children. We may, perhaps, think it wonderful that he should doubt, even for a moment, what to choose; but we must not forget that, after all, his choice was *Christ;* for he chose life, that he might be the means of winning more souls. Compare Rom. ix. 3, " For I could wish that myself were accursed from Christ for my brethren, my kinsmen according to the flesh."

St. Chrysostom says[z], 'The blessed Paul placing before himself the alternative of living upon earth, and departing and being with Christ, decides for the former."

23. For I am in a strait betwixt two,

συνέχομαι ἐκ τῶν δύο, 'coarctor ex his duobus;' (compare 2 Sam. xxiv. 14;) i.e. I am perplexed, held in, kept back from decision by *the* two, (the article being highly emphatic,) viz. τὸ ζῆν and τὸ ἀποθανεῖν, for it is about these two that he has already been speaking. The meaning is, I am drawn in two different directions; on the one hand by the desire of being with Christ, on the other, by the love of the brethren. For συνέχομαι in this sense, see Luke xii. 50; Acts xviii. 5. See also St. Augustine, *De doctr. Christ.*, lib. iii. c. 2. It is just possible that the use of this word may have been suggested to the Apostle by the circumstance of his being at this time a prisoner, and bound to two soldiers. Compare Acts xii. 6.

having a desire to depart,

τὴν ἐπιθυμίαν ἔχων εἰς τὸ ἀναλῦσαι; literally, 'having *my* desire towards,' τὴν ἐπιθυμίαν ἔχων being much stronger than the simple ἐπιθυμῶν. In order to make the English

---

[z] In Gal. i. 4.

Version correct, the reading should be ἐπιθυμίαν ἔχων τοῦ, hence the delicacy of the sense is lost. The Apostle here gives the reason for his being 'in a strait;' he does not, however, say, 'to die,' but 'to depart,' ἀναλῦσαι, Vulg. 'dissolvi,' the idea probably being that of *unharnessing* the spirit, as opposed to ἐπιμένειν ἐν τῇ σαρκί, 'to remain in the trammels of the flesh.' The plain word 'die' is very seldom used of Christians. As the heathen used scrupulously to avoid it, so St. Paul (a classical scholar) seems to prefer using another word whenever he can. 'Depart, decease, sleep, rest, cease,' &c., are the words which find most favour with him. Bp. Andrewes remarks beautifully on 1 Cor. xv. 20 : " Christ is risen from the *dead*, the firstfruits not of the *dead*, but *of them that sleep.* You see His rising hath wrought a change." We should never forget, therefore, the important bearing which the word 'depart,' and kindred terms, should have upon Christian doctrine, since they teach that the change involved in death is but of place, not of company. 'What do I here?' i. e. in the world, was a favourite saying of St. Augustine's holy mother. Camerinus ordered in his will that the following line should be inscribed on his tomb :—

" Vita mihi mors est ; mors mihi vita nova est."

The 'strait' in which St. Paul felt himself may be illustrated by the words of Pontius, the deacon and biographer of St. Cyprian, who, speaking of his martyrdom, says, "What shall I here do? between joy at his passion and grief at bereavement my mind is divided, and two sorts of feelings oppress a breast too straitened for them. Shall I grieve that I was not his companion? but his triumph is to be celebrated. Shall I celebrate his triumph? but I am in grief that I am not his companion. To you, however, the truth is to be avowed, and simply, as you know it, that it was in my purpose to be so. In his glory I exult much and more than much, and yet I grieve more that I remain behind."

and to be with Christ,

This must be connected closely with 'to depart,' since

death *by itself* is not a thing to be desired or chosen, but only in so far as it unites us to Christ. The faithful in this life are 'in Christ,' and Christ is in them [a], but only those who are actually present in glory can be said to be 'with Christ [b].'

St. Chrysostom [c] shews that St. Paul's longing to depart is our example, and represents him as saying, "'I have tasted of the grace, and I cannot contain myself in the delay. I have the first-fruits of the Spirit, and I press on towards the whole. I have ascended to the third heaven; I have seen that glory which is unutterable; I have beheld the shining palaces; I have learnt what joys I am deprived of while I linger here, and therefore do I groan.' For suppose any one had conducted thee into princely halls, and shewn thee the gold glittering everywhere on the walls, and all the rest of the glorious show; if from thence he had led thee back afterward to a poor man's hut, and promised that in a short time he would bring thee back to those palaces, and would there give thee a perpetual mansion: tell me, wouldest thou not indeed languish with desire, and feel impatient, even at these few days? Thus, then, think of heaven and of earth, and groan with Paul, not because of death, but because of the present life!"

which is far better:

πολλῷ μᾶλλον κρεῖσσον, the comparative is doubled, by a common Hebraism, to shew the exceeding earnestness of the Apostle. Compare Mark vii. 36, and 2 Cor. vii. 13. St. Ambrose [d] mentions three reasons why the faithful Christian should desire to be 'dissolved,' or 'depart,' because there are three chains which bind us down to earth: (1) the pains and suffering of the body; (2) lusts and sinful affections; (3) the eager pursuit of worldly objects. Death breaks these chains, and so sets us free. As might be expected, this is a very favourite passage with the Fathers for consolation on the death of friends. Tertullian says [e], "He

---

[a] 2 Cor. xiii. 5; Eph. iii. 17; 1 John iv. 13.
[b] 2 Cor. v. 8.
[c] On the Statues, v. 5.
[d] De Bono Mortis.
[e] De Patientiâ, ix.

that goeth before us is not to be mourned, but altogether to be longed for; and even this longing must be tempered with patience. For why shouldest thou not bear with moderation that he hath departed whom thou shalt presently follow? But impatience in such a matter augureth ill for our hope, and is a double dealing with our faith. Besides, we injure Christ, when, as each is called away by Him, we bear it impatiently, as though they were to be pitied. How 'much better' does the Apostle shew the desire of the Christian to be! Wherefore, if we impatiently mourn for others who have obtained this desire, we are unwilling to obtain it ourselves."

St. Chrysostom [f] makes use of this passage against sorcerers and those who professed to have dealings with the inhabitants of the other world; shewing that disembodied spirits are not allowed to roam about at pleasure. "It is evident," he says, "that after their departure hence our souls are led away into some place, having no more power of themselves to come back again, but awaiting that dreadful Day."

24. This verse contains the reason why St. Paul chose life; viz. that by his continued presence among his spiritual children he might further their faith.

Nevertheless to abide in the flesh

i. e. in this mortal body, as above, v. 22.

is more needful for you.

ἀναγκαιότερον δι' ὑμᾶς; the English Version misses the delicate sense contained in these words, which is, 'my remaining in the flesh is the more needful of the two alternatives *because of you;*' i. e. for your sake; and it is to be observed that the Apostle does not say to 'remain in the flesh' is less good, or less desirable; but, as if it were neither good nor desirable in itself, he says, 'more needful *because of you.*'

---

[f] Hom xxviii. 3, in Matt.

So Seneca, "Vitæ suæ adjici nihil desiderat suâ causâ, sed corum quibus utilis est [g]."

Speaking of the intensity of St. Paul's loving self-denial, St. Chrysostom says [h], 'Let one fast and deny himself, and be a martyr, and be burnt to death; but let another delay his martyrdom *for his neighbour's edification;* and let him not only delay it, but let him even depart without martyrdom; who will be the more approved after his removal hence? We need not have many words, nor a long circumlocution, for the blessed Paul is at hand, giving his judgment and saying, 'to depart and be with Christ is better, nevertheless to abide in the flesh is more needful for you;' even to his removal unto Christ did he prefer his neighbour's edification. For this is in the highest sense 'to be with Christ,' even to be doing His will; but nothing is so much His will, as that which is for one's neighbour's good."

What an admirable example does the Apostle here set for Christ's ministers to follow! Instead of seeking benefices and honours, to choose the lowest room; to deny themselves worldly honour and glory, for the edification of their flock! St. Chrysostom well describes the love that a minister should have for his people; "Oh! that I could always be with you. Yea rather, am I always with you; though not by bodily presence, yet by the power of love. For I have no other life but you, and the care of your salvation. As the husbandman hath no other anxiety but about his seeds and his harvests, and the pilot about the waves and the harbours, so the preacher is anxious with respect to his auditors and their progress, even as I am at this present time. Wherefore I bear you all upon my mind, not only here, but also at home. For if the multitude be great, and the measure of my heart be narrow, yet love is wide, and ye are not straitened in us [i]."

25. The Apostle here begins to treat of his grace in bonds, and the defence and confirmation of the Gospel, relatively to the Philippians.

---

[g] Ep. 98.   [h] Hom. lxxvii. 6, in Matt.   [i] On the Statues, ix. 1.

And having this confidence,

i. e. that my continued life in the flesh is needful for your spiritual welfare.

I know that I shall abide and continue with you all

Not that he had any absolute or certain source of knowledge; but he spoke from reasonable conjecture. Sedulius, however, says, "Spiritu prophetico promittit."

for your furtherance and joy of faith;

i. e. that I may promote your spiritual interests[j], and fill you with that holy joy which results from a living faith. It is to be observed, that *advance* in the faith is inseparable from *joy*. The more we are penetrated with faith the more we rejoice[k], and gloom and moroseness are pretty certain signs that vital religion is absent. 'Furtherance and joy' are a hendiadys for 'joyful advance.'

This verse proves that the Epistle was written during St. Paul's *first* imprisonment, as he was put to death in his second. Bengel says, "Non dubium est quin Paulus ex priore captivitate in illa climata redierit." The use of the expressions 'abide' and 'continue' would seem to point out that the Apostle anticipated a lengthened sojourn among the Philippians, on his release from prison.

There is a remarkable passage in Seneca, Epist. 104, which illustrates this verse. "Indulgendum est enim honestis affectibus, et interdum, etiamsi premunt causæ, spiritus in honorem suorum vel cum tormento revocandus, et in ipso ore retinendus est: cum bono viro vivendum sit, non quamdiu juvat, sed quamdiu oportet. Ille qui non uxorem non amicum tanti putat ut diutius in vitâ commoretur, qui perseverat mori, delicatus est. Hoc quoque imperet sibi animus, ubi utilitas suorum exigit; nec tantum si vult mori, sed si cœpit, intermittat, et suis se commodet. Ingentis animi est alienâ causâ ad vitam reverti; quod magni viri sæpe fecerunt."

---

[j] Rom. i. 11.   [k] Rom. v. 1—5.

26. That your rejoicing may be more abundant

Τὸ καύχημα ὑμῶν, somewhat stronger than 'rejoicing.' It is probably equivalent here to ἀγαλλίαμα, *exultatio*, or perhaps *gratulatio*, or *gloriatio*, i.e. boasting, in a good sense. Estius says the meaning of the passage is, "Ut cum liberatus et vobis restitutus fuero, possitis affatim de me Apostolo vestro gloriari, vobisque gratulari, sed hoc in Christo Jesu." Others, however, understand it to mean, That I may the more abundantly boast myself of you in Christ Jesus, when I have returned to you, and seen how much you have advanced in Christian doctrine and discipline during my absence. The former meaning is probably the correct one; being more in harmony with the general tone of the Apostle's character and his language throughout this Epistle, which is to ignore *self*.

The difference between καύχημα and καύχησις must not be overlooked, καύχημα being the *thing boasted of*, the object of boasting; καύχησις the *act* of boasting[1]. This difference (a very important one) is often lost sight of by translators, e. g. κήρυγμα[m] *is the thing preached*, not 'preaching,' as translated in the English version; this would be κήρυξις. The 'foolishness of preaching,' then, does not mean a *bad sermon*, but a subject which seems unphilosophical. And so in this place τὸ καύχημα ὑμῶν means that *the reason you have for boasting* may abound through my restoration to you. See also 1 Cor. v. 6, οὐ καλὸν τὸ καύχημα ὑμῶν, 'the reasons you give for glorying are not good.'

in Christ Jesus for me

St. Paul never even for a moment separates himself from Christ. He is the Central Figure in all his thoughts. See Commentary on the Ephesians, pp. 127, 141.

by my coming to you again.

i. e. that from my unexpected return to you, you may be able to see how great is the care which God has for His people.

---

[1] Rom. iii. 27.   [m] 1 Cor. i. 21.

27. Only

From an intense desire of receiving good fruits from among the Philippians, he passes on to exhortation, calling upon them to *shew* themselves such as he believes them to be. As if he had said, Dismiss all your anxiety on my behalf; this is the one thing that I have to ask of you in the prospect of my speedy return, viz. that your life be answerable to the holiness of your profession.

let your conversation be

Πολιτεύεσθε, 'play the citizen.' There is great force and beauty in this word as used here, because πολίτευμα was applied to the *imperfect citizenship* (municipium) of the Romans. See chap. iii. 20; compare also Acts xxiii. 1. As if he had said, "Play the citizen of heaven, though your heavenly citizenship is as yet necessarily *imperfect*[n]." At the last day we shall be made 'full citizens' (*Quirites*, καλοὶ κἀγαθοί) of the celestial Jerusalem.

as becometh the gospel of Christ:

See Commentary on the Ephesians, pp. 216, 217. "To walk worthily in the Gospel is to believe in Christ and to teach Him according to the precepts of the Gospel; to live according to His commands, to trust in His promises, and to do all things according to His will[o]."

that whether I come and see you, or else be absent,

Shewing that he did not feel certain how his imprisonment would end. See above, verse 25.

I may hear of your affairs,

This is explained by what immediately follows, where he tells them what he desires to see when present among them, and to hear of when absent, viz. :—

that ye stand fast in one spirit,

"Ecce societas gratiæ spiritualis[p]." In using the word

---

[n] Heb. xiii. 14.   [o] Haymo.   [p] Caietan.

'stand,' the Apostle borrows a figure from wrestlers and others who contended in the Grecian games. See remarks in Commentary on Eph. vi. 11, 13, 14.

He here exhorts the Philippians to *unity*. As the Spirit is one, he would say, so must they who are under His blessed influence be *one* also. See Acts iv. 32, and Commentary on Ephesians iv. 3. Zanchius remarks, "He well shews that perseverance is not of our own strength or merit, but is the free gift of the Holy Ghost." It is not necessary, however, to restrict the meaning of 'one Spirit' to the Holy Ghost. It may also mean that identity of thought and feeling which should ever exist among Christians.

with one mind

Μιᾷ ψυχῇ, "quasi vobis omnibus una tantum esset anima charitatis [q]." Aristotle calls a friend ἄλλος αὐτός. See remarks on chap. ii. 20, and compare 1 Cor. i. 10.

striving together

συναθλοῦντες, a very emphatic word. He still preserves the metaphor taken from wrestling. "Ecce societas ad confirmationem Evangelii [r]." 'Striving,' not *amongst* each other, or *against* each other; but helping one another, and me also, in spreading the common faith.

for the faith

Τῇ πίστει, i. e. ὑπὲρ τῆς πίστεως. See Jude 3, "that ye should earnestly contend for the faith." It may also be rendered *per fidem*, being that by means of which the conflict is to be carried on.

of the gospel;

i. e. "which faith rests on the Gospel as its foundation, and consequently upon the unconquered strength of Christ [s]." This shews that it is not for trifles that Christians have to contend, but for the Truth of the living God.

---

[q] Corn. à Lap.   [r] Caietan.   [s] Beza.

28. And in nothing terrified by your adversaries:
Compare with this verse Ps. iii. 6, "I will not be afraid for ten thousands of the people: that have set themselves against me round about."

'Terrified,' πτυρόμενοι, "is a word properly used of horses[t]," and thence transferred to men. The figure is taken from gladiators, who with a fierce assault and savage gestures rush upon their antagonists in order to terrify them. "Ecce societas ad defensionem Evangelii[u]." The Apostle would say, Let not persecutions excited by wicked men disturb or terrify you. There is no real cause for alarm; since the affliction which they endeavour to bring upon you will cast them down to hell, but will be the means of exalting you to heaven. Compare 1 John v. 4: "This is the victory that overcometh the world, even our faith."

which is to them an evident token of perdition,

"Quod vos terrent et affligunt perditionis illis causa est, vobis salutis, et hoc Dei gratia[x]." The English Version 'evident token' seems hardly to express the force of the original ἔνδειξις. From the way in which the verb ἐνδεῖξαι is used elsewhere (see 2 Tim. iv. 14, 'Ἀλέξανδρος ὁ χαλκεὺς πολλά μοι κακὰ ἐνεδείξατο), it is plain that the word 'token' inadequately translates its substantive ἔνδειξις. It must be taken, therefore, not so much for a *token*, as a *cause*, q. d., the malice of the Gentiles is the *cause* of their destruction, and at the same time the *cause* of your salvation. For that affliction is not only a *token*, but also a *cause* of salvation, appears from 2 Cor. iv. 17. If the English Version 'token' is accepted, ἔνδειξις will be a *shewing* by signs or tokens, as opposed to ἀπόδειξις, logical proof; and then the meaning will be, 'the opposition of your adversaries is a proof of their being lost, and of your being saved by a salvation which comes of God, because you suffer as Christ did.'

and that of God.

Since this freedom from terror is not to be acquired by

---

[t] Bengel. [u] Caietan. [x] Gagneius.

our own natural powers it is well said to be 'of God,' "Who wills that His Own children should be crowned when proved, as Job is permitted to be tempted [y]."

Zanchius says, "There is therefore no reason why the stronger should wax insolent, or the weaker become fearful, since they are able to seek and obtain from God fortitude and perseverance." And Hemmingius, "The Apostle ascribes the victory to God as its Author for two reasons; viz. that the faithful should not faint in their minds if anything is to be suffered for the Gospel, and may not become insolent and be puffed up, as if they could effect anything through their own excellence."

The word 'terrified,' used in this verse by the Apostle, is suggestive of a very solemn line of thought, as shewing the nature of the devices of the adversary with whom we have to contend. In the first instance he endeavours to overcome our constancy by bringing to bear upon us all *pleasurable* things, thereby enticing us to gratify our appetites to the full; but at last, when these have failed, he brings all *painful* things. He first knocks at the door of *desire*, and when he finds that closed against him, at the door of *fear*. It was so with our blessed Lord, as will be seen by comparing the temptation of the wilderness with the temptation of the garden. See especially the words "for a season [z];" implying that there was another and a fiercer temptation still to come.

29. For unto you it is given in the behalf of Christ, not only to believe on Him, but also to suffer for His sake;

St. Paul here ascribes the very highest position to sufferings endured for the sake of Christ, a position even above faith itself, and the power of working miracles, and as conferring such an honour as the most exalted angel in heaven is not permitted to enjoy:—"Non solum ut fidei

---

[y] Sedulius. [z] Luke iv. 13.

meritum, sed etiam martyrii meritum præmium habeatis, dum vos tentari Deus patitur ut vincatis [a]."

We learn hence (1), That to suffer for Christ's sake is grace and favour, ("it is given," ἐχαρίσθη,) and that if the grace be used aright it merits the highest rewards. (2) That they who infer from these words that faith is so exclusively the gift of God, that men are merely the passive recipients of it, have just as much reason for pronouncing that we can possibly be considered to have suffered for the name of Christ without the concurrence of our own wills; the expression 'given' being applied equally to both.

St. Augustine in a passage of singular beauty [b] shews how persecution and suffering helped to propagate the Faith. "Let the Jews," he says, "rage madly, and be filled with jealousy; Stephen be stoned, Saul keep the raiment of them who stone him, Saul, one day to be the Apostle Paul. Let Stephen be killed, the Church of Jerusalem dispersed in confusion; out of it go forth burning brands, and spread themselves and spread their flame. For in the Church of Jerusalem, as it were, burning brands were set on fire by the Holy Spirit, when they had all one soul and one heart to God-ward. When Stephen was stoned that pile suffered persecution: the brands were dispersed, and the world was set on fire. . . . Let the nations hear, let the nations believe, let the nations multiply, let the Lord's empurpled spouse spring forth from the blood of martyrs."

Speaking of suffering for the sake of Christ, St. Chrysostom says that it is a gift "far more wonderful than raising the dead or working miracles, as there I am a debtor to Christ, but here I have Christ as my debtor." "Your cruelty is our glory," said the primitive martyrs. "I had rather be a martyr than a monarch," said St. Ignatius. "It is to my loss if you defraud me of anything in my sufferings," said another holy martyr. And St. Augustine testifies that Crispina rejoiced aloud when she was apprehended, when she was brought to trial, when she was condemned, and when she was led away to execution.

---

[a] Sedulius. [b] Hom. lxvi. 6, in Nov. Test.

And this, surely, when rightly considered, should be the ground of the deepest and holiest Christian joy, viz. that God thinks us worthy to suffer *anything* for the love of Him who suffered *everything* for love of us. In the case of St. Paul persecution followed close upon persecution,— there were tumults, fightings, scourgings, stonings[c],—the devil only relaxed his efforts for a moment to gain strength for a new assault, and yet these things only excited in him a *deeper rejoicing*. And so with the other Apostles: *suffering* was the groundwork of their most fervent joy; the utmost malice of their enemies was their source of triumph. It was in the inner prison, with their feet fast in the stocks, that SS. Paul and Silas sang hymns of victory[d]; and when St. Peter and the rest were dismissed by the council, their backs having been torn by rods, they rejoiced, not indeed because God had vouchsafed to them the power of working miracles, but because "they were counted *worthy to suffer shame* for His Name[e]."

30. **Having the same conflict**

St. Paul uses the word ἀγών ('conflict') in describing the sufferings of Christians to shew that he who suffers aright ever *strives* manfully lest he be overcome by an impatient spirit.

St. Cyprian[f], speaking of the fortitude of the martyrs, and the glorious strife between the tortures and the tortured, continues:—"The crowd of by-standers witnessed wondering the heavenly conflict, the conflict of God, the spiritual conflict, the battle of Christ; that His servants stood with voice unfettered, with minds unbroken, with courage given of God, of secular weapons indeed naked, but armed and trustful in the armour of faith. The tortured stood more resolute than the torturers, and the racked and mangled limbs vanquished the grappling-hooks that racked and mangled them. Long though it raged, the oft-renewed blow could not vanquish a faith invincible, although the closure of their bowels was

---

[c] 2 Cor. xi. 23—28.   [d] Acts xvi. 25.
[e] Acts v. 41.   [f] Ep. x. 1.

torn open, and now in God's servants not limbs, but wounds, were tortured. There flowed blood, that might extinguish the blazes of persecution, quench the flames and fires of hell by its glorious gore. Oh! what a spectacle was that to the Lord, how sublime, how great, how acceptable to the eyes of God, the fealty and devotion of His soldiery!"

which ye saw in me, and now hear to be in me.

He proposes himself as a pattern to them (as it were a *speculum fortitudinis*) of the way in which they should withstand all adversaries, so that they should not be crushed beneath the weight of the cross, nor cast aside their profession through the bitterness of affliction. He reminds them of the sufferings endured by himself, of which they had been eye-witnesses (see Acts xvi.), there being special stress on the words 'in me,' i.e. 'in me not terrified or cast down,' as a proof of what may be borne by one sustained by the grace of God. "Let it not therefore be thought unworthy in you to suffer those things wherein you behold us glorying [g]."

It appears from this verse that verse 29 must be parenthetical, and explanatory of 'to you of salvation, and that of God,' since the Greek is τὸν αὐτὸν ἀγῶνα ἔχοντες, and not ἔχουσι (dative), which it would be if this verse were connected with ὑμῖν in ver. 29. We gather from this passage, that after the departure of St. Paul the Philippian Christians were exposed to persecution, although no account of it is given in Holy Scripture.

---

[g] Sedulius.

SUMMARY OF CHAPTER II.

With many arguments and much fervour, St. Paul exhorts the Philippians to unity, humility, and perseverance. He promises that he will send Timothy and Epaphroditus, whom he separately commends to them.

The chief parts of this chapter are two :—

(1.) Hortatory, in which he encourages the Philippians to the practice of virtues worthy of the Christian calling, and takes occasion to dwell specially on the humiliation and exaltation of Christ, ver 1. to 18.

(2.) Commendatory, in which he specially commends St. Timothy and Epaphroditus to their love: ver. 19 to 30.

CHAP. II.

Ver. 1. See with what amazing earnestness the Apostle here entreats the Philippians, with love surpassing even that of the fondest parent! Estius has not done more than justice to this exhortation, when he calls it "oratio vehemens ac mira pathetica." Another writer, speaking of the exquisite tenderness of this verse, says, " Persuasion itself could not speak more persuasively." Nor shall we wonder at the exceeding earnestness of the Apostle's language when we consider the importance of the matters he is about to introduce, viz., four great points of the Christian life, which he proceeds severally to unfold.

St. Chrysostom remarks upon the affectionate fervour of the Apostle's language, and goes on to say, " We indeed remind men of our *carnal* claims; for example, if a father were to say to his son, 'If thou hast any reverence for thy father, if any remembrance of my care in nourishing thee, if any affection towards me, if any memory of my kindness, be not at enmity with thy brother. This is what I ask in return for all those things.' But Paul does not so; for he calls to our remembrance no carnal, but all of them *spiritual* benefits."

If there be therefore

It is to be observed that the use of the word 'if' in such a construction as this implies a strong and earnest affirmation.

any consolation in Christ,

q. d. If you are willing to afford to me, who am bound for the sake of Christ, any such consolation as it becomes one Christian to offer to another. The words 'in Christ' are added to shew that it is *spiritual* consolation which he asks at their hands, and that he is not actuated by mercenary motives. It may also mean, if you feel in yourselves any consolation arising from a sense of God's love and your forgiveness through Christ; but the former is the best interpretation.

It may well be thought that there is a notion of *entreaty* included in the word 'consolation' (παράκλησις) in this place, παρακαλεῖν meaning 'to entreat,' see Matt. xviii. 32, and the sense would then be, 'if you can be entreated in Christ.' "Si exhortatio nomine Christi instituta locum apud vos habere potest[1]." See also 2 Cor. v. 20: ὑπὲρ Χρίστου οὖν πρεσβεύομεν ὡς τοῦ Θεοῦ παρακαλοῦντος δι' ἡμῶν.

if any comfort of love,

παραμύθιον ἀγάπης, i. e. comfort furnished by love; 'of love' being the subjective genitive. The primary meaning of παραμύθιον is an 'address' or 'exhortation'—*alloquium*, and then by an easy transition it comes to mean that particular form of address whereby we comfort the afflicted (the word is so used John xi. 19, 1 Thess. ii. 11, and v. 14), and so it has been well translated here, *locutio super cor*; for to speak to the heart is to speak those things by which the heart may be cheered and refreshed. The meaning of the Apostle is plain, viz. if you are willing to shew your love by consoling me. "There is," says Caietan, "among those who suffer in fellowship for Christ a mutual consolation also in Christ." For if God so loved the world as to give His Only

---

[1] Rosenmüller.

Son, and the eternally Begotten was willing to die for His enemies, surely Christians are bound by the closest ties to love one another, and to abound in mutual consolation. Though the above is most probably the Apostle's meaning, it is possible that παραμύθιον ἀγάπης may be nearly the same as the preceding words, q. d. 'if ye can be persuaded by love,' which should ever be the highest and most forcible persuasion to a Christian[k].

if any fellowship of the Spirit,

εἴ τις κοινωνία πνεύματος, literally 'if there be any fellowship of spirit,' (the word 'the' before 'spirit' in the English Version being gratuitous,) i. e. of human sympathy and kindly affection between us. See chap. i. 27. But this interpretation need not of course exclude the higher sense, 'if there be any fellowship *between us and the Holy Spirit,*' in union with Whom alone all true fellowship consists. For if they were of old called 'Pagani' who were accustomed to drink from the same fountain, how much more intimate is the connexion of those who drink of the same Spirit? See 1 Cor. xii. 4. Gagneius paraphrases these words thus: " Si mecum aliquam Spiritus Sancti communicationem accepistis."

if any bowels and mercies,

σπλάγχνα καὶ οἰκτιρμοί. In Col. iii. 12 we meet with σπλάγχνα οἰκτιρμῶν. σπλάγχνα means the feelings generally, (see chap. i. 8); οἰκτιρμοί feelings of *pity* towards the distressed. The meaning is, If you feel any tenderness and compassion towards me a prisoner of the Gospel[l].

St. Chrysostom paraphrases the whole verse thus: " If I can obtain consolation from you, if I can obtain any comfort from your love, if I can communicate with you in the Spirit, if I can communicate with you in the Lord, if I can find mercy and pity at your hands, shew by your love the return of all this."

[k] ἀγάπης ψυχαγωγίαν.—Theodoret.
[l] "Viscera vocat viscerales affectus, puta tenerrimam, intimam, et ex imis quasi visceribus miserationem et compassionem, q. d. si qua erga miseros et afflictos, ac præsertim erga me Apostolum vestrum vinctum, tenerâ et viscerali commiseratione tangimini."— Corn. à Lap.

2. Fulfil ye my joy,

πληρώσατέ μου τὴν χαράν. "Cumulum afferte gaudio meo." "So macht meine Freude dadurch vollkommen[m]." The same kind of expression occurs John iii. 29[n]. That the exhortation might not be thought to be directed to people who were altogether deficient in the qualities which he has mentioned, observe how he does not say, 'cause me to rejoice,' but *fulfil* (complete) 'my joy.' As much as if he had said, You have already inspired me with some portion of holy joy and peacefulness, (see chap. i. 4,) but I desire nothing less than to arrive at its *fulness*; and what that fulness is he immediately proceeds to explain.

Aretius takes occasion to remark here upon the thorough *unselfishness* of the Apostle, which indeed is a conspicuous feature in all his Epistles, and goes on to say, "He had reasons for grieving rather than rejoicing, if he regarded his own condition,—closely confined in prison, expecting the sentence of death and the sword of the executioner every moment,—but despising all this, he is wholly bent on furthering the affairs of the Philippians, so that they may be as happy as possible."

that ye be like-minded,

'That' (ἵνα) is expletive; as if he had said, 'ye will fulfil my joy if ye be like-minded,' &c.

'Like-minded,' τὸ αὐτὸ φρονῆτε, see Rom. xii. 16, and xv. 5; 2 Cor. xiii. 11. This expression appears to be somewhat more *general* than τὸ ἓν φρονοῦντες below. And this is all that can reasonably be said of the difference between them; for, as Alford well remarks, in the more fervid portions of such an Epistle as this we must be prepared for something very nearly approaching to tautology. Rosenmüller, however, observes the following distinction between τὸ αὐτὸ φρονεῖν and τὸ ἓν φρονεῖν. He thinks that the former denotes consent *in doctrine*, as chap. iii. 15, while the latter denotes consent *in life* and mutual offices of charity, as

---

[m] Rosenmüller.
[n] "Adhuc suspensa hæret sententia, hic tandem absolvitur."—*Aretius.*

Rom. xv. 5. This distinction is highly fanciful. According to Estius the expression means "ut eadem velint, cademque credant." Gagneius explains it " non divisi affectionibus aut opinionibus."

having the same love,

i. e. let it not be in *faith* alone, but in all other things; for it is easy to contemplate a case where there may be like-mindedness, but not love. " Having the same love, that is, love and be loved alike; do not thou enjoy much love and shew less love to others, so as to be covetous even in this matter; and though there be that do this, yet do not thou suffer it in thyself º."

This precept must also be understood to include love of the Church, its doctrines, institutions, ministers, &c., and requires (how hard, alas!) that the same measure of love be shewn to the poor as to the rich, to the stranger as to one living under the same roof; and perhaps in no particular that could be mentioned does the doctrine of Christ stand in broader contrast to the custom of the world than in this. The world loves and cherishes *its own*. The Christian loves *all*, even enemies and persecutors.

It has been well said, "Magnes amoris est amor." " Hoc est," said Seneca, "philtrum sine veneficæ carmine cogens etiam hostes ad redamandum; si vis amari, ama."

being of one accord,

σύμψυχοι, equivalent to μιᾷ ψυχῇ in chap. i. 27 and Acts iv. 32. Aretius says of this, "It springs from unity of doctrine and flows through love into all parts." " Unanimity is the effect of love," says Hemmingius. " Behold, how good and joyful a thing it is : brethren, to dwell together in unity ᴾ ! " St. Chrysostom explains the expression thus : " Deeming the bodies of all to be your own; not in substance, for that is impossible, but in purpose and intention. Let all things proceed as from one soul."

of one mind.

See remarks on 'like-minded' above.

º St. Chrysostom.   ᴾ Ps. cxxxiii. 1.

Observe with what exceeding earnestness the Apostle here exhorts to unity. The near approach to tautology in the different expressions in this verse is the strongest evidence of the fervour of his soul. He foresaw the dreadful mischief that would arise from Christians forsaking the traditions of the Church, and walking in ways of their own devising,— hence his burning language. It is impossible to read the opening verses of this chapter without being struck with the importance that ought to be attached to unity of purpose and action among Christians, as contrasted with our present feelings on the subject. So much fervour with the Apostle! so much coldness among ourselves! It is one of the most dreadful signs of the times in which we live that the principle of unity is so little understood amongst us. It may truly be said that even the *desire* for it is nearly extinct in those bodies of Christians which at present are not in communion with the Church. And yet even heathens have seen the necessity of this corporate unity which modern Christians so much despise, but which was the subject of our Redeemer's prayer of agony; for Scipio, when he had conquered Numantia, asked the king for what reason it had before remained unconquered, but was now captured and overthrown? He replied, in words which it would be well for Christians to remember, " Concordia victoriam, discordia exitium præbuit." Micipsa, also, being at the point of death, exhorted his sons, with all the fervour of a father's affection, to be united. His dying words have passed into a proverb, and have formed a motto for some of the noblest of our commercial enterprises: " Concordiâ parvæ res crescunt ; discordiâ autem maximæ dilabuntur." And to turn to Christian writers, from whose writings it would be easy to select enough to fill volumes on this subject, St. Augustine [q] says, " Give oneness, and it is a people; take oneness away, and it is a crowd." And Tertullian, speaking of the love of the early Christians, says, " Animo animâque inter se miscebantur."

---

[q] Serm. liii. 4, in Nov. Test.

For more on this subject, see Commentary on Ephesians, pp. 100, 224, 226, 227, 256.

3. **Let nothing be done through strife or vainglory;**

He proceeds to illustrate his former precepts by mentioning their contraries. 'Through strife,' i. e. not trying *enough* to please others. 'Vainglory,' i. e. trying *too much* to please others. For ἐριθεία see chap. i. 16. Conybeare translates it 'selfish party intrigue, conducted in a mercenary spirit,' and more generally 'selfish cunning,' being derived from ἐριθεύομαι, 'to undertake a work for hire.' The same word occurs also in 2 Cor. xii. 20, Gal. v. 20, and James iii. 16. Ἐριθευόμενοι is used for 'intriguing partizans' by Aristotle [r]. The history of this word seems to bear a strong analogy to that of our term 'job [s].' Aretius well calls ἐριθεία 'mater sectarum.'

Haymo says that this exhortation of the Apostle was suggested by the conduct of certain Judaizing teachers at Philippi, whose thoughts were occupied, not in saving souls, but in subtleties of speech for the sake of procuring for themselves the reputation of wisdom. Be this as it may, he points out here, as St. Chrysostom well remarks, "the cause of all evil. Hence come fightings and contentions. Hence come envyings and strifes. Hence it is that love waxes cold, when we love the praise of men, when we are slaves to the honour which is paid by the many; for it is not possible for a man to be the slave of praise and to be a true servant of God." It has been truly said that the desire of praise and glory is innate in man, and, according to Plato, is the very last thing which is laid aside from the soul. Hence the special mention of it by the Apostle in this place.

---

[r] Polit., v. 3.
[s] Estius renders the word 'per contentionem,' and explains it as "cam verborum pugnam et concertationem quae non veritatis aut justitiae, sed gloriae studio suscipitur. Unde rectè Theophyl. annotat Apostolum continuò subjungere matrem hujus *inanem gloriam*. Ex hâc enim, inquit, illa nascitur."

but in lowliness of mind

He opposes this to the two vicious frames of mind of which he has just been speaking. For ταπεινοφροσύνη, 'lowliness of mind,' see remarks on Eph. iv. 2. On this subject St. Augustine[1] says, "In order therefore that each be not puffed up by reason of that which he sees clearly that he can do, let him humbly consider that he knows not that there is perchance something more excellent which he cannot do; but that some who neither have nor profess that of which he is lawfully self-conscious are able to do this, which he himself cannot do. Thus will he be kept, not by feigned, but by true humility."

let each esteem other better than themselves.

i. e. be not inflated and puffed up with self-importance, but let each suppose that his neighbour is superior to himself in something, that is to say, let every one consider that every other person has his own points of excellence, so that he cannot pronounce himself to be absolutely superior in the aggregate, and this "Non minus verè quam humiliter," as says St. Bernard.

Respecting the way in which this is to be effected, Bengel remarks, "Fieri id potest, non externè tantum, sed per veram ταπεινοφροσύνην, cùm quis per abnegationem oculos avertit à suis prærogativis, et alterius dotes, quibus prior est, studiosè contemplatur."

This is a good remark of Bengel, for ταπεινοφροσύνη does not consist, as some suppose, in disparaging one's own gifts and privileges, but in humble estimate of the way in which they are used. It would have been absurd for Sir I. Newton to have considered his servant a better astronomer than himself; the question would be whether Newton used his gifts so much to God's glory as his servant did his lesser gifts. And so the pious Christian does not enquire, 'What *is* that man as compared with me?' but, 'What would he have been with my advantages?'

St. Chrysostom says of this passage, "Oh how full of true

---
[1] De Virg., 47.

wisdom, how universal a gathering-word (συγκρότημα) of our salvation, is the lesson he (St. Paul) has put forth! If thou feelest, he means, that another is greater than thyself, and persuadest thyself so; yea, more, if thou not only sayest it, but art fully persuaded of it, then thou assignest him the honour, and if thou assignest him the honour, thou wilt not be displeased at seeing him honoured by another. Do not then think him simply *greater* than thyself, but *better*, which is a very great superiority, and thou wilt not think it strange, nor be pained thereby, if thou seest him honoured. Yea, though he treat thee with scorn, thou wilt bear it nobly, for thou hast esteemed him greater than thyself. Though he revile thee, thou wilt submit. Though he treat thee ill, thou wilt bear it in silence. For when once the soul is fully persuaded that he is greater, it falls not into anger when it is ill-treated by him, nor yet into envy [u]."

"Esteem not thyself better than others," is the wholesome advice of St. Thomas à Kempis [x], "lest perhaps in the sight of God, Who knoweth what is in man, thou be accounted worse than they." "If there be any good in thee, believe that there is much more in others, that so thou mayest conserve humility within thee. It is no prejudice unto thee to debase thyself under all men, but it is very prejudicial to thee to prefer thyself before any one man [y]." And again, "Do not think that thou hast made any progress unless thou esteem thyself inferior to all [z]."

St. Gregory [a] lays great stress on the word 'each' in this verse, and says, "Lest, when one person humbles himself before another, this humiliation should tend to the pride of the other, he (St. Paul) rightly admonished both parties, saying, 'each esteeming other better than themselves, in

---

[u] Respecting the difficulty that may arise in carrying out this precept of the Apostle in the case of a person guilty of open and notorious sin, Estius says, "Sed quæres, quid si videam alium manifeste graviterque peccantem? Respondeo, quod et illum te meliorem reputare debeas, eo judicii modo quem superius exposui, (i. e. as possibly being endowed with higher excellencies than yourself, in spite of that particular sin of his which you s e and condemn); maximè quia potest in corde tuo latere vitium superbiæ, quo revera sis illo deterior. Deinde, quia forte ille te melior est secundum prædestinationem divinam quæ nobis est occultissima."

[x] De Imit. Christi, lib. i. c. 7.
[y] Ibid., lib. i. c. 7.
[z] Ibid., lib. ii. c. 2.
[a] Moral. xxxiv. 43.

order that in the thoughts of the heart I should prefer him to myself, and he in turn should prefer me to himself; so that when the heart is kept down on either side, no one may be elated by the honour bestowed upon him.'"

It was one of the rules of St. Ignatius, left for the guidance of his Order,—

"Nulli vel minimo quavis ratione repugnes,
Cedere te potius quam superare juvet."

The bearing of David towards Saul[b] when he had him in his power in the cave of Engedi, and had cut off the skirt of his robe, is a remarkable example of the Apostle's precept carried into practice. On the other hand, the conduct of our Lord's brethren[c] furnishes us with an example of persons acting from a desire of vain-glory. "His brethren therefore said unto Him, Depart hence and go into Judæa, that Thy disciples also may see the works which Thou doest. For there is no man that doeth anything in secret and he himself seeketh to be known openly. If Thou do these things, shew Thyself to the world."

4. Look not every man on his own things,

See 1 Cor. x. 24, and xiii. 5. The Apostle here shews how the precept of the former verse may be carried into practice, viz. by looking 'not every man,' &c. The word 'look' must not be understood as being for purposes of *curiosity*, or to find food for a diseased mind, but as relating to a sincere desire to render to a neighbour the same amount of loving assistance that we should desire to have returned to ourselves. There must be no 'looking' but that prompted by affection. Haymo well says, "Not merely ought men to seek their own interest and welfare, but that of others also; for the welfare of many profits many, while the welfare of one profits only one."

The expression 'his own things' refers, (1) to parts and gifts, and (2) to private interest and advantage, φιλαυτία in all its aspects being the most fruitful source of dissensions.

[b] 1 Sam. xxiv. 4—22.   [c] John vii. 3—5.

but every man also on the things of others.

'Also' (καὶ) is here highly emphatic, for in giving this precept the Apostle by no means intended to imply that we are to neglect ourselves and our own concerns in order to serve other people, but that care for ourselves and thoughtfulness for our neighbour are to run side by side. See 1 Tim. v. 8.

The sentiment embodied in this verse was not unknown to the ancients. Cicero[d] says, "Non nobis solum nati sumus, sed ortus nostri partem patria, partem parentes vendicant, partem amici." Hemmingius[e] cautions us not to confound this most necessary virtue with the odious vice πολυπραγμοσύνη, 'meddlesomeness;' a most salutary caution for days like the present.

St. Cyprian[f], complaining of the laxity of discipline in his day, makes the following remarks illustrative of this verse: "Our Lord fulfilled the will of the Father, and we do not fulfil the will of our Lord; eager about our property and our gains, seeking to exalt ourselves, giving ourselves up to emulation and dissension, careless about single-mindedness and the faith, renouncing the world in words only not in deeds, each of us pleasing himself, and displeasing all men."

5. Let this mind be in you, which was also in Christ Jesus:

Τοῦτο γὰρ φρονείσθω ἐν ὑμῖν κ.τ.λ. There is another reading, φρονεῖτε, which if correct would be much more simple than the commonly received φρονείσθω.

Our Blessed Lord was pleased to set Himself before His disciples as their pattern[g]: "Take My yoke upon you, and learn of Me; for I am meek and lowly in heart: and ye shall find rest unto your souls." St. Paul now does the same, and in exhorting the Philippians to humility brings

---

[d] De Off., (quoting probably from a well-known passage in Plato).
[e] "Illa sancta quædam cura est, qua quisque proximi studiis perinde atque suis studet. Hæc profana temeritas est, qua quis nunc aliena munera invadit, nunc alios calumniandi studio observat. De hâc rectè dicitur—τῆς πολυπραγμοσύνης οὐδὲν χερεώτερον ἄλλο."—Hemmingius, in loc.
[f] Ep. xi. 1.
[g] Matt. xi. 29.

forward the example of his Divine Master, as well in the precept which he had given concerning the preservation of humility towards all, as in preferring a neighbour's good to private advantage[h]. St. Paul might have cited *himself*, if he had desired to do so, for in chap. i. 24 we have a remarkable instance of his self-denying humility[i],—an example, too, which the Philippians would be sure to appreciate,—but he was content to set before them as a pattern no less a Person than Christ Himself, (see Rom. xv. 2, 3; 2 Cor. viii. 9; and Eph. v. 2,) for "Nothing," says St. Chrysostom, "will rouse a soul to the performance of good works so much as learning that in this it is likened to God. What encouragement is equal to this?" This verse, then, teaches us that we should daily strive to express Christ to the world; not merely as a picture does a man, in outward lineaments, but as a child does his father, in affections and actions. For as Moses was commanded by God, when about to build the tabernacle, "See that thou make all things according to the pattern shewed to thee in the mount[j]," so Christians ought always to set before themselves as their pattern Christ crucified on Calvary.

This verse also may be used to refute the heresy of Nestorius, who assigned to Christ a double Person and Nature; for the expression 'let this mind' relates to His Humanity, while what follows, about 'the form of God,' belongs to His Divinity. And yet the former is assigned by St. Paul to One and the self-same Person as the latter.

St. Augustine[k] shews that true humility was taught by Christ, and not by the wisest heathens. He says, "This is the water of confession of sin, this is the water of humiliation of heart, this is the water of a life leading unto salvation, abasing itself, presuming nothing of itself, attributing nothing proudly to its own power. This water is not in any of the books of the Gentiles; not in the books of the Epicureans, not of the Stoics, not of the Manichæans, not of the Platonists. Even where the best precepts of

---

[h] Estius, in loc.   [i] See also Commentary on Ephesians, p. 183.
[j] Heb. viii. 5.   [k] In Ps. xxxii. Exp. 2.

morals and discipline are found, yet is not found that humility. The way of that humility flows from another source; it comes from Christ. This way is from Him, Who when He was high, came lowly."

6. St. Chrysostom remarks that this one verse overthrows some of the most pernicious heresies that had arisen up to his time against the Nature and Person of our Lord, viz. those of Arius, Paul of Samosata, Marcellus of Galatia, Sabellius, Marcion, Valentinus, Manes, Apollinarius, Photinus, Sophronius and others. "Rouse yourselves, then," he says, "to behold so great a spectacle, so many armies falling by one stroke, lest the pleasure of such a sight should escape you. For if when chariots contend in the horse-race there is nothing so pleasing as when one of them dashes together and overthrows whole chariots with their drivers, and after throwing down many with the charioteers that stood thereon, drives by alone towards the goal, and the end of the course, and amid the applause and clamour which rises on all sides to heaven, with coursers winged as it were by that joy and that applause, sweeps over the whole ground; will not the pleasure be much greater here, when by the grace of God we overthrow at once and in a body the combinations and devilish machinations of all these heresies together with their charioteers?"

Who, being in the form of God,

2 Cor. iv. 4; Col. i. 15; Heb. i. 3. ἐν τῇ μορφῇ equivalent to ἐν τῇ οὐσίᾳ καὶ τῇ φύσει. Strictly speaking, μορφή signifies what may be termed the externals of the Godhead—the blessedness, the majesty, the glory, the adoration of others (sc. angels), since the word in composition, such as μεταμόρφωσις, signifies rather change of appreciable condition than change of essential nature. Polus says, "*Μορφή, forma*, designat essentiam et naturam, et proprietates naturæ; idemque est quod οὐσία et φύσις nisi quod οὐσία *nudam* essentiam denotat, cui φύσις addit proprietates essentiales et naturales, quales in Deo justitia, potentia, &c.; eisque μορφή addit *accidentia naturam rei consequentia*, et quibus quasi

lineamentis οὐσία et φύσις confirmantur et depinguntur, ut, in homine, esse facie in cœlum conversâ, &c.; in Deo autem (in quo nulla sunt accidentia) immensa ejus gloria, majestas, &c. Μορφή ergo denotat essentiam Dei non nudam sed suis vestitam qualitatibus, et proprietatibus essentialibus, gloriâ, majestate," &c. Strigelius[1] says, " Μορφή significat essentiam et proprietates naturæ." This is a subject of very great difficulty. For further information see St. Athanasius against the Arians, Disc. 3, c. 23; also Bull, " Primitive Tradition of the Catholic Church," p. 302 and following, Oxford Edition.

Μορφή Θεοῦ, as opposed to μορφή δούλου, might with great propriety be rendered the *condition* of God and the *condition* of a slave[m].

It is to be observed that Christ's *Divinity* is here most strongly asserted, and that *antecedent to His humiliation*, as the *terminus à quo*, the term of elevation from which His humiliation takes its rise, from which it derives great increase. Heretics have endeavoured to find in these words a proof that the Son is not equal to the Father. It would be wearisome and unprofitable to follow them through their reasonings; suffice it, therefore, to say that μορφή, which the English Version renders ' form,' undoubtedly means ' forma quæ dat esse rei.' Hence, ' the form of God' is the Nature of God—His Divinity, i. e. God Himself, as by the form of man is signified the nature of man[n]. All the Fathers who wrote against the Arians are unanimous on this point, arguing rightly that Christ was really and truly God before He took the form of a servant.

Cornelius à Lapide, in answer to the question, " Dices cur clarè non dixit Apostolus, ' Qui *cum esset Deus?*' " replies,

---

[1] ὑπομνήματα in libros N. T.

[m] Bp. Pearson says, " By the word ' form' is certainly understood *the true condition* of a servant, and by the likeness is infallibly meant the *real nature* of man; nor doth the *fashion* in which He was found destroy, but rather assert the truth of His humanity. And, therefore, as sure as Christ was really and essentially man, of the same nature with us, in whose similitude He was made, so certainly was He also really and essentially God, of the same nature and being with Him in Whose Form He did subsist."

[n] Haymo says, " In formâ Dei, id est in æqualitate Paternæ Divinitatis consubstantialis et coæqualis omnibus Illi."

"Id dixit, et amplius dixit; per formam enim significat gloriam et majestatem Dei, eamque opponit formæ, id est, infirmitati et vilitati humanæ."

St. Chrysostom, writing against those heretics who wished to limit the meaning of 'being in the form of God' to suit their own unworthy conceptions of the Nature of Christ, happily contrasts the expression 'form of God' with 'the form of a servant,' which follows. "Tell me," he says, "the form of a servant, is it the *energy* of a servant, or the *nature* of a servant? Thou wilt say, truly the nature of a servant. Thus, too, the 'form of God' is the Nature of God, and therefore not an energy." Gagneius says, "Qui cùm in formâ Dei esset, id est, in eâdem cum Patre substantiâ. Formam enim hoc loco, et Græcum verbum μορφὴν, interpretatur Chrysostomus formam substantialem."

It is very important to notice the use of the word ὑπάρχων, 'being,' and not γενόμενος, in this sentence. Its occurrence here may be compared with Exod. iii. 14: "And God said unto Moses, I AM THAT I AM: and He said, Thus shalt thou say unto the children of Israel, I AM hath sent me unto you."

thought it not robbery to be equal with God:

'Robbery,' ἁρπαγμός, means the *act* of seizing or snatching; not so much snatching *from* another as snatching *for* oneself[o]. The meaning then is that our Lord thought it not robbery to assert that He was equal to God, as when He said[p], "I and My Father are one;" whereas, on the other hand, if the blessed Forerunner, instead of saying, 'I am not the Christ[q],' had affirmed, 'I am the Christ,' He would have been guilty of the 'robbery' contemplated by the Apostle, an offence actually perpetrated by Simon Magus, when he blasphemously dared to assert, "I am the Son of God; I am the Paraclete."

The eternal pre-existence of the Only Begotten is most

---

[o] "Rapina est," says Haymo, "quando quilibet homo alienam rem per violentiam sibi usurpat, quæ illi non competit."
[p] John x. 30; see also John v. 18.   [q] John i. 20.

clearly set forth in these words; for that of which a man has become the possessor through fraud and violence he dares not lay aside even for an instant, lest he should lose it altogether. The Son of God, however, feared not to descend from His right, for He thought not Deity a matter of acquisition. He was not afraid that any would strip Him of that Nature, or that right, therefore He laid it aside, being confident that He should take it up again.

'To be equal with God;' τὸ εἶναι ἴσα Θεῷ. Tertullian translates the expression *pariari*.

'With God,' i. e. the Father, declaring the equality of Person[r].

It is obvious that the word 'God' is here used in a different sense from 'being in the form of God;' for there 'God' signifies absolutely the Essence common to the Three Persons of the ever-adorable Trinity, whereas in this place it refers to the *First* Person, God the Father.

Primasius paraphrases this verse as follows:—"Non rapuit quod habebat, id est, equalitatem Patris, quam naturaliter habebat, non rapuit."

Justin Martyr, in his Epistle to Diognetus, gives a striking testimony to the Eternal Godhead of our Lord: "The Almighty and all-creating and invisible God hath Himself from heaven established the Truth, and the holy and incomprehensible Word amongst men; and hath fixed It in their hearts, not, as one might suppose, by sending unto men a *minister*, either angel, or prince, or any one of those who order things on earth, or any one of those to whom hath been entrusted the administration of things in heaven; but *the very Framer and Creator* of the universe Himself, by Whom He founded the heavens, by Whom He shut in the sea within its proper bounds, Whose mysteries all the elements do faithfully observe, from Whom the sun hath received to observe the due measures of the course of the day, Whom the moon obeys when He bids her shine by night,

---

[r] "The very memorable words of a celebrated ancient Synod of the third century afford an excellent comment here: 'Ἐν τῇ ἐκκλησίᾳ τῇ ὑπὸ τὸν οὐρα- | νὸν πάσῃ Χριστὸς πεπίστευται Θεὸς, κενώσας ἑαυτὸν ἀπὸ τοῦ εἶναι ἴσα Θεῷ.'— Concil. *Antioch*. (*Wordsworth, Greek Test.*)

Whom the stars obey as they follow the course of the moon, by Whom all things have been arranged, and determined, and placed in due subjection, the heavens and all that is in the heavens, the earth and all that is in the earth, the sea and all that is in the sea, fire, air, and the abyss; all that is in the heights above, all that is in the depths beneath, and all that is in the region that lies between. This One sent He unto them. Was it then, as any one of men might suppose, for despotic sway, and fear, and terror? In no wise, but rather in clemency and meekness; even as a King sending His Son, a King He sent Him; as God He sent Him; as unto men He sent Him; as willing to save He sent Him."

7. But made Himself of no reputation,

'Ἑαυτὸν ἐκένωσε: 'Semet ipsum exinanivit:' literally, 'EMPTIED *Himself.*' "Humiliavit, et quasi contraxit et minoravit[s];" i.e. from a Master became servant; from God, man; from Creator, creature. "Non tantum aliunde nihil rapuit, verum etiam quod habuit abdicavit[t]." He Who had all riches voluntarily led the life of a poor man[u]. Unfortunately the English Version, 'made Himself of no reputation,' loses much of this meaning.

Haymo describes this act of our Blessed Lord, whereby He emptied Himself, as "quando res magna et incomprehensibilis in parvâ formulâ comprehenditur," and proceeds to say, that if an artist were to represent on a small scale, in a picture, birds and beasts and fishes, and the different objects of nature, it would give some idea of the humiliation of the Son of God, Who being everywhere by His Godhead, though not discerned by sense, deigned to become visible in the small form of man, and so emptied, and as it were contracted Himself. No doubt allusion is intended in this verse to Dan. ix. 26.

Bp. Pearson justly complains of our translation of this passage[v]. We have two copulative conjunctions, neither of

---

[s] Haymo.
[u] Matt. viii. 20; see also 2 Cor. viii. 9.
[t] Wetstein.
[v] Art. ii.

which is in the original text, and three distinct propositions, without any dependence of one upon the other, whereas all the words together are but an expression of Christ's exinanition, with an explication shewing wherein it consists.

As might be expected, this astounding act of humiliation, whereby the eternal Son, remaining *full*[x], carried Himself among men as *empty*, is a theme on which the Fathers delight to dwell, as what loving, reverent soul will not? St. Jerome, in particular, was so devoted to the contemplation of this strange humility of his Master, that he spent many years of his life near the spot where the manger stood. It will be well to quote a few passages from their writings; no easy task, however, when we remember how allusions to this wondrous mystery run through nearly every page.

"Emptied Himself," says St. Augustine[y], "not that that Wisdom was changed, seeing that It is altogether unchangeable, but because in so humble a guise He willed to be made known unto men." Again[z], he uses the humiliation of our Lord to exhort teachers to mildness and gentleness with their pupils; specially with those who are dull of understanding, and when it becomes wearisome to dwell so long on first principles: "Let us meditate on what we have received from Him who has shewed us an example that we may follow His steps. For however much our articulate speech may differ from the vividness of our perception, much more does mortal flesh differ from equality with God." The same Father[a] makes Elisha restoring the dead child a type of our Lord's humiliation. By the 'staff' sent by the hand of the servant he understands the Law. "If," he says, "there had been a Law given which could give life, the boy might have been raised to life by the staff; but seeing that the Scripture hath concluded all under sin, he still lies dead. But why hath it concluded all under sin? That the promise by the faith of Jesus Christ might be given to them that believe. Let, then, Elisha come, who sent the staff by the servant to prove that he was dead; let him come himself,

---

[x] John i. 14.
[z] De Catechizandis Rudibus, 15.
[y] De Fid. et Symb., 18.
[a] Serm. lxxxvi. 6, in Nov. Test.

come in his own person, himself enter into the woman's house, go up to the child, find him dead, conform himself to the members of the dead child, himself not dead but living. For this he did; he laid his face upon his face, his eyes upon his eyes, his hands upon his hands, his feet upon his feet; he straitened, he contracted himself; being great, he made himself little. He contracted himself; so to say, he lessened himself."

St. Gregory [b] also uses Elisha as a type of Christ. He says: "He, (Elisha,) when he sent his servant with a staff never a whit restored life to the dead child; but upon coming in his own person, and spreading himself upon the dead body, and contracting himself to its limbs, and walking to and fro, and breathing seven times into the mouth of the dead body, he forthwith quickened it to the light of new life through the ministering of compassion. For God, the Creator of mankind, as it were grieved for His dead son, when He beheld us with compassion killed by the sting of iniquity. And whereas He put forth the terror of the Law by Moses, He as it were sent the rod by the servant. But the servant could not raise the dead body with the staff, because, as Paul bears witness, 'the Law made nothing perfect.' But when He came in His own Person, and spread Himself in humility upon the dead body, He contracted Himself to match the limbs of the dead body to Himself. He 'walks to and fro' also, in that He calls Judæa nigh at hand, and the Gentiles afar off. He breathes upon the dead body seven times, in that by the publishing of the Divine Gift He bestows the Spirit of seven-fold grace upon those that lie prostrate in the death of sin. And afterwards it is raised up alive, in that the child, whom the rod of terror could not raise up, has been brought back to life by the Spirit of Love."

The same illustration occurs in St. Augustine, in Ps. lxxi. 19.

St. Augustine [c] says: "If He had avoided poverty, we should not have been rid of poverty."

---

[b] Moral. ix. 63.   [c] Serm. cxix. in Nov. Test.

Again [d]: "'Emptied Himself;' not by losing what He was, but by taking to Him what He was not."

Again [e]: "In that sort emptying Himself that He appeared less here than He remained with the Father; for in truth the form of a servant was taken, not the form of God forsaken; this was assumed, not that consumed. In regard of this He saith, 'The Father is greater than I;' but in regard of that, 'I and the Father are one.'"

St. Gregory [f], after speaking of the evils of pride, says, "To this end the Only-begotten Son of God took on Him the form of our infirmity; for this the Invisible appeared not only visible, but even despised; for this He endured the jests of contumely, the reproaches of derisions, and the torments of sufferings, that God in His humility might teach man not to be proud. How great, then, is the virtue of humility, since for the sole purpose of truly teaching it He Who above estimation is great became little, even to suffering? For since the pride of the devil caused the origin of our fall, the humility of God was found out as the instrument of our redemption. For our enemy who was created great among all things, wished to appear exalted above all things. But our Redeemer, remaining great above all things, deigned to become little among all things."

St. Augustine [g]: "So great, truly, is the benefit of man's lowliness, that even God's loftiness was pleased to enforce it by His own pattern; because proud man should be for ever lost, had not a lowly God found him. For the Son of Man came to seek and save that which was lost. Lost by following the pride of the deceiver, let him follow the lowliness of the Redeemer, being found."

St. Bernard [h] has the following, the delicate beauty of which would be lost in a translation:—"In Christo agnoscitur longitudo brevis, latitudo angusta, altitudo subdita, profunditas plana, lux non lucens, Verbum infans, aqua sitiens, panis esuriens. Videas, si attendas, potentiam regi, sapientiam instrui, virtutem sustentari, Deum denique lac-

---

[d] Hom. xvii. 16, in Joh.   [e] Hom. lxxviii. 1, in Joh.
[f] Moral. xxxiv. 54.   [g] Hom. lv. 7, in Joh.   [h] Serm. ii. Super Missus est.

tantem, sed angelos reficientem; vagientem, sed miseros consolantem. Videas, si attendas, tristari lætitiam, pavere fiduciam, salutem pati, vitam mori, fortitudinem infirmari; sed est hæc tristitia lætificans, pavor confortans, mors vivificans."

and took upon Him the form of a servant,

i. e. He took man's nature upon Him in truth; for the words μορφὴ δούλου signify the true nature of man, and not a shadowy resemblance. It is to be remembered that our Lord was predicted by the Prophets under the name of 'servant,' (see Isa. xlii. 1; Ezek. xxxiv. 23; Zech. iii. 8); and constantly in the Psalms, especially Ps. xxii., where, together with Isa. liii., our Lord is fully described under this character.

The words 'took upon Him' indicate that this was a voluntary act on our Lord's part, and that He was under no constraint. And not only did He take upon Him the 'form of a servant,' but He also performed a servant's work, (see John xiii. 1—17,) washing not the hands, but the feet of the disciples, even of the traitor. If anything can enhance His surpassing lowliness, surely it is this, that He disdained not even to wash the feet of him whose hands He already saw in the act of wickedness. Bp. Andrewes[i] well says, "The shame of being put out of the number of free-born men He despised, even the shame of being in *formâ servi.*"

and was made in the likeness of men:

ἐν ὁμοιώματι ἀνθρώπων γενόμενος. "Id est, similis hominibus factus. Similitudinem accipe, non accidentalem, non apparentem et phantasticam; sed substantialem, qua omnes homines dicuntur esse similes specie, seu natura humana[k]." It must be observed, however, that the 'likeness' was of *nature,* not of *sin.*

"Made," says Caietan, "non ex humano semine, sed divinâ efficientiâ." The word γενόμενος translated 'made' in this place is especially to be observed; it is literally

---

[i] Serm. iii. on the Passion.   [k] Corn. à Lap.

'born,' of course not ὤν or ὑπάρχων. The continual distinction between εἶναι and γένεσθαι in St. John i. should be carefully noticed in connection with this passage.

The plural, 'of men,' (ἀνθρώπων,) is used to express the *nature of man*, as in Heb. ii. 16 ἀγγέλων ἐπιλαμβάνεται is used to express *angelical nature*. Hooker[1] says, "That which deceived him (Nestorius) was want of heed to the first beginning of that admirable combination of God with man. The Word dwelt *in us*. The Evangelist useth the plural number, men for manhood, *us* for the nature whereof we consist;" and then he goes on to refer to Heb. ii. 16.

St. Chrysostom enquires, "What means this which he says, 'Being made in the likeness of men?' He had many things belonging to us, and many He had not; for instance, He was not born of wedlock. He did no sin. These things had He which no man has. He was not what He seemed only, but He was God also; He seemed to be a man, but He was not like the mass of men, though He were like them in flesh. He means, then, that He was not a mere man. Wherefore he says, 'in the likeness of men.' For we indeed are soul and body, but He was God, and soul and body; wherefore he says, 'in the likeness.' For lest when you hear that He emptied Himself, you should think that some change, and degeneracy, and loss is here; he says, whilst He remained what He was, He took that which He was not, and being made flesh He remained God, in that He was the Word." This interpretation is materially strengthened by Rom. viii. 3, where it is said, "God sending His Own Son *in the likeness of sinful flesh*," since there was in Him no 'sinful flesh,' but only the 'likeness of sinful flesh.'

For some excellent remarks on the relative meanings of εἰκών, ὁμοίωσις, and ὁμοίωμα, see Trench, "Synonyms of the New Testament," p. 56 and following.

8. And being found in fashion as a man,

It is to be observed that μορφὴ and ὁμοίωμα, ver. 7, and

---

[1] Eccl. Pol. v. 52.

σχῆμα in this verse, are not synonyms, though they are words of kindred meaning. The force of σχῆμα may be gathered from Aristotle[m], a *material quality*. Aristotle makes it *nearly* synonymous with μορφή. Of course the Apostle does *not* do so, but uses σχῆμα *only* in the Aristotelian sense. The Deity can have no σχῆμα. Bengel translates these words respectively by *forma, similitudo,* and *habitus,* and explains them as follows: " 'Forma' dicit quiddam absolutum; 'similitudo' dicit relationem ad alia ejusdem conditionis; 'habitus' refertur ad aspectum et sensum."

'Being found,' εὑρεθείς. Εὑρίσκεσθαι is often = γίνεσθαι[n]. This expression means that our Lord shewed and carried Himself as man, and was openly recognised as such.

'In fashion;' i.e. "Agnitus est verus homo[o]." Christ had not merely the *inner* nature of man, but also his *outward* form[p].

It is well known that St. Augustine and others have interpreted this passage to mean, that Christ being clothed with our nature exhibited Himself as man. Not, however, that it is to be inferred from this, as some have erroneously done, that they considered Christ's Human Nature as an 'accident,' such as a garment would be, and so that Christ was not a man *substantialiter*. Their meaning is, that the Eternal Son of God, without any change in Himself, was made man, just as the person who puts on a garment is in no respect changed, whether we regard his 'substance' or 'accidents.'

'As a man.' This may mean 'as the Pattern Man,' the archetype of Adam, or 'as any ordinary man[q];' or, perhaps better, 'as a *true* man.' It is to be observed that the adverb of resemblance, 'as,' in this place does not signify mere likeness, but truth and identity. See John i. 14: "And we beheld His glory, the glory as of the Only-begotten of the Father."

[m] Categ. vi. 14.
[n] " Experientiam significat corporalium actionum et passionum, comedendi, bibendi, laborandi, patiendi, et hujusmodi."—*Caietan.*
[o] Estius.
[p] " ' Habitu inventus ut homo;' i.e. in formâ hominis, perinde ac unusquisque ex hominibus, quod ad naturam attinet, non ad contractum vitiorum."—*Gagneius.*
[q] " Ad exprimendum corpus simile corporibus reliquorum hominum."— *Caietan.*

He humbled Himself,

Not by constraint, but willingly, 'Himself' being emphatic. And how deep was this humiliation! Not only, being God, did He take upon Himself man's nature; but also, in that nature He humbled Himself to the lowest depth, even the death of the Cross. The Sun of Righteousness went ten degrees back on the dial of His Father, that He might come to us with healing in His wings.

and became obedient unto death,

These words explain the *manner* of our Lord's humiliation. " Ne perderet obedientiam perdidit vitam[r]." The obedience here contemplated is that by which He cheerfully submitted His own will to the eternal decree of the Father[s]. Although all the actions of our Lord as Man proceeded from *obedience*, (see John vi. 38, xiv. 31,) yet in a higher and more special sense does the Apostle in this place commend His example to us in undergoing death for our sake. See John x. 18.

The expression 'unto death' is of course not to be taken as limiting our Lord's obedience to the act of dying upon the Cross, but is to be regarded as inclusive of His whole life. It is not *in morte*, but *usque ad mortem*, i. e. from the moment of His Incarnation to His last sigh of agony upon the Cross.

Heretics have used this passage to prove that Christ is not equal to the Father. They consider His obedience a token of His inferiority. But they did not reflect that it is quite possible to be *obedient* (in the highest sense of the word) without being *inferior*. Common life will supply us with many cases in point. "Christ," says St. Chrysostom, "became obedient willingly as a Son to His Father; He fell not thus into a servile state, but by this very act above all others guarded His wondrous Sonship, by thus greatly honouring the Father. He honoured the Father, not that thou shouldest dishonour Him, but that thou shouldest the rather admire and learn from this act, that He is a true Son, in honouring His Father more than all besides."

---

[r] St. Bernard. [s] Estius.

even the death of the Cross.

i. e. a death of the lowest shame. "It pleased God that as by means of a tree man sinned, so by means of a tree man should be redeemed[t]." Wonderful is that act of humiliation by which Christ became a servant; more wonderful still that by which He underwent death; but most wonderful of all that by which He underwent the death of the Cross. It is this which overwhelms us with wonder at His *obedience*. "All deaths are not alike; His death seemed to be the most ignominious of all, to be full of shame, to be accursed; for it is written, 'Cursed is every one that hangeth on a tree.' For this cause the Jews eagerly desired to slay Him in this manner, to make Him a reproach, that if no one fell away from Him by reason of His death, yet they might from the *manner* of His death. For this cause two robbers were crucified with Him, and He in the midst, that He might share their ill-repute, and that the Scripture might be fulfilled, 'And He was numbered with the transgressors.'" So St. Chrysostom, *in loc.*

How our Lord, though God, could be thus humbled is very happily expressed by St. Irenæus[u]: '*Ἡσυχάζοντος τοῦ Λόγου ἐν τῷ πειράζεσθαι καὶ σταυροῦσθαι καὶ ἀποθνήσκειν.* "The Word being *silent*" is a most felicitous phrase, which perhaps only finds a parallel in the language of St. Chrysostom on Matt. xv. 23, "He answered her not a word," where he says, "The Word has no word; the Fountain is sealed; the Physician withholds His remedies."

9. Wherefore

Διὸ: "propter quod." "Observe," says Cornelius à Lap., "that this expression does not denote consequence or event, but *merit* and recompence. The exaltation of Christ was *merited* by His humiliation." St. Paul dwells on this, so that by the hope of a future exaltation to glory he might

---

[t] Haymo.
Neale (Commentary on the Psalms, p. 159) mentions the following beautiful legend: "When Adam had fallen sick of the sickness of which he died, he sent Seth to the place where he was wont to pray, and desired healing from God. An angel gave three seeds into the hand of the son, and 'Place them,' he said, 'in your father's mouth; when they bear fruit he shall recover of his sickness.' From these seeds grew the tree whereof the Cross was made."

[u] Adv. Hæres., iii.

stimulate the Philippians to present humility. " Exinanitionis præmium justissimum est exaltatio. Luke xxiv. 26; John x. 17 ˣ."

God also

i. e. the Father. " Christum Christus exinanivit; Christum Deus exaltavit. Cf. 1 Pet. v. 6 ʸ."

hath highly exalted Him,

See observations on Eph. i. 20, 21. Not only ὕψωσεν, but ὑπερύψωσεν, ' super exaltavit ;' His exaltation being one above all height. " In summam extulit sublimitatem ᶻ." Compare Heb. xii. 2.

We must be careful to observe that the words 'humbled' and 'exalted' are spoken of Christ's *Human Nature*, in which alone it was possible for Him either to be humbled or exalted; the exaltation being represented in Scripture as the *reward* of His most salutary Passion. See Heb. ii. 9; Rev. v. 12.

and given Him a Name

Contrast this with "made Himself of no reputation," ver. 7. 'Given' is not spoken of Christ as the Everlasting Word, but as *Man*. The Word gives as God, what He receives as Man. St. Athanasius well remarks, " It is not for *His* sake, but for *ours*, that this is said of Him; for as He died and was exalted as *Man*, so, as man, is He said to take what, as God, He ever had, that even this so high a grant of grace might reach even to us." And St. Augustine ᵃ : " To Christ in *His Human Nature*, to Christ Who died in the flesh, arose, ascended, He hath given a Name which is above every name."

The notion of 'grace' which is involved in the use of the word ἐχαρίσατο, 'given,' in this place must not be overlooked. As Vorstius truly remarks, " Hoc verbum emphaticum est, significans totam Christi exaltationem à gratiosâ Dei voluntate sive ordinatione dependere."

Christ was full of *grace* ᵇ when He dwelt here; and the Father ὑπερύψωσε, highly exalted Him, and gave a *further grace* of superiority, when He left this world.

ˣ Bengel.   ʸ Bengel.   ᶻ Estius.   ᵃ In Ps. cx 7.   ᵇ John i. 14.

which is above every name :

See above, τὸ ὄνομα,—*the* Name, the article being emphatic,—the Name of God Himself; and this very Name, which He bore in His humiliation, is now the highest and most glorious of all names. His own words from glory are, "I am *Jesus* Whom thou persecutest[c]." The expression 'name' includes, of course, all the *dignity* and worship belonging to it. See Commentary on Ephesians, p. 331.

St. Athanasius[d] says, "For as He was ever worshipped as being the Word, and existing in the Form of God, so being what He ever was, though become Man and called Jesus, He still has, as before, the whole creation under foot, and bending their knees to Him in this Name, and confessing that the Word's becoming flesh, and undergoing death in flesh, hath not happened against the glory of His Godhead, but "to the Glory of God the Father." For it is the Father's glory that man, made and then lost, should be found again; and, when the prey of death, that he should be made alive, and should become God's temple. For whereas the powers in heaven, both angels and archangels, were ever worshipping the Lord, *as they are now worshipping Him in the Name of Jesus*, this is our grace and high exaltation, that even when He became Man, the Son of God is worshipped, and the heavenly powers are not startled at seeing all of us, who are of one body with Him, introduced into their realms. And this had not been, unless He who existed in the form of God had taken on Him a servant's form, and had humbled Himself, permitting His Body to reach unto death."

St. Bernard[e] speaks thus: "Jesus is honey in the mouth, in the ear a honied strain, exultation in the heart; yea, and a balm no less. Doth any sorrow? Let Jesus come into his heart, and from its fulness the mouth will speak. Lo! let the light of that Name but gleam, the clouds are scattered, and the sky is bright. Does any sin and meditate destruction in despair? Let him invoke the Name of Life; he breathes again and lives. When hath ever hardness of heart, which

---

[c] Acts ix. 5. [d] Against Arians, Disc. i. c. xi. [e] Serm. xv. 6, in Cant.

so often broods upon the Christian, or slothful indolence, or irksome weariness, resisted the presence of this healthful Name? What dried-up fount of tears has not gushed forth afresh, and still more plentifully, by invoking Jesus? What like this checks the rage of anger, soothes the swelling of pride, heals the wound of envy, puts out the flame of lust, slakes the thirst of avarice, and allays all itching lust of shame? When I name Jesus, I set before me One Who is meek and lowly of heart, kind, temperate, chaste, pitiful, the Pattern of all that is virtuous and holy; yea, Who is also God Almighty; Who heals me by His example, and strengthens me by His help. All this I hear when I hear 'Jesus.' I take examples from Him as Man, help from the Mighty One; *those* as healthful aromatics; *this* as that which draws out their hidden strength; and so I make up a confection, such as no physician's art can equal. This, my soul, is thy electuary, laid up in the vessel of the Name of Jesus; and truly it is wholesome, and there is no sickness of thine which it cannot cure."

In such language as this have holy men spoken of the most sacred Name, but words would be altogether wanting to describe the wondrous beauty of the Church's Litany of the Holy Name of Jesus. There He is invoked by every term of grace and mercy by which He has ever been pleased to make Himself known to His people. So also in the following hymn, (dear to every Catholic heart,) with what exquisite simplicity is the sweetness of the Holy Name set forth:—

> " Jesu, Who dost true joys impart,
>   Sweet is Thy memory :
>   More sweet than honey to the heart,
>   To know and feel Thee nigh.
>
> There's nothing sweet in sweetest sound,
>   In hearing nothing heard,
> In sweetest thought nought sweet is found
>   As Jesus, God and Lord.
>
> Of penitents sole hope and stay ;
>   To wandering sinners kind ;
> To those that seek Thou art the way,
>   But what to those that find ?

Sweetness of heart, and living Fount,
Of souls the light and fire,
All joys we know dost Thou surmount,
And all that we desire.

No tongue of man hath power to tell,
No written words can prove,
But he who loveth knoweth well
What Jesus 'tis to love.

Thee would I seek upon my bed,
In chamber of my breast,
In private and in public led,
By anxious love possessed.

I seek the tomb, wherein Thou art,
With Mary in the morn,
Not with the eye, but with the heart,
And sorrow's plaint forlorn.

There with my tears bedew Thy tomb,
And fill with sighs the place;
There fall before Thee in the gloom,
And Thy loved feet embrace.

There with love's tender offices,
I to Thy feet would flee,
Nor shall my sighs and sorrows cease,
Till I am filled with Thee.

Jesu, great King adorable,
Of all Thy saints admired,
The sweetness which no words can tell,
All and alone desired."

10. That at the Name of Jesus every knee should bow,

'That' denotes the *intent* of our Blessed Lord's exaltation; q. d. so that all recognising in that *Man*, Who is called Jesus, the Son of God, and the true and eternal God, may submit themselves to Him, and adore Him as Lord of all, 'bowing the knee' being expressive of the deepest veneration. It appears from this text, therefore, that the *Humanity* of Christ is to be adored with the same degree of worship as His Divinity. See Commentary on Ephesians, p. 95.

It must not be forgotten that the Greek is ἐν τῷ ὀνόματι,

'*in* the name,' and the bowing the knee *in* the Name of Jesus signifies that all prayer, to be acceptable, must be offered *in His* Name and through Him. See John xvi. 23; Acts iv. 12. Of course the Human Name is given, because He intercedes for us not only as God, but as *Man*.

It has always been the custom of the faithful to shew a sign of worship to the sacred Name, whenever they pronounced it themselves, or heard it pronounced by others. This practice of adoration is so old that it is hard to fix upon the time when it commenced, and we shall be safe in referring it to the age of the Apostles. The Council of Lyons in the thirteenth century formally sanctioned it; and in the following age two councils granted special privileges to those who observed the sign of adoration. The English Church also [f] has enjoined upon her children the solemn observance of this sign, as follows: "Likewise, when in time of Divine Service the Lord Jesus shall be mentioned, *due and lowly reverence shall be done by all persons present, as it hath been accustomed.*"

For remarks on St. Paul's and St. Augustine's deep reverence and love for our Lord's Name, see Commentary on the Ephesians, p. 143.

The following extract from Bp. Andrewes [g] is well worthy of attention: "God, though He have so exalted It, (i. e. the Name of Jesus,) yet reckons it not exalted, *unless we do our parts also*, unless our exaltation come too. At which words comes in our duty, the part that concerns us. Thus, to esteem it *super omne nomen*, above all; and in sign we do so, to declare as much. And therein He leaves us not to ourselves, but prescribes the very manner of our declaration, how He will have it, namely these two ways; the knee to bow to it, the tongue to confess it. Now these are outward acts both. So then, first we are to set down this for a ground, that the exalting of the soul within is not enough. More is required by Him, more to be performed by us. He will not have the inward parts only, and it skills not for the outward members, though we favour our knees,

---

[f] Canon xviii.   [g] Serm. ix. on the Resurrection.

and lock up our lips. No, mental devotion will not serve, He will have both corporal and vocal to express it by. Our body is to afford her part to His glory; and the parts of our body, and namely, these two, the knee and the tongue. Not only the upper parts, the tongue in our head, but even the nether also, the knee in our leg. The words be plain, I see not how we can avoid them."

of things in heaven,

i. e. angels and celestial powers. For remarks on the different orders of angels see Commentary on Ephesians, pp. 93, 94.

and things in earth,

i. e. men still living.

and things under the earth;

i. e. either the souls of the departed, who are in Hades; or devils, and lost spirits; for even in the nethermost hell that dread Name is acknowledged and adored[h]. It is well known that the Jews were accustomed to describe all creation under the terms heaven, and earth, and the parts under the earth, with all things contained in them[i]; and the New Testament writers adopted the same idea[k]. Compare with this verse Rom. xiv. 9; Eph. i. 21; 1 Pet. iii. 22.

St. Chrysostom[l] makes use of this passage to show that there is no room for saving repentance after death. "If unbelievers," he says, "are after death to be saved on their believing, no man shall ever perish. For all will then repent and adore. And in proof that this is true, hear Paul saying, 'Every tongue shall confess, and every knee shall bow, of things in heaven, and things in earth, and things under the earth.' And, 'the last enemy that shall be destroyed is death.' But there is no advantage in that submission, for it comes not of a rightly disposed choice, but of the necessity of things, as one may say, thenceforth taking place."

---

[h] James ii 19
[i] Exod. xx. 4; Deut. iv. 17, 18; Ps. xcvi. 11; Ezek. xxxviii. 20.

[k] Acts iv. 24; Rev. v. 13.
[l] Hom. xxxvi. 3, in Matt.

11. This universal confession (relating most probably to the day of judgment) is partly spontaneous, and partly wrung from unwilling lips; for as they who pierced our Lord will be obliged to look on Him, so also will the devils to confess Him, and the damned to acknowledge the justice of their doom.

And that every tongue should confess

The use of the word ἐξομολογήσεται in this place should be compared with Rom. xiv. 11, γέγραπται γάρ· Ζῶ ἐγώ, λέγει Κύριος· ὅτι ἐμοὶ κάμψει πᾶν γόνυ, καὶ πᾶσα γλῶσσα ἐξομολογήσεται τῷ Θεῷ· whence it appears that the same honour is to be paid to Christ as to God, because He is God. The expression 'every' seems decisively to point to the day of judgment, since many *now deny* Him. These words are evidently quoted from Isa. xlv. 23.

that Jesus Christ is Lord,

No longer as He appeared on earth in "the form of a servant [m]," but surrounded with every attribute of majesty, the Lord of the quick and dead, the Origin and Source of all life, the Object of adoration to men and angels.

to the glory of God the Father.

εἰς δόξαν, literally 'unto the glory;' i.e. His dignity and the recognition of it redounding to the Father's glory, the advancement of which is the great object of our Lord's work, (see 1 Cor. xv. 24—28,) and should be the all-absorbing thought of His followers. See Commentary on Ephesians, p. 76. Observe, then, that this confession of the Lordship of Christ, so far from diminishing the lustre of the Father's attributes, is glory to Him. "Seest thou," says St. Chrysostom, "how wherever the Son is glorified, the Father is also glorified? Thus, too, when the Son is dishonoured, the Father is dishonoured also. If this be so with us, where the difference is great between fathers and sons, much more in respect of God, where there is no difference, doth honour

---

[m] Verse 7.

and dishonour pass on to Him. If the world be subjected to the Son, this is glory to the Father."

Bp. Bull[n] says, "The Father gave Christ His judicial power, because, for the salvation of mankind, He vouchsafed to become the Son of man, that is, Man; and, although He was God, to take upon Himself human life, and expose it to death for man's salvation. Wherefore by that so great humiliation of Himself, by which He was willing to become man, and die for men, He merited this great exaltation to judicial power, in order that He, who was the Saviour of all, might be the Judge of all." He then goes on to paraphrase the Apostle's language from verse 6 to 11, and gives an excellent summary of the whole. "The Apostle exhorts the faithful to humble-mindedness, by an argument drawn from the example of Christ, Who being in the form of God, (that is, being God,) and so equal to God the Father in respect of His Nature, yet did not arrogate to Himself that equality with God, did not carry Himself as God, did not make a show of it openly, being alien from ostentation and pomp; but of His own accord lowered and humbled Himself, taking on Him the form of a servant, and being made man, &c.; and therefore to Him has been given by His Father a Name which is above every name, &c.; exactly as it is said in the passage of John[o] that the authority of judging is given to the Son, because He is the Son of Man."

12. The Apostle having referred to the example of obedience shewn by Christ, now returns to exhortation.

Wherefore, my beloved,

ὥστε; i.e. as a consequence of this pattern set before you by Christ.

as ye have always obeyed,

i.e. from the day of your conversion. See chap. i. 5, "For your fellowship in the Gospel *from the first day* until now." He praises them for the steady obedience which they had

---

[n] Primitive Tradition of the Catholic Church, vi. 19.   [o] Chap. v. 27.

uniformly shewn; and a very high commendation this is. It is worthy of observation that he does not set *other* people before them as an example, but cites their own case as a pattern of this virtue. After 'obeyed' must be understood either 'the Gospel [p],' or 'Word [q].'

not as in my presence only,

The word 'as' in this sentence is emphatic, q. d. ye did not obey as merely regarding my presence among you, when your obedience was shewn under my very eye, but &c.

but now much more in my absence,

And this indeed was their highest praise. When St. Paul's bodily presence was removed from among them, and the excitement attending the first preaching of the Word had died away, and persecution began to arise, they still remained stedfast. They continued to be in the Apostle's *absence* what they had been in his *presence*.

work out your own salvation

'Work out,' κατεργάζεσθε; not merely 'work,' but 'work out,' implying a continuous and persevering work, to be accomplished only with much care and earnestness. For a similar use of the word see Rom. vii. 18. This word must be carefully distinguished from ἐνεργεῖν, which is God's action, and by Him inspired into man, (see next verse). Κατεργάζεσθαι is a word used of artificers; see Ex. xxxv. 33, LXX.; Demosth. *Aphob.* i. p. 816, ἐλέφαντα καὶ σίδηρον ὧν κατειργάζοντο.

The word ἐνέργεια is used by Aristotle to denote actual action as opposed to δύναμις or ἕξις, *potentiality* or power of acting. Philosophically speaking, therefore, in the Deity there is no mere δύναμις or ἕξις, because He is always in action (συνεχῶς ἐνεργεῖ). But, besides this, the word ἐνεργεῖν has another signification; it is ἐν ἐργεῖν, to work anything in another. Thus God ἐνεργεῖ, works by His own power, or, as we might say, *energy*, and He also ἐν ἐργεῖ, works by the same power *in* man; and thus God,

---

[p] 2 Thess. i. 8.   [q] 2 Thess. iii. 14.

inspiring man with His own power, enables *him* also ἐνεργεῖν, (in the first sense,) to *energise*, and act, and use those capacities before given him by God, (Who really has them in Himself and gives them to man); and man, when so energising, κατεργάζεται, carves or chisels out, as a workman does, his own salvation [r].

Aristotle would tell us that a man, having by *nature* δύναμις, works (ἐνεργεῖ) by the sole operation of his own will.

The Pelagian, admitting that the δύναμις comes originally from God, still maintains, with the heathen philosopher, that man ἐνεργεῖ, works with this δύναμις, by the sole operation of his own will.

While the Churchman believes with the Pelagian that God gives to man δύναμις, the power of working (one grace), but, besides this, he is aware that God must grant him a second grace, *the working upon his will*, which may incite him to use the first grace, and so κατεργεῖν σωτηρίαν, to work out by imparted energy his means of grace; for σωτηρία does not mean final salvation, but, as it were, the rough material of salvation which we have to work out for ourselves. Hence the expressions in our collects, " Who workest in us both to will and to do of Thy good pleasure," "special grace preventing us to put into our minds good desires," together with " enabling us to bring the same to good effect," " stirring up our wills," " the spirit to do and to think such things as be rightful," &c. For more on the subject of ἐνέργεια see Commentary on the Ephesians, p. 88.

'Your own;' the work cannot be done by proxy. These words give us a view of the *individual* self-denial and zeal required in the Christian life. Compare Ps. xlix. 7, " But no man may deliver his brother: nor make agreement unto God for him."

with fear and trembling.

See Ps. ii. 11, " Serve the Lord in fear: and rejoice unto Him with reverence." See also 1 Pet. i. 17.

---

[r] For a distinction between the way in which God ἐνεργεῖ and that in which the devil 'energizes,' see Commentary on Ephesians, p. 113.

'With fear,' μετὰ φόβου; i. e. the fear of failure.
'And trembling,' καὶ τρόμου; i. e. an eager anxiety to please God. For a similar combination of words see 1 Cor. ii. 3; 2 Cor. vii. 15; Eph. vi. 5 ; see Commentary on this last place. The two expressions when taken together obviously indicate a high state of anxiety and self-distrust, as opposed to *carnal security*. Hemmingius well describes the condition here indicated by the Apostle as "sollicitus tremor," and goes on to say of it, "with which doubt is not nourished, but by means of which the neglect of God, the false way of worshipping God, carnal security, idleness, and pride are excluded."

St. Paul earnestly exhorts the Philippians to maintain this state of mind, since it is impossible for one who lives devoid of fear to reach a high point of Christian excellence. If anxiety and fear are necessary elements in *worldly* success, how much more so in *spiritual*, where the contest lies not with objects that may be discerned by sense, but with "principalities and powers, and the rulers of the darkness of this world[s]." St. Chrysostom says, "I desire to know who ever learnt his letters without fear? who ever became a proficient in any art without fear? But if, when the devil does not lie in the way, where indolence is the only obstacle, so much of fear is necessary merely in order that we may master that indolence which is natural to us; where there is so fierce a war, so great hindrances, how can we by any possibility be saved without fear?"

How deeply the Apostle himself was sensible of this salutary fear will be seen from 1 Cor. ix. 27, where he says, "I keep under my body, and bring it into subjection: lest that by any means, when I have preached to others, I myself should be a castaway."

The 'fear' which the Apostle here speaks of must be carefully distinguished from the *slavish fear* which attaches itself to sin. The former fear "is the beginning of wisdom," it "is clean and endureth for ever;" the latter "hath torment," and, therefore, finds no place in those who are "made per-

---

[s] Eph. vi. 12.

fect in love." "Fear, so to say, prepares a place for charity. But when once charity has begun to inhabit, the fear which prepared the place for it is cast out. For in proportion as this increases, that decreases; and the more this comes to be within, is the fear cast out. Greater charity, less fear; less charity, greater fear. But if no fear, there is no way for charity to come in. As we see in sewing, the thread is introduced by means of the bristle; the bristle first enters, but except it comes out the thread does not come into its place; so fear first occupies the mind, but the fear does not remain there, because it enters only in order to introduce charity[t]."

The same Father[u], shewing the danger of prosperity if not accompanied with fear, says again, "There is then fear in gladness. How can there be gladness, if fear? Is not fear wont to be painful? There will hereafter be gladness without fear, now gladness with fear; for not yet is there perfect security, nor perfect gladness. If there is no gladness, we faint: if full security, we rejoice wrongly. Therefore may He both sprinkle on us gladness, and strike fear into us, that by the sweetness of gladness He may lead us to the abode of security; by giving us fear, may cause us not to rejoice wrongly, and to withdraw from the way[v]."

St. Chrysostom, *in loc.*, very beautifully shews how this 'fear and trembling,' so necessary to the Christian, may be produced and stimulated. "If," he says, "we but consider that God is everywhere present, that He heareth all things, that He seeth all things, not only whatsoever is done or said, but also all that is in the heart, and in the depth of the soul, for He is 'a Discerner of the thoughts and intents of the heart;' if we so dispose ourselves, we shall not do, or say, or imagine, aught that is evil. For, tell me, if thou hadst to stand constantly near the person of a ruler, wouldest not

---

[t] St. Aug. in 1 Joh. iv. 18.
[u] In Ps. lxxxvi. 16.
[v] "The Schoolmen have distinguished four kinds of fear: the fear of man, by which we are led rather to do wrong than to suffer evil; servile fear, through which we are induced to avoid sin only from the dread of hell; and this fear, taken by itself, was, till later and laxer times, always held to be sinful: thirdly, initial fear, in which we avoid sin partly from the fear of hell, but partly also from the love of God, which is the fear of ordinary Christians; and filial fear, when we are afraid to disobey God only and altogether from the love we bear Him, which is the fear of saints."—*Neale, Commentary on the Psalms,* pp. 100, 101.

thou stand there with fear? And how, standing in God's presence, dost thou laugh, and throw thyself back, and not conceive fear and dread? Let it never be that thou despisest His long-suffering, for it is to bring thee to repentance that He is long-suffering; and when thou doest aught, never allow thyself to do it without being sensible that God is present in all things, for He *is* present. So then, whether eating, or preparing to sleep, or giving way to passion, or robbing another, or whatever thou art about, consider that God is standing by, and thou wilt never be led into laughter, never inflamed with rage."

Gerard Vossius concludes from this text (coupled with Matt. xxv. 21, 23, 34, 35; Rev. vii. 14, 15; 2 Cor. iv. 17; Gal. vi. 8) that they do not go far enough who think the promise of reward is made to good works *merely as signs of faith*; since it is plain from these passages, to which many more might easily be added, that in the matter of salvation our works are viewed as the indispensable cause or condition precedent, which carries with it inseparably the promise of eternal life.

13. For it is God which worketh in you

ἐστὶν ὁ ἐνεργῶν is stronger than the simple ἐνεργεῖ. For the use of this word see observations on verse 12. The *in-working* of God, which, as St. Augustine [x] says, is efficacious, when rightly considered, is the foundation of true humility. The work of grace in the soul is God's work, but yet, though energetic and effective, not wrought in such an irresistible manner as that it is impossible for those in whom He is pleased to work to retard, and finally to destroy, His work. If this were so, the Apostle's exhortation in the preceding verse, 'work out your own salvation with fear and trembling,' could have no bearing upon Christians. But God works *in* us, not *against* us; not by physical determination of the will, not by destroying the nature of His creature, but morally, by illumination, persuasion, and inspiration. As St. Augustine[y] says, "Through thee and in thee He worketh good." The fact, therefore, that it is 'God which

---

[x] De Gratiâ, xvi.   [y] In Ps. ciii. 29.

worketh,' &c., supplies us with the *reason* why our share of the work should be accompanied by 'fear and trembling,' since the good which we may possess is not of ourselves, but of God, Who resists the proud (the self-confident and careless), but gives grace to the lowly. St. Augustine[z] says, "If therefore God worketh in thee, by the grace of God thou workest well, not by thy strength. Therefore if thou rejoicest, fear also, lest perchance that which was given to a humble man be taken away from a proud one." And again[a]: "Thou sayest, O Paul, work: thou commandest us to work: wherefore with trembling? For it is God, he saith, which worketh in you. For this reason then with trembling, because God worketh in you. Because He gave, because what thou hast cometh not from thee, thou shalt work with fear and trembling, for if thou fearest not Him He will take away what He gave."

'In you;' observe the force of these words. Not *among* you, but *in* you. See 2 Cor. iv. 12; Eph. ii. 2; Col. i. 29.

both to will and to do

St. Augustine[b] says, "The will is prepared by the Lord." And again[c]: "We may understand that even what we do well should be ascribed to God's grace." "Deus operatur," says Estius, "velle et perficere, per sanctas inspirationes, illuminationes, affectiones, ostendendo bonum, ad illud alliciendo et trahendo, absque tamen ulla impressione quæ voluntatem prædeterminet." St. Bernard[d] shews how God works in us these three things: "Primum, scilicet cogitare, sine nobis; secundum, scilicet velle, nobiscum; tertium, scilicet perficere, per nos facit."

Speaking on this subject, Bp. Andrewes[e] says, "Now of ourselves, as of ourselves, we are not fit so much as to think a good thought. Not so much as to will, 'for it is God that worketh in us to will.' If not these two, (1) neither think, nor (2) will, then, not to work. No more we are; neither to begin; nor having begun, to go forward, and bring it to an end. Fit to none of these. Then made fit we must be; and

---

[z] In Ps. lxvi. 5.
[a] In Ps. civ. Serm. iv. 16.
[b] In Ps. cxix. Serm. xi.
[c] In Ps. cxix. Serm. xxv.
[d] De Grat. et Lib. Arbitrio.
[e] Serm. xviii. On the Resurrection.

who to reduce us to this fitness but this God of peace that brought again Christ from the dead?"

of His good pleasure.

ὑπὲρ τῆς εὐδοκίας. Conybeare puts a stop after ἐνεργεῖν, and, connecting εὐδοκία with the next verse, takes it in the same sense as at chap. i. 15 and Luke ii. 14. He translates, "Do all things for the sake of good-will," and says, "It is strange that so clear and simple a construction, involving no alteration in the text, should not have been before suggested [f]." St. Chrysostom, however, connects these words with what has gone before, and takes them to mean, "works in us to fulfil His good pleasure concerning us."

The use of the preposition ὑπὲρ in this place for κατὰ, as Eph. i. 9, (and for διὰ, as 2 Thess. ii. 1,) is probably a Hebraism; ὑπὲρ indeed is often used in the sense of ὑπὸ, 'by,' 'by reason of.' No doubt εὐδοκία may be used of men, as chap. i. 15, but still it is a word which more generally is applied κατ' ἐξοχὴν to God, see Matt. xi. 26. What God's εὐδοκία is, is explained in Eph. i. 9, 10, (see observations there); viz. the final salvation of His elect through Christ. Consequently, whether we render ὑπὲρ 'according to,' or 'by reason of,' the sense will be the same, viz. that God, because He has predestined His people to eternal glory, will continue to help them with good inspirations and means of grace to attain this end.

Bp. Andrewes [g] says, "The Greeks distinguish between the will of God by both the words of θέλημα and εὐδοκία. When we do God's will without any regard how, so it be done, that is His θέλημα, but when God's will is done with a *sicut*, and in such sort as He requireth, that is His good pleasure, and εὐδοκία."

14. The Apostle here continues the exhortation which he commenced in verse 3, "Let nothing be done through strife or vain-glory."

Do all things

These words are very important, following so closely as

---

[f] Conybeare and Howson, Life and Epistles of St. Paul, ii. 441, note.
[g] Serm. xii. On the Lord's Prayer.

they do upon the statement in verse 13, that 'it is God which worketh,' &c., and shew that the *inworking* of *God* by no means excludes effort on the part of man.

without murmurings and disputings :

γογγυσμός probably means murmuring against men, i. e. amongst one another, (see 1 Pet. iv. 9 ; Jude 16,) and not against God. Zanchius, with more truth than elegance, distinguishes between 'murmurings' and 'disputings' thus,—'murmurings,' secret complaints one of another, like the grunting of hogs; 'disputings,' open contentions and quarrels. It is most probable, however, that this last word has special reference to the subtleties of philosophers, more especially of the Aristotelian school, many of whom were in Macedonia.

St. Chrysostom aptly remarks, " The devil, when he finds that he has no power to withdraw us from doing right, goes about to spoil our reward by other means. For he has taken occasion to insinuate pride or vainglory ; or if not this, then murmuring ; or, if none of these, misgivings."

15. That ye may be blameless

ἄμεμπτοι, *sine querelâ*, see Luke i. 6 ; i. e. concerning whom no one can justly complain, inasmuch as ye afford no opportunity for the enemy to blaspheme. In Eph. i. 4 St. Paul uses the word ἄμωμοι : see remarks there. This 'blameless' character will result from the virtues which the Apostle has already mentioned—unity, love, humility.

and harmless,

ἀκέραιοι, derived from κεράω, 'to mingle,' and the sense of the word is *simplex, sincerus*, i. e. without any alloy. " As God is simple, so His children ought to walk with a pure and simple heart [h]," and this according to our Lord's own words, Matt. x. 16, " Be ye therefore wise as serpents, and harmless as doves." See also Rom. xvi. 19. Some, however, derive the word from κέρας, 'a horn,' as if it were ἀκέρατος, i. e. 'without horns,' and so ' harmless.' But whichever derivation is followed, the idea is the same.

---

[h] Haymo.

the sons of God,

See Rom. viii. 16, 29, and ix. 8; Gal. iv. 28; Eph. v. 1. He mentions their *dignity* to enforce a more careful discharge of duty. What an exalted idea do these words, when rightly considered, give us of the Christian calling. See remarks on Eph. iv. 1.

without rebuke,

ἀμώμητα, (see Commentary on Ephesians, p. 39,) i.e. without sin, which causes rebuke, for Christians should excel in virtue, and, as being "followers of God," should lead blameless lives [i]; they should be higher than others, as Saul was by the head and shoulders; being without blemish from head to foot [k].

in the midst of a crooked and perverse nation,

(These words are taken from Deut. xxxii. 20.) i.e. among wicked and self-willed men. He here alludes to the manners of the Gentile world, which, as having deviated from the law of God's commandments, were truly 'crooked.' See Acts ii. 40, where the word rendered 'untoward' in the English Version is the same as that used here.

Caietan very properly says that there is the greater reason that Christians should strive to be 'blameless and harmless,' since they live in the midst of a world that industriously twists their words and actions to a wrong end, being itself crooked and perverse.

St. Gregory [l] says of Job, "He was good among bad men, for it is no very great praise to be good in company with the good, but to be good with the bad; for as it is a greater offence not to be good among good men, so is it immeasurably high testimony for any one to have shewn himself good even among the wicked." Compare 2 Pet. ii. 7, 8.

And again [m], the same Father beautifully shews that sinners are mingled with the righteous to try them: "Thus in the threshing-floor the grains are squeezed under the chaff,

---

[i] Eph. i. 4, and v. 27; Col. i. 22; 2 Pet. iii. 4; Jude 24; Rev. xiv. 5.
[k] 1 Sam. ix. 2.   [l] Moral. i. 1.   [m] Moral. xx. 76.

thus the flowers come forth between thorns, and the rose that smells grows along with the thorn that pricks. Thus the first man had two sons, but one was elect, the other refuse. The three sons of Noah, too, did the ark contain, but while two continued in humility, one went headlong into the mocking of his father. Two sons Abraham had, but one was innocent, the other the persecutor of his brother. Two sons also Isaac had, one saved in humility, while the other even before he was born was cast away. Twelve sons Jacob begat, but of these one was sold in innocency, while the rest were through wickedness the sellers of their brother. Twelve Apostles, too, were chosen in Holy Church; but that they might not remain untried, one is mixed with them, who by persecuting should try them. For to a just man there is joined a sinner together with wickedness, just as in the furnace to the gold there is added chaff along with the fire, that in proportion as the chaff burns the gold may be purified." Compare with this verse Rev. ii. 13.

among whom ye shine as lights in the world;

φαίνεσθε, some prefer to take this as the imperative, 'among whom shine as,' &c., but there appears to be no sufficient reason why the English Version, which makes it the indicative, should not be received.

'As lights,' φωστῆρες; not merely 'lights,' but 'luminaries,' i.e. heavenly bodies. See Eph. v. 8; 1 Thess. v. 5. "The Apostle desired that the faithful should so live, that as the sun dispels the darkness, and the moon and other heavenly bodies illuminate the night, so they by shining with faith, hope, and doctrine, might scatter by their example the darkness of error and the mists of unbelief from the hearts of those who receive not the truth[n]."

Schleusner says φωστήρ in its *general* sense means "that which has, and scatters, light, (from φῶς and τηρέω,) but in its *special* sense stands for the "heavenly bodies." Thus Gen. i. 14, 16: Καὶ ἐποίησεν ὁ Θεὸς τοὺς δύο φωστῆρας τοὺς μεγάλους, τὸν φωστῆρα τὸν μέγαν εἰς ἀρχὰς τῆς ἡμέρας, καὶ

---

[n] Haymo.

τὸν φωστῆρα τὸν ἐλάσσω εἰς ἀρχὰς τῆς νυκτός. See also Wisd. xiii. 2; Ecclus. xviii. 7. The word φωστήρ, therefore, will signify not merely lights, but light-keepers and dispensers, those to whom light has been committed for the purpose of transmitting it to others, as when our Lord said, "Ye are the light of the world[p]." The doctrine therefore is, that all who have received graces of any kind from Heaven have received them not exclusively for their own salvation, but in order that they might transmit them to others, as the sun which received light not for itself alone, but for the purpose of illuminating the world.

Conformably with this interpretation, Tertullian[q] says, "We are both temples of God, and His altars, and *lights*, and vessels."

St. Chrysostom has a passage of extraordinary beauty on this subject: "For the stars, too, give light in the night, they shine in the dark, and receive no blemish to their own beauty; yea, they even shine the brighter; but when light returns, they no longer shine so. Thus thou, too, dost appear with the greater lustre, whilst thou holdest straight in the midst of the crooked."

St. Augustine[r] shews that holy men are "stars," and continues, "These stars God counteth; all who shall reign with Him, all who are to be gathered into the Body of His Only-begotten Son, He hath counted, and still counteth them. Whoso is unworthy is not even counted. . . . Let each one of you consider whether he shineth in darkness, whether he refuseth to be led astray by the dark iniquity of the world; if he be not led astray nor conquered, he will be as it were a star which God already numbereth."

St. Anselm says, "He desires that Christians should be like stars, which being fixed in heaven care not for earthly things, but are wholly occupied with fulfilling their courses, and shedding light upon the world." It is a well-known saying, "Nec Hesperus nec Lucifer ita admirabilis est ut justus." The woman in Rev. xii. 1, who is regarded as a type of the Church, is represented as "clothed with the sun,

---

[p] Matt. v. 14.   [q] De Cor. ix.   [r] In Ps. cxlvii. 9.

and the moon under her feet, and upon her head a crown of twelve stars." And how appropriately Christians are likened to stars will be further seen from Dan. xii. 3, " And they that be wise shall shine as the brightness of the firmament; and they that turn many to righteousness as the stars for ever and ever."

It has been thought, however [s], that the word φωστῆρες cannot be properly applied to the heavenly bodies in this place, since they do not shine in the midst of what is *crooked and perverse*, but of what is clear and glorious. Nor do they guide any one through the midst of winding intricacies. Discarding this idea, then, some prefer to consider the figure as taken from the custom of carrying torches to guide passengers along the dark and narrow streets of ancient cities, perhaps of Rome itself, which was at this time remarkable for its narrow and winding streets, soon to be destroyed by Nero's conflagration, which changed the aspect of the city. It must be felt, however, that the former interpretation, which connects the word with the heavenly bodies, gives a very beautiful sense, and one which we cannot hastily part with.

16. Holding forth

i. e. as an ensign; or rather, as the hand does a torch, or a watch-tower the light, to point out the harbour to weather-beaten sailors. Ἐπέχοντες properly contains the notion of holding out, and so *applying*, just as a nurse may be said to ἐπέχειν her breast to the infant. For this use of the word see *Iliad*, xxii. 83, where Hecuba says to Hector εἴποτέ τοι λαθικηδέα μαζὸν ἐπέσχον, 'have held out,' *porrexi*. The Apostle's meaning will then be, making others partakers of grace which you yourselves enjoy. St. Chrysostom understands ἐπέχοντες as 'holding fast,' (= κατέχοντες,) but this mode of interpretation entirely destroys the beauty of the figure.

the word of life;

This shews what sort of light it is that Christians are to

---

[s] See Wordsworth's Greek Test., *in loc.*

hold forth, viz. the doctrine of the Holy Gospel, which is pre-eminently 'the word of life,' as being the revelation of Him Who is Life itself, and as working eternal life in those who embrace and believe it. In Eph. i. 13 it is called "the word of truth." See remarks there.

that I may rejoice

εἰς καύχημα ἐμοί: εἰς here implies the effect. It is to be observed that he does not say εἰς δόξαν, as if he wished to receive *glory* or honour on account of what he had done for the Philippians, but εἰς καύχημα, q. d. "that I may have ground for honest exultation in you, as being so eager to hand on to others that light of the Gospel which you received in the first instance from me your Apostle."

It must be observed that 'rejoice' is not strong enough to give the Apostle's meaning; it rather stands for 'boasting' in a good sense. See observations on chap. i. 26.

in the day of Christ,

i. e. the day of judgment, which is specially Christ's day. See remarks on chap. i. 6.

that I have not run in vain,

He here gives the ground of his exultation. The figure is an agonistic one, and one which would be very impressive as addressed to persons who were familiar with Roman games. This figure is expanded in chap. ii. 12—14.

It is obvious that the expression 'in vain' does not relate to the *Apostle*, as if he would lose *his own* reward through anything the Philippians might do; but to the Philippians, lest they should fail of *theirs*. This appears from 1 Cor. iii. 8, "Every man shall receive *his own reward according to his own labour;*" where it is to be observed that it is not said according to the *fruit* of his labour, since this is altogether out of man's control, and even after the most patient care and toil it is possible that no appreciable result may follow. Still, whether the fruit is much or none, the reward will follow in proportion to the exertion bestowed, and the spirit of love in which the work has been undertaken.

neither laboured in vain.

A figure borrowed from husbandry. The Philippian Church is the field in which the Apostle has been toiling, (his labour being that of "planting and watering[1],") and he expects to see some fruit springing up in it as the result of his labour.

The work of preaching the Gospel is likened to a *course* in Acts xx. 24; Gal. ii. 2; 2 Tim. iv. 7; and to *laborious toil* in Acts xx. 35; 1 Cor. xv. 10; 1 Tim. iv. 10, and v. 17; Rev. ii. 3.

17. Not only does the Apostle rejoice for the exemplary conduct of the Philippians, but he goes on to say that even if it should be needful for him to seal his testimony to the faith with his blood, it will not abate the holy exultation of which he has been speaking, but he will still rejoice. In order the better to enforce his meaning, he uses a very striking illustration borrowed from sacrificial rites. The figure is a Jewish one, (see Exod. xxix. 40, 41,) though the words which are used in connection with it are classical.

Yea, and if I be offered

This is the *second* member of the alternative. See chap. i. 22.

The word σπένδομαι ('offered') is used not only of the blood of the victim shed in sacrifice, but also of the libation of wine which was poured over it, when it was set apart for slaughter. In this sense the word is taken here and 2 Tim. iv. 6, ἐγὼ γὰρ ἤδη σπένδομαι, and the use of the *present* tense is emphatic, shewing that the Apostle looked upon the laying down of his life as a *certainty;* the afflictions which he was even then undergoing being the preparatory libation.

upon the sacrifice and service of your faith,

ἐπὶ τῇ θυσίᾳ καὶ λειτουργίᾳ τῆς πίστεως ὑμῶν. A sacrifice (θυσία) was first killed, and then prepared by the Priests

---

[1] 1 Cor. iii. 6.

and Levites, this last operation being the λειτουργία. St. Paul combines both expressions in order to shew the *perfectness* of the sacrifice he was willing to make of himself. When applied to the Philippians, their faith, i. e. their receiving the Gospel and being baptized, is this θυσία, and the labour afterwards bestowed upon them in confirming them and fitting them for being offered a living sacrifice to God, is the λειτουργία. And then, the spending of the Apostle's life, and probable shedding of his blood in the employment, is the pouring out the wine on the sacrifice. The whole sentence is highly emphatic, as shewing the perfect willingness of the Apostle to lay down his life for the Gospel. Compare Rom. xv. 16.

Haymo well remarks, in reference to the sacrificial word 'offered,'—" Nero himself was the priest of Peter and Paul, because he sacrificed them. He sacrificed them indeed, but *offered* them not, since they offered themselves."

St. Chrysostom, on this place, says, " He is both consoling them about his own death, and instructing them to bear death gladly for Christ's sake. I am become, he says, as it were a libation and a sacrifice. O blessed soul! His bringing them to God he calls a sacrifice, which teaches us that it is much better to present a soul than to present oxen; if now then, over and above this offering, he says, I add myself likewise, as a drink-offering, I have joy in my death!"

Thorndike[u] expands this declaration of the Apostle, and shews how it may be referred to ourselves. He says, " It appeareth that by submitting to the Gospel men become a sacrifice to God, inasmuch as they die to the world; and that they who bring them to Christianity are the priests that offer this sacrifice."

I joy,

On my own account, since my death will bring its reward.

and rejoice with you all.

i. e. congratulate you, as those to whom the benefit of my death will reach.

---

[u] Principles of Christian Truth, chap. xv. § 16.

St. Chrysostom [v] points out how the prospect of death, even martyrdom, is a source of joy and gladness to the Christian: "And if thou disbelievest our sayings, hearken to them that have seen the countenances of the martyrs in the time of their conflicts, how when scourged and flayed they were exceeding joyful and glad, and when exposed upon hot irons rejoiced and were glad of heart, more than such as lie upon a bed of roses. Wherefore Paul also said, when he was at the point of departing hence, and closing his life by a violent death, 'I joy, and rejoice with you all.' Seest thou with what exceeding strength of language he invites the whole world to partake in his gladness? So great a good did he know his departure hence to be, so desirable and lovely, and worthy of prayer, that formidable thing, death!"

18. For the same cause also do ye joy, and rejoice with me.

His meaning is, The joy must not be only on *my part*. My desire is that you should share in my joy, and congratulate me on the prospect of my martyrdom, since it is well said [x] of the martyrs that they enter at once upon their reward, "leaving the world to seek heaven; quitting men to stand amidst angels; breaking through all worldly impediments to stand free in the sight of God; to gain a heavenly kingdom without any delay; to become the colleague with Christ in suffering for the Name of Christ; by the Divine mercy to be made the judge of one's own judge." We gather from this verse that it is necessary that the affections of the people should answer to the affections of their teacher. See Acts xx. 31 and 37, where the 'tears' of the Apostle are responded to by the 'tears' of the elders of Ephesus.

19. He here affords further consolation to the Philippians, by promising to send St. Timothy to them. He had said [y],

---

[v] Hom. xxxviii. 4, in Matt. Ep. lviii. 2—4.   [y] Ver. 4.

[x] St. Cyprian, Ep. xxxi. 3. See also

"Look not every man on his own things, but every man also on the things of others," and he now puts this doctrine into practice, by depriving himself of the services of Timothy, at a time when he much needed them, for the good of the Philippians.

But I trust in the Lord Jesus to send Timotheus shortly unto you,

"See how he refers everything to Christ, even the mission of Timothy [z]." He does not absolutely promise, but his meaning is, I have a *good hope* that God will grant me this. Compare James iv. 15, a formula that should ever be adopted by Christian people.

The use of the particle δὲ (ἐλπίζω δὲ) in this sentence is worthy of observation. The Apostle breaks off his discourse and proceeds to something fresh, as if he said, I am unwilling to spend more time in exhorting you to unity, love, and humility, *because* Timothy will come to you, who will enter fully upon these topics, and will correct by word of mouth anything among you that may require amendment.

that I also may be of good comfort,

"Again he joins his own good with that of the Philippians [a]."

when I know your state.

γνοὺς τὰ περὶ ὑμῶν, "quæ circa vos sunt;" i. e. when I know that all is going on well, and that you are making steady progress in the doctrine of Christ; for as long as I have no intelligence, fear and anxiety possess me, lest some evil should have happened to you.

It is to be observed that the sending of St. Timothy at this particular juncture was " a proof of excessive care; for when he could not himself be with them, he sent his disciples, as he could not endure to remain, even for a little time, in ignorance of their state. For he did not learn all things by revelation of the Spirit [b]."

---

[z] St. Chrysostom.   [a] Estius.   [b] St. Chrysostom.

The example of St. Paul should teach ministers that it is only when they postpone all considerations (more particularly their own private griefs and crosses) to the good of their flock that they can hope to receive abundant fruit.

20. For I have no man like-minded,

Wordsworth[c] well remarks on the use of the word 'for' at the commencement of this verse, that it is "a remarkable reason. St. Paul in the time of his trial sends Timothy away from himself at Rome to Philippi, *because* he has *no one who is like-minded* with himself, and therefore no one will be so earnest and affectionate in his love and care for them. He gives to *others* what he *loved best* and what he *needed most* for himself."

The notion of ἰσόψυχος ('like-minded') among Greek writers appears to be the same as ἴσος ἐμῇ ψυχῇ, 'equal to my own soul,' such, for example, as Patroclus was to Achilles. And this is the meaning here; not to express what love St. Timothy had for the Philippians, but how highly he was valued by St. Paul, being, as it were, *his second self*; so that when he came to them they should believe a second Paul had come. There is also a reading ἰσόζυγον. Hammond prefers the marginal translation 'so dear to me.' But this gives an inferior sense. Compare Aristotle, *Eth. Nic.*, xxix. ix. §§ 4, 5, ἐστὶ γὰρ ὁ φίλος ἄλλος αὐτός.

It is plain that the Apostle's words, 'I have no man,' &c., must be understood only of those who were *then present with him*, and cannot be referred to Titus, Luke, or Clement, who were his disciples and companions, but who doubtless were absent at this particular time.

St. Augustine[d] says, "In the midst of hirelings the shepherd groaned; he sought some one who would sincerely love the flock of Christ, and about him, among those who at that time were with him, he found none. Not that in the Church of Christ there was then, save Paul the Apostle and Timothy, no man who would naturally care for the flock; but it so fell out, that at the time when he sent Timothy, he had not

---

[c] Greek Testament.   [d] Hom. xlvi. 5, in Joh.

about him any other of his sons; only hirelings were with him, men 'seeking their own, not the things which are Jesus Christ's.' And yet he, naturally caring for the flock, chose rather to send his son, and to be left in the midst of hirelings."

who will naturally care for your state.

'Naturally,' γνησίως, "germane, vere, cordate et realiter[e];" i. e. with genuine affection. It means that St. Timothy would take care of the Philippians as if he were one of them. Or, better, as having an interest in St. Paul's *spiritual relationship* to them: possibly also because Timothy was with St. Paul at the time when he first converted the Macedonians. The same word occurs 2 Macc. xiv. 8.

21. For all seek their own,

Compare 1 Cor. x. 24. 'All.' This word must be understood with some limitation. It is intended to shew the *general* rather than the *entire* state of self-seeking into which they had unhappily fallen [f]. The Apostle is referring to those (a very numerous body, alas! in all branches of the Church) who seek for ease and quiet at the expense of truth, and who are indisposed to suffer anything in mind, body, or pocket, for the sake of Christ. There is also, no doubt, a reference to those who only profess Christianity for the sake of *gain;* seeking for the prizes and honours which the Church has to give.

St. Chrysostom refers the expression 'their own' to *their* own *comfort*, their own *safety*. "But why," he asks, "doth he lament such things as these? To teach us, his hearers, not to fall in like sort, to teach his hearers not to seek for remission from toil; for he who seeks remission from toil seeks not the things that are Christ's, but his own. We ought to be prepared against every toil, against every distress."

---

[e] Cornelius à Lap.
[f] " Non absolutè et simpliciter; nec enim Paulus et Apostoli quærebant quæ sunt sua, sed quæ Jesu Christi. 'Omnes,' ergo, id est, plerique omnes, passim omnes, plurimi."—*Cornelius à Lap).*

Bengel exclaims, " O quam multi sui causâ pii sunt, quanquam non sunt ' hostes,' " chap. iii. 18.

St. Augustine [g] says of self-seekers, "They preach mercy and truth, and do not mercy and truth. But by preaching it they know it, for they would not preach it unless they knew it. But he that loveth God and Christ, in preaching the mercy and truth of the same doth himself seek her for Him, not for himself; that is, not in order that himself may have by this preaching temporal advantages, but in order that he may do good to His members, that is, His faithful ones, by ministering with truth of that which he knoweth, in order that he that liveth no longer for himself, may live but for Him that for all men hath died."

The same Father [h], commenting on the words, "O God, my life I have told out to Thee," continues, "If therefore thou livest, and livest not by thyself, because that thou shouldest live He hath granted; tell out thy life, not for thyself, but for Him; not thine own things seeking, not for thyself living, but for Him that for all men hath died. For of certain reprobate men what saith the Apostle? 'For all men seek their own things, not the things which are of Christ Jesus.' If for this reason thou tellest out thy life, in order that it may profit thee, and other men it may not profit, for thyself thou tellest it out, not for God; but if so thou tellest out thy life, in order that other men also thou mayest invite to receive life, which thou, too, hast received, thou tellest out thy life to Him from Whom thou hast received, and thou shalt have a reward more ample, because even out of that which thou hast received not ungrateful thou hast shewn thyself."

And again [i]: "Many men seek to learn His (God's) mercy and truth in His books. And when they have learned, for themselves they live, not for Him; their own things they seek, not the things which are of Jesus Christ; they preach mercy and truth, and do not mercy and truth."

not the things which are Jesus Christ's.

i. e. which tend to His honour and glory in the salvation of souls.

---

[g] In Ps. lxi. 9.   [h] In Ps. lvi. 14.   [i] Ps. lxi. 9.

22. **But ye know the proof of him,**

We meet with the word δοκιμή Rom. v. 4; 2 Cor. ii. 9, viii. 2, ix. 13, and xiii. 3. 'That I am not speaking at random,' he says, 'ye yourselves *know* how many *proofs* of his faith he has already given.' Compare 1 Cor. xvi. 10. St. Timothy had laboured among them at the first. See Acts xvi. 1—3, xvii. 14, xviii. 5, xix. 22. This is one of the many passages that shew the depth of St. Paul's affection for him.

that, as a son with the father,

The Apostle would have written 'as a son a father, so he served *me*,' but changes it to 'so he served *with* me;' and this he does from modesty and reverence, seeing that we are not servants one of another, but all of God, in the Gospel[1]. Compare Nehem. vii. 2.

"Concinnè loquitur, partim ut de filio, partim ut de collegâ; sic iii. 17 se ut typum sistit, et tamen συμμιμητάς, 'una imitatores,' non merè 'imitatores' esse jubet[m]."

he hath served with me

The force of the word 'served' (ἐδούλευσε) must not be overlooked. It means 'served as a slave,'—a Roman mode of expression, the father having by Roman law the same power over a son as over a slave.

in the Gospel.

εἰς τὸ εὐαγγέλιον, 'unto the Gospel;' i.e. in teaching and promoting the spread of the Gospel. Younger ministers should learn from the example of St. Timothy to shew that reverence to their elder brethren, particularly the bishops, which becomes their years and experience, while the spiritual rulers of the Church should remember that those who are entrusted to their charge stand to them in the relation of *sons*. It is forgetfulness of this hallowed bond of connection that is the fruitful source of so much oppression on the part of those who govern, and of disobedience in the

---

[1] Alford. [m] Bengel.

governed. No form of Church government can ever be successful where the notion of *paternity* is lost sight of.

St. Chrysostom[n] says that "Paul's humility is shewn here, by thus associating Timothy with himself;" and Caietan well remarks that the Apostle commends him thus highly in order that the Philippians may the better understand the greatness of the favour he has done in sending him.

23. **Him therefore I hope to send presently, so soon as I shall see how it will go with me.**

i. e. how my imprisonment shall end,—ὡς ἂν ἀπίδω, "I shall have seen, as *from* a point from which I am able to contemplate the things around and concerning me; not only the issue of my trial, but also my own consequent movements." Compare Jonah iv. 5, where it is said that the prophet went out of the city, and took his seat in front of it, ἕως οὗ ἀπίδῃ τὸ ἔσται τῇ πόλει.

'How it will go with me,' τὰ περὶ ἐμέ—"quæ circa me sunt." It is plain from these words that the Apostle was by no means certain what the result of his imprisonment would be; and it is probable that the departure of St. Timothy was delayed for the present, in consequence of his assistance being indispensable to him.

St. Bernard draws a beautiful spiritual lesson from these words : "Whatsoever," he says, "relates to the body, whether good or evil, is external, and cannot touch him who is within. Wherefore the Apostle lying in filth of body and in chains, and, as far as his body was concerned, crowned with tribulation, says, I will send Timothy unto you, that ye may know the things which are around me. 'The things which are around me,' he says, that is, in the outward man, in the outward clothing of the flesh, but which do not touch me myself, who am within."

24. **But I trust in the Lord that I also myself shall come shortly.**

Compare chap. i. 25. "See how he depends in all on God[o]." This verse is evidently added to confirm what he

---

[n] Hom. i. in 2 Cor.   [o] St. Chrysostom.

had already said in ver. 15, lest they should think that because he sent Timothy he did not intend to come himself.

25. **Yet I supposed it necessary**

i. e. for your comfort, while the journey of Timothy was delayed.

to send to you Epaphroditus,

He is not mentioned elsewhere, except in chap. iv. 18. The name was a common one. Some have supposed him to be identical with Epaphras, (see Col. i. 7, iv. 12; Philem. 23,) but the grounds for such a supposition appear to be insufficient.

Here follow five titles of commendation which St. Paul applies to Epaphroditus.

my brother,

(1.) A fellow Christian, in the sense in which all the baptized make up one great family, and so are brethren; or (2.) in the still higher sense in which all who have been called to the ministry of the Church are brethren.

and companion in labour,

i. e. in preaching the Gospel: συνεργός means 'colleague.'

and fellow-soldier,

συστρατιώτην, (see Philem. 2); this expresses more than συνεργόν, ('colleague,') it implies a fellowship in contests and dangers for the cause of Christ, a brotherhood in arms. There are many who will *work* zealously enough in time of peace, but are not prepared to *fight* when the time of peril comes. The faithful Christian must be prepared to do both. See 2 Tim. ii. 3.

but your messenger,

ἀπόστολον. It is commonly inferred from the use of the term 'Apostle,' which is here applied to Epaphroditus, that he was *Bishop* of the Church at Philippi, and, as such, set over those who in the opening of the Epistle are called 'Bishops and Deacons.' This is the opinion of Theodoret, and it has been largely adopted. Hilary says of Epaphroditus, "he was their apostle, made so by the Apostle;" i. e. he was constituted their Apostle (Bishop) by St. Paul. But, as he was also the *messenger* of the Church at Philippi, having carried their contributions to St. Paul, it is not impossible that the word ἀπόστολος may have been purposely used in this place, to express the *twofold* character of Epaphroditus, messenger *and* bishop.

It is to be observed that the word ἀπόστολος means originally 'one sent.' It was translated into Hebrew by the word *malach*, signifying 'messenger.' This, when re-translated into Greek, became ἄγγελος. Hence we see why the oriental St. John calls the *Bishops* by the name of ἄγγελοι [p].

and he that ministered to my wants.

καὶ λειτουργὸν τῆς χρείας μου. The word λειτουργός is applied to Epaphroditus, as if he were discharging a *public* office, the person so called being properly a citizen who undertook a λειτουργία. See remarks on ver. 30. This is the last, but not least honourable, commendation of the services of Epaphroditus. The Philippians had sent money by his hand, in the first place to supply the needs of St. Paul himself, and then to enable him to help the poor at Rome. This is called χρεία Acts ii. 45, iv. 35, vi. 3, xx. 34, xxviii. 10; Eph. iv. 28; Phil. iv. 16.

26. For he longed after you all,

ἐπιποθῶν ἦν, (ἰδεῖν must be supplied here: it is found Rom. i. 11 and 2 Tim. i. 4). The expression signifies such a vehement desire as is impatient of delays. His heart was among his flock at Philippi. He did not merely desire to see those of *his own* household, but *all* the Philippians, shewing how wide his affections were.

and was full of heaviness, because that ye had heard that he had been sick.

It was not on account of *his own sufferings* that Epaphroditus grieved, but for the distress and anxiety which he knew the report of his dangerous sickness would cause

---

[p] Rev. i. 20.

among the Philippians. An admirable example of devoted zeal for the welfare of his flock which it will be good for ministers to have constantly before their eyes!

St. Chrysostom [q] quotes this among other passages of Holy Scripture to shew that the saints had infirmities, lest they should exalt themselves above measure, or lest they should be exalted, and, as it were, deified by others. "For if," he says, "when this was the case, (i. e. when they were liable to sickness, &c.) the people accounted them to be gods, and prepared to do sacrifice to them, saying the gods are come down to us in the likeness of men [r], had such infirmities not existed, to what extent of impiety might not men have proceeded when they beheld their miracles?"

27. For indeed he was sick nigh unto death:

This sickness of Epaphroditus was caused by his assiduous attendance upon St. Paul, hence the marked way in which he makes mention of it.

but God had mercy on him;

i. e. by restoring him to health, no doubt in answer to the Apostle's prayers, though with his usual modesty he suppresses all mention of this. We gather from this place that, since Epaphroditus was not recovered by the gift of healing, then frequent in the Church, that gift was not exercised by those to whom it was given simply at their own pleasure, but in obedience to a special and Divine instinct.

St. Paul here shews how recovery from sickness is a *mercy*, especially against those who held that life was an evil in itself. In answer to those who might object, that "if to depart and be with Christ is far better," how does the Apostle say that he obtained mercy, St. Chrysostom replies, "I would rather ask why the same Apostle says that to abide in the flesh is more needful for you? For as this was needful for him, so too for this man, who would hereafter depart to God with more exceeding riches, and greater boldness. Hereafter that would take place, even if it did not

---

[q] Hom. x. 7, on the Statues. [r] Acts xiv. 11.

now, but the winning souls is at an end for those who have once departed thither. In many places, too, Paul speaks according to the common habits of his hearers, and not everywhere in accordance with his own heavenly wisdom, for he had to speak to men of the world who still feared death."

It is plain that St. Paul is speaking in this place of death *considered by itself.*

and not on him only, but on me also, lest I should have sorrow upon sorrow.

The second 'sorrow' refers of course to his imprisonment, and the sufferings consequent upon it. He would doubly grieve if, as Grotius says, "ad vincula accessisserit jactura amici." This verse plainly shews that God does not require of men the ἀπάθεια of the Stoics, but the συμπάθεια of Christians.

28. I sent him therefore the more carefully,

σπουδαιοτέρως,—*festinantius,—diligentius.* St. Ambrose renders it *sollicitius,* others *studiosius.* The meaning is, that the Apostle took the earliest possible opportunity of despatching him.

that when ye see him again,

'Again,' i.e. after his sickness, and on his return amongst you.

ye may rejoice,

as it was most natural they should.

and that I may be the less sorrowful.

When I hear of his safe arrival, and so become partaker of your joy. This is an unusual form of expression, and it should be observed that he does not say 'that I should be altogether without sorrow,' but 'less sorrowful,' evidently implying that as long as he was in the flesh his soul could never be wholly free from sorrow. See Rom. ix. 1, 2; 2 Cor. xi. 29.

29. Receive him therefore in the Lord

'In the Lord,' *propter Dominum* ; i. e. as an ambassador of Christ. 1 Cor. iv. 1.

with all gladness ;

With deep and fervent Christian joy. The Apostle may be supposed to distinguish between the gratification of simply seeing a friend, and the holy joy which would be superadded in the case of those who are brethren in the faith. This expression must not be regarded so much as a *command*, (for they were not likely to fail in joy at the arrival of Epaphroditus,) as a token of *approval* at what they would do.

and hold such in reputation :

See 1 Cor. xvi. 18; 1 Thess. v. 12 ; 1 Tim. v. 17. Not merely Epaphroditus himself, but all ministers who are like him in zeal and love, are to be esteemed for their work's sake. "All," says Haymo, "who have the same faith, and persevere in good works, as he."

How sadly the command of the Apostle contrasts with the practice of the present day, when people have mostly learnt to say, "ministris eorum nihil vilius !"

30. Because for the work of Christ he was nigh unto death,

'The work of Christ ;' i. e. work done for the honour and glory of Christ, but specially here visiting St. Paul in prison. All works of mercy are well called ' works of Christ,' since they are done for His sake, and He reckons them as done to Himself[a].

Observe, the Apostle does not say 'for my sake,' but 'for the work of Christ ;' which shews that it was from love of God that Epaphroditus acted. "It is probable," says St. Chrysostom, "that on his arrival at the city of Rome, he found Paul in such great and urgent peril, that those who were accustomed to resort to him were unable safely to do so, but were themselves in peril by their very attendance, and that Epaphroditus, being of a noble nature, despised all

---

[a] Matt. xxv. 36.

danger, that he might go in unto him and minister unto him, and do everything which need required."

not regarding his life,

Παραβουλευσάμενος τῇ ψυχῇ. "Non habitâ ratione vitæ [t]." Παραβουλεύομαι properly signifies 'I take counsel contrary to my interest;' and is a word used of those who place themselves in jeopardy.

There is a reading, παραβολευσάμενος, which has found much favour; it means, "having staked his life." Either reading gives a good sense.

to supply your lack of service toward me.

Ἵνα ἀναπληρώσῃ τὸ ὑμῶν ὑστέρημα τῆς πρός με λειτουργίας; i. e. inasmuch as you were at a distance, and so were unable to minister to my temporal necessities, Epaphroditus, acting as your messenger, supplied your place. See Philem. 13. "That which you were unable to fulfil, on account of the distance that intervened between you, he fulfilled in your stead [u]." The service (λειτουργία) was the contribution of money which the Philippians sent by the hand of Epaphroditus. The 'lack' (ὑστέρημα) in this affectionate 'service' was their inability through absence to minister to the Apostle themselves; but this Epaphroditus filled up, (see 1 Cor. xvi. 17,) and in so doing risked his life.

There is a catachresis in the use of the word λειτουργία, which properly signifies *the administration of a public office*, (see verse 25, where Epaphroditus is called λειτουργός,) the magistracy, for instance, or priesthood; but it is here used to signify the *private* offices of kindness shewn towards St. Paul. As the word λειτουργία contains the notion of discharging a *public duty*, it is probable that St. Paul employed it in order to check any feelings of pride that might arise among the Philippians from having exercised towards him a liberality greater than that shewn by other Churches.

Photius gives the following explanation of this verse:— "Misistis quæ mihi opus erant, et absentis meministis, ac vestram beneficentiam ostendistis; supererat ad hæc omnia

---

[t] Rosenmüller.   [u] Haymo.

ut à vobis ad me missa recuperarem, et hoc solum deerat: et hoc ille (Epaphroditus) implevit quando vestra ad me munera allaturus ad mortem usque accessit."

SUMMARY OF CHAPTER III.

THE Apostle cautions the Philippians to beware of the snares of false apostles, and of carnal confidence, setting himself before them as a living example of piety, which he earnestly exhorts them to imitate.

The chief parts of this chapter are three:—
(1.) Dissuasive. He cautions them to beware of all corrupters of true doctrine, with a special reference to Judaizing teachers: ver. 1 to 3.
(2.) Demonstrative. He sets himself forward as a pattern, and by reference to his own case shews that nothing pertaining to perfection is to be sought for out of Christ: vers. 4 to 16.
(3.) Hortatory. After he has spoken of himself as one who was to be followed, he exhorts them to true piety: vers. 17 to 21.

In his treatment of these three heads we find many remarkable passages, e.g. concerning the true joy of believers, circumcision (concision), Christian perfection, the Advent of Christ, the ultimate glorification of the body, &c.

CHAP. III.

NEARLY the whole of this chapter is taken up with warnings against false teachers.

Ver. 1. Finally, my brethren,

τὸ λοιπὸν, "quod superest."

The Apostle seems to have intended to conclude his Epistle here, as he is wont to do, by the word τὸ λοιπὸν, or λοιπὸν, or τοῦ λοιποῦ, as 2 Cor. xiii. 11; Gal. vi. 17; Eph. vi. 10; 2 Thess. iii. 1; and by the word χαίρετε, 2 Cor. xiii. 11; 1 Thess. v. 16; but afterwards, when he had had a little more time for reflection, to have added what follows. His meaning is, I have already described to you in what your salvation consists, viz. in Christ alone; and now what remains but that ye rejoice in Him as in your chief good? &c.

There would be peculiar force in this expression if we believe that this was actually the *last* Epistle ever written by St. Paul.

rejoice in the Lord.

'Rejoice' is the sum and substance of the Epistle. See remarks on ver. 3, and on chap. i. 4. But it is of *spiritual* joy that he is speaking, as indicated by the addition of 'in the Lord,' 'propter Dominum,' "Whether therefore ye eat, or drink, or whatsoever ye do, do all to the glory of God [v];" or, "according to the will of the Lord," see 1 Cor. vii. 39; or, "with joy which is *worthy* of the Lord."

Some regard the words χαίρετε ἐν Κυρίῳ merely as a form of salutation, and translate, "Dominus vobis quævis fausta evenire jubeat." The same expression occurs chap. iv. 4.

We can easily understand why the Philippians should need this exhortation to *joy*. There were many circumstances likely enough to depress them. Epaphroditus their Bishop was away, and it was doubtful whether they would ever see him again. St. Paul, to whom they were fervently attached, was in prison at Rome, living in daily prospect of a painful death, so that distresses and difficulties seemed to be rising on all sides; and, therefore, in writing to them the Apostle endeavours to revive their drooping spirits. "You no longer have," he says, "cause for despondency. You have Epaphroditus, for whose sake you were grieved. You have Timothy; I am myself coming to you; the Gospel is gaining ground. What is henceforth wanting to you? Rejoice [x]!" Compare St. Paul's exhortation to the Ephesians, chap. iii. 13, "Wherefore I desire that ye faint not at my tribulations for you, which is your glory," and see Commentary, *in loc.*

St. Chrysostom remarks that St. Paul calls the Galatians 'children [y],' but the Philippians 'brethren,' and assigns as

---

[v] 1 Cor. x. 31.
[x] St. Chrysostom.
[y] Gal. iv. 19. "My little children, of whom I travail in birth again until Christ be formed in you."

a reason that when he aims to correct anything, or to shew his fondness, he calls them 'children,' but when he addresses them with greater honour, 'brethren' is the title.

To write the same things to you,

Some suppose that the expression, 'the same things,' refers either (1) to a lost Epistle; this opinion is supposed to derive confirmation from a well-known passage in St. Polycarp's Epistle to the Philippians; or, (2) to the instruction which he communicated to them by word of mouth whilst he was among them. Either of these explanations may be true; but, since *joy* is the groundwork of the whole Epistle, it seems better to refer 'the same things' to the words 'rejoice in the Lord,' which he has just used, and so we get a sense in accordance with the general bearing of the Epistle. Hence it will appear that St. Paul thought it good for the spiritual advancement of the Philippians to be constantly speaking about *joy*; it was a topic that could not too often be repeated; and so St. Augustine[z] is careful to admonish preachers to continue repeating the same topic, till by the gesture and countenance of their hearers they perceive that they understand it. That this was the plan which he himself adopted in his discourses may be gathered from the following[a]: "We have often impressed upon you, beloved, what we do not fear to reiterate frequently; in order that, since many of you possibly cannot read, either because they have no leisure or know not letters, at least by constantly listening they may not forget their healthful faith. Certainly by repeating them we may appear troublesome to some, while, however, we may be building up others. For we are well assured that there are many of retentive memory, and careful reading in Holy Writ, who know what we are about to say; and perhaps they wish us to say what they do not know. But if they are quicker, let them see that they are travelling with others not so quick; for when two persons of different speed are travelling in company, it is in the power of the quicker, and not of him who is more

---

[z] De Doctr. Christ. [a] In Ps. xci. Serm. 2.

slow, to give or deny his company; because if the swifter is pleased to do his utmost, the slower will not keep up with him, and so he must needs rein in his own speed, in order not to leave his fellow-traveller behind."

So also St. Chrysostom, who says [b], "The nature of man is slothful, and needs much reminding. The earth, when it has once received the seed, straightway gives forth its fruits and needs not a second sowing; but with our souls it is not so, and one must be content, after having sown many times, and manifested much carefulness, to be able once to receive fruit." The same Father also says [c], "Physicians often use the same remedy."

It is a well-known saying of Socrates, οὐ μόνον ἀεὶ ταυτὰ, ἀλλὰ καὶ περὶ τῶν αὐτῶν.

to me indeed is not grievous,

ἐμοὶ μὲν οὐκ ὀκνηρόν—"Me quidem neutiquam piget," or, "nunquam id per desidiam aut torporem omiserim." There seems, however, to be a notion of *cowardice* involved in the word ὀκνηρόν, and then the meaning will be that for him to write what he is about to write next, viz., cautions against 'dogs,' &c., does not arise from *cowardice* on his part, but from regard to their safety, it being for their spiritual good to be thus warned and admonished by him.

but for you it is safe.

i.e. useful and salutary; so that the constant repetition may have the effect of confirming you in the faith.

Seneca [d] well remarks, "Etiam aperta monstrare plurimum prodest. Interdum enim scimus, nec attendimus. Licet nil doceat admonitio, excitat tamen et continet memoriam, nec patitur elabi."

2. Beware of dogs,

Βλέπετε τοὺς κύνας, literally, '*the* dogs,' the article seeming to point to persons who were *well-known*. The Jews were accustomed to call the Gentiles by this name; and so our Blessed Lord, speaking according to the common practice

---

[b] Hom. xviii. 1, in Joh.   [c] Hom. li. in Joh.   [d] Ep. 95.

of the country, used the word [e]: "It is not meet to take the children's bread, and to cast it to *dogs*." (Compare Deut. xxiii. 18, and Matt. vii. 6.) But now the Apostle hurls back the name, and all the odium belonging to it, to the *Jews*. Henceforward God's relation with them is reversed; *they* are the 'dogs,' as they have shut themselves out of the covenant, and the *Gentiles* are the 'children.' Compare with this verse Rev. xxii. 15.

St. Chrysostom asks, "Whom does he style 'dogs'?" and then replies, "there were at this place some of those, whom he hints at in all his Epistles, base and contemptible Jews, greedy of vile lucre and fond of power, who, desiring to draw aside many of the faithful, preached both Christianity and Judaism at the same time, corrupting the Gospel. As then they were not easily discernible, therefore he says 'beware.'"

Cornelius à Lap. says such false teachers are well likened to 'dogs,' "because they bark after us, and bite like dogs."

And so Caietan, "He calls the false apostles 'dogs,' because after the fashion of dogs they barked against Paul."

beware of evil workers,

Τοὺς κακοὺς ἐργάτας, literally, '*the* evil workers,' not so much the Gnostics, as the Judaizing teachers. The Apostle points out a class of people who actually *worked*, and that professedly for the Gospel, but who all the while were working amiss [f]. St. Irenæus [g] well describes these people as like those who offer water mixed with chalk instead of milk. They adulterate the pure word of God.

Observe, there is a distinction to be drawn between 'evil-workers' and 'evil-doers.' The former expression denotes far more activity and zeal, and implies a kind of propagandism of evil.

In another place [h] St. Paul calls these people 'deceitful workers;' and again [i], "For they that are such serve not our Lord Jesus Christ, but their own belly; and by good words and fair speeches deceive the hearts of the simple."

---

[e] Matt. xv. 26.
[f] "Eos quos quo ad verba descripsit canes, quo ad facta describit malos operarios."—*Caietan.*
[g] Adv. Hær., lib. iii. c. 19.
[h] 2 Cor. xi. 13.
[i] Rom. xvi. 18.

By the threefold use of the word 'beware' (βλέπετε) in this verse the Apostle wishes to indicate the exceeding watchfulness that should be shewn on the part of Christians against the machinations of those whom he is describing.

The way in which he uses the words 'dogs,' 'evil workers,' 'concision,' is very remarkable. His object in the opening verses of this chapter is to put the Philippians on their guard against false teachers, whom he prefers not simply to mention by name, but to designate by epithets which would have the double effect of putting them in the most unfavourable light, and affording an insight into the nature of their devices. It has been thought that the terms which he here applies to these Judaizing teachers point out this Epistle as the last which was written by St. Paul. In earlier Epistles he had spoken of the same things with greater gentleness, but now, since ample warning had been given, and it was possible he might never be able to testify against them again, he adopts a severity of tone suited to the magnitude of the danger.

beware of the concision.

Βλέπετε τὴν κατατομήν. The Jews are frequently called "the circumcision [k]," (the abstract being put for the concrete,) but St. Paul no longer allows them the dignity that of old used to belong to this name; and while claiming for Christians the glorious title of the *true* circumcision, by a most felicitous form of expression he designates the Jews as the κατατομή, or 'the sham-cision,' (if such a word might be allowed,) since they did nothing else than cut off the flesh. No doubt also the notion of cutting themselves off from Christ is contained in this word, (see Gal. v. 2, 3,) and also of cutting up the Church into factions, since κατατέμνειν means *in partes lacerare*.

3. For we are the circumcision,

i.e. *the true* circumcision; q.d. 'if you wish to seek for circumcision, you will find it among us.' See Rom. ii. 28, 29,

---

[k] Rom. iii. 30, iv. 9; Gal. ii. 9.

and iv. 11, 12. Haymo says, "All we who believe aright are spiritually circumcised," i. e. in heart and affections. This is, of course, in strong contrast with 'the concision' in verse 2.

St. Augustine[1] points out why the Apostle says "we *are* the circumcision," instead of "we *have* the circumcision." "Understand that he intended hereby to express this, 'We are righteousness.' For circumcision is righteousness. But it sets forth the value of it more that he expresses it by saying that we are righteousness, than by saying that we are righteous; yet so as that when he says that we are righteousness, we should understand righteous."

which worship God in the spirit,

Οἱ πνεύματι Θεῷ λατρεύοντες. This might be rendered 'who worship God the Spirit,' and would then (according to St. Ambrose[m]) furnish a proof of the Divinity of the Holy Ghost; the use of the word λατρεύοντες giving additional force to this interpretation. Some MSS. read Θεοῦ, and then the sense would be, 'who worship the Spirit of God.' St. Augustine[n] favours this; but adds that most of the Greek codices read Θεῷ. There is, however, no satisfactory reason why the Apostle should be thought to be speaking in this place of the Holy Ghost, not to mention that the article is omitted before πνεύματι. The expression seems to = πνευματικῶς, being in direct contrast to ἐν σαρκί which follows. In this case the sentence will run, 'who worship God spiritually,' (see John iv. 24; Rom. vii. 6,) and not with fleshly ordinances only as the Jews, (see Isaiah xxix. 13,) 'the spirit' referring to the *inner man*[o].

and rejoice in Christ Jesus,

Not in Moses, the Jewish lawgiver, as St. Anselm says, nor yet in our own merits, but in Christ, do we boast ourselves; so that not only do we 'worship God in spirit,' but we glory in Jesus as our Messiah, from which it appears again that we are 'the circumcision.'

---

[1] Serm. cxix. 2, in Nov. Test.
[m] De Spir. Sanct. 2. c. 6.
[n] Serm. cxix. 1, in Nov. Test.
[o] Rom. vii. 22; 2 Cor. iv. 16.

and have no confidence in the flesh.

To have confidence in the flesh is to rely on external ordinances as things which will commend us to God; particularly such grounds of confidence as are mentioned by the Apostle in verse 5. Haymo explains this of *circumcision*, which no doubt is referred to primarily, though not exclusively. St. Augustine[p] says, "He had his eye on some who had confidence in the flesh; these were they who gloried of the circumcision of the flesh."

St. Chrysostom shews with what propriety St. Paul could contrast spiritual with carnal circumcision, since "if being of the Gentiles, he had condemned the circumcision, and not only the circumcision, but all those that adopted it out of place, it would have seemed that he was denying it because he wanted the high ancestry of Judaism, as being a stranger to its solemn rites, and having no part therein;" and therefore he immediately proceeds to shew that he has ample ground for confidence, or boasting, in the flesh, whenever he is pleased to use it.

4. Though I might also have confidence in the flesh.

The expression καὶ ἐν σαρκί, '*even* in the flesh,' is emphatic; shewing that the Apostle *had* grounds for boasting, according to the judgment of men, if he chose to use them. See 2 Cor. xi. 18, 21.

His object is to point out to the Philippians (against Judaizing teachers), that though he possessed those very advantages which a Jew would prize most highly, yet he willingly laid them all aside for Christ's sake. His example, therefore, would be the best possible answer to those who might endeavour to bring them into bondage to legal observances.

If any other man thinketh that he hath whereof he might trust in the flesh, I more:

"Do not imagine," saith he, "that I despise what I have

---

[p] Serm. cxix. 3, in Nov. Test.

not. What great thing is it if a mean, common, ignoble man despise nobility, and then make a show of real humility ᑫ ?"

The 'I' in this verse is highly emphatic, for though some Jews may have possessed *single* advantages superior to St. Paul, yet none could have surpassed him in the aggregate; and the word 'thinketh' is probably used to shew that there was no real ground for glorying.

"It was well to say 'thinketh,' either inasmuch as they really had no such confidence, or as that confidence was no real confidence, for all was by necessity, and not of choice ʳ."

Here follow seven particulars in which the Apostle might have gloried " in the flesh."

5. Circumcised the eighth day,

He mentions circumcision first of all, as it was the thing above all others on which Israelites prided themselves; and he adds 'the eighth day' (περιτομῇ ὀκταήμερος—abstract for concrete) to shew that the rite was duly performed according to God's ordinance, and that he was a true-born Jew, and not a proselyte, having been circumcised as Isaac and his descendants were. "That is," says St. Augustine ˢ, "not a proselyte, not a stranger joined to the people of God, not circumcised at an advanced age, but of my parents born a Jew, I have the circumcision of the eighth day."

of the stock of Israel,

Understand 'born;' compare 2 Cor. xi. 22, "Are they Israelites? so am I?" As the circumcision on the eighth day shewed that he was not a proselyte, so this expression points out that he was not born of proselyte parents, and that he was not of the descendants of Ishmael and Esau who were circumcised.

of the tribe of Benjamin,

See Rom. xi. 1, "For I also am an Israelite, of the seed of Abraham, of the tribe of Benjamin." He adds this to

---

ᑫ St. Augustine, Serm. cxix. 4, in Nov. Test.   ʳ St. Chrysostom.
ˢ Serm. cxix. 6, in Nov. Test.

augment his dignity, for it was a high distinction to belong to this tribe, (the descendants of Jacob's well-beloved son,) since the first king was chosen from it, and when the rest revolted it remained loyal. In addition to which, Jerusalem was situated within its bounds.

an Hebrew of the Hebrews;

Not merely a Jew, but one of pure descent, whose family had never been defiled by a forbidden marriage. Compare 2 Cor. xi. 22. Caietan says, "Non ex Samaritis, non ex admistis parentibus, sed ex parentibus Hebræis, unde Abraham originem duxit." So that these words must not be considered as a mere repetition of what has gone before.

as touching the law, a Pharisee;

"He is coming now to the circumstances dependent *on his own will*," says St. Chrysostom, "for all those things were apart from the will; for his being circumcised was not of himself, nor that he was of the stock of Israel, nor that he was of the tribe of Benjamin." Compare Acts xxiii. 6, "I am a Pharisee, the son of a Pharisee;" and xxvi. 5, "After the most straitest sect of our religion I lived a Pharisee." The word 'law' means as far as *discipline* is concerned.

6. Concerning zeal, persecuting the Church;

'Zeal,' i.e. for the traditions of the Fathers. See Rom. x. 2. The word ζῆλος ('zeal') is sometimes used in Scripture in a good sense [t] and sometimes in a bad sense [u]. It is plain that it must be taken here in a *good* sense, as signifying the honourable emulation, with the consequent imitation, of that which presents itself to the mind as excellent.

For more on this subject see Trench's "Synonyms of the New Testament," p. 101 and following.

He mentions his 'zeal,' because it would be quite possible to be a Pharisee, and yet only a cold and indifferent one. It was not so, however, with him; for he had 'zeal,' and he

---

[t] John ii. 17; Rom. x. 2; 2 Cor. ix. 2.
[u] Acts v. 17; Rom. xiii. 13; Gal. v. 20; James iii. 14.

shewed it by 'persecuting the Church.' Compare 1 Cor. xv. 9.

St. Augustine[x] has the following upon this verse: "Among his merits he enumerates that he was a persecutor; 'according to zeal,' he says. What zeal? I was not, says he, an inactive Jew; whatsoever it was that seemed contrary to my law I bore impatiently, I followed up vehemently. This was, with the Jews, nobility; but with Christ is sought humility."

touching the righteousness which is in the law, blameless.

i. e. such righteousness as the Law can give to those who obey its precepts. The Apostle keeps for the last place that which was of the highest importance, viz. the exact fulfilment of the Law; see Acts xxiii. 1; 2 Tim. i. 3. He is careful in this place to mention 'righteousness,' "since it is possible to be adventurous, or to act thus (i. e. shew zeal, as he had done in persecuting) from *ambition*, and not out of zeal for the Law, as the high priests did." So St. Chrysostom.

It is plain that 'blameless' must be taken in a limited sense, as far as human observation could go, but not before God[y]. He did not say absolutely 'without *sin*,' but 'without *blame*,'—Rosenmüller explains, "Nihil unquam feci morte aut verberibus dignum,"—shewing that although he sinned, yet his sins were not of such a character that any one could fairly find fault with him on the score of legal observances. Bp. Wilson interprets, "So as the Law never took hold of me." After citing the examples of Zacharias and Elisabeth[z], St. Augustine[a] goes on to say of St. Paul, "He walked in the Law without blame, and what in him was without blame, this made great matter of blame concerning him."

It is highly interesting and instructive to notice in passing the widely different way in which St. Paul speaks of his state *before* and *after* his conversion. *Before* his conversion his

---

[x] Hom. cxix. 5, in Nov. Test.   [y] 1 Tim. i. 13, 14.   [z] Luke i. 6.
[a] Hom. cxix. 6, in Nov. Test.

estimate of himself was "touching the righteousness which is in the Law *blameless.*" *After,* "This is a faithful saying, and worthy of all acceptation, that Christ Jesus came into the world *to save sinners; of whom I am chief* [b]." Just as a man that has acquired wealth may be a rich man with respect to himself, but on mixing with other people may, by comparison, appear only poor, so St. Paul, as long as he was wrapped up in himself, and did not know God truly, could never learn how great his poverty really was.

7. But what things were gain to me, those I counted loss

It is well worthy of observation that although 'gain' (κέρδη) in this verse is *plural,* 'loss' (ζημία) is *singular.* It is as if it was but this *one* 'loss' that he saw in all the 'gains' of which he has been speaking. The antithesis between the two words is very remarkable; he *depresses* his former position and attainments as much as he had previously exalted them. It is also to be observed, as St. Ambrose, Augustine, and Œcumenius point out, that he is not speaking absolutely here of the *Law,* but of the 'righteousness which is in the Law.' And this is plain from verse 9, where he says, "not having mine own righteousness which is of the Law," &c. It was this 'righteousness,' which he had achieved in the Law, and not the Law itself, which he calls 'loss' and 'dung.'

for Christ.

i.e. 'that I might embrace Christ as my Saviour.' It would have been in vain that the Apostle abandoned the Jewish ritual unless something better had been substituted for it.

St. Gregory Nazianzen, who was famous for his learning, used to rejoice like the Apostle that he had something of value that he might count 'loss' for Christ's sake. A noble ground of boasting.

8. Yea doubtless, and I count all things but loss

The Apostle rises in fervour. Not merely did he count

---

[b] 1 Tim. i. 15.

his Jewish birth and education and his other past-'gains' to be 'loss;' but he reckons *all possible things*, including life itself, to be but 'loss.' Not only what he has already possessed, or still has, but what it is *possible* for him in any way to acquire, all this he counts but 'loss.'

The use of the present tense, ἡγοῦμαι, ('I count,') is emphatic. As Caietan says, "I not only *have* counted, but at the present time *continue* so to count;" i. e. after long experience my conviction remains unshaken. The expression ἀλλὰ μενοῦνγε, 'yea doubtless,' *veruntamen etiam*, is very strong, and denotes great vehemence on the part of St. Paul; it is a correction of any possible or actual mistake. Compare Luke xi. 28, μενοῦνγε μακάριοι, κ.τ.λ.

for the excellency of the knowledge of Christ Jesus

διὰ τὸ ὑπερέχον τῆς γνώσεως, instead of διὰ τὴν γνῶσιν τὴν ὑπερέχουσαν. It was the ardent longing for this knowledge that inspired the Apostle with contempt for all besides.

'For,' i. e. in comparison of. St. Chrysostom says, "When the sun hath appeared, it is loss to sit by a candle; so that the loss comes by comparison, by the superiority of the other. You see that Paul makes a comparison from superiority, not from diversity of kind; for that which is superior is superior to somewhat of like nature with itself. So that he shews the connection of that knowledge by the same means by which he draws the superiority from the comparison."

my Lord:

See the wonderful ardour of his affection in speaking of Christ! as if He were in a special sense *his* Lord[c]. See remarks on chap. i. 3.

for whom I have suffered the loss of all things,

δι' ὃν τὰ πάντα ἐζημιώθην—" propter quem omnium jacturam feci;" i. e. I have not merely *counted* them as loss, but I have actually *deprived myself of them* by a voluntary act of surrender; for the words will bear this meaning, and

---

[c] John xx. 28.

so a beautiful sense is obtained. He had said before, 'I *count* all things but loss;' he now goes a step further and says, 'I have *made* them but loss,' according to the commandment of Christ, Matt. xvi. 24, "If any man will come after Me, let him deny himself, and take up his Cross, and follow Me."

We learn from this verse that he who desires to return to Christ must come *naked*, and the remark of Aretius is very forcible, "Moses ornatum te facilè fert, at nudum Christus te vult conspicere."

and do count them but dung,

See Isa. lxiv. 6. An intensification of verse 7, "I count all things but *loss*." And here again the Apostle is evidently not speaking of the Law in itself, but of his own righteousness which is of the Law. The word σκύβαλον ('dung') means offal or refuse of any kind. Photius, however, explains the expression (σκύβαλα) to mean *stipula frumenti*, and then proceeds to apply it to the Law in the following manner: "Quemadmodum enim necessaria est stipula donec creverit triticum, et separatum inde fuerit, ita Christo, Qui fuit verum granum frumenti, nondum nato, et in legis stipulâ latente, utilis erat lex. Ubi autem per Passionem et Resurrectionem collectum est nobis hoc granum, et per Ascensionem in horrea æterni Patris reconditum, ad nihil amplius utilis fuit legis culmus et stipula [d]." But whatever the precise meaning of the word may be, it is highly emphatic, and is probably the strongest that the Apostle could select in order to express his contempt for what he once prized so highly.

that I may win Christ,

He here furnishes the reason for what he has said before [e], "That I may obtain the benefits offered in Christ [f]."

---

[d] Aretius has a curious way of explaining this word: "Σκύβαλα sunt si Grammaticis credimus, duriora excrementa, quæ vix purgationibus ab ægris expellunt medici, quæ mihi significatio hic perplacet: nam revera ægros nos significat, et purgationibus nos indigere ad expellenda illa σκύβαλα: et sanè optimus sit medicus oportet, qui hæc stercora à nobis expulerit."

[e] "Ut Christi gratiam, justitiam, amicitiam, virtutes ac dona, tandem gloriam lucrifaciam." — *Cornelius à Lap.*

[f] Bp. Wilson.

St. Chrysostom [g] has the following passage about contempt of worldly things which forms an excellent illustration to this verse :—" Let us look into the nature of human things, that we may kindle with the longing desire of things to come; for in no other way is it possible to become humble, except by the love of what is divine, and the contempt of what is present. For just as a man on the point of obtaining a kingdom, if instead of that purple robe one offer him some trivial compliment, will count it to be nothing; so shall we also laugh to scorn all things present, if we desire that other sort of honour. Do ye not see the children, when in their play they make a band of soldiers, and heralds precede them, and lictors, and a boy marches in the midst in the general's place, how childish it all is? Just such are all human affairs; yea, and more worthless than these; to-day they are, and to-morrow they are not. Let us therefore be above these things; and let us not only not desire them, but even be ashamed if any one hold them forth to us. For thus casting out the love of these things, we shall possess that other love which is divine, and shall enjoy immortal glory."

9. And be found in Him,

'Found' is a Hebraism for 'that I may be in Him,' (see chap. ii. 8, καὶ σχήματι εὑρεθεὶς ὡς ἄνθρωπος,) as the branch in the Vine, John xv. 5; see also Gal. ii. 17, "We ourselves also are *found* sinners;" i.e. we are sinners. Compare 2 Cor. v. 3, and Rev. xii. 8. A very beautiful sense, however, would be obtained from these words even if 'found in Him' were understood in their simple English meaning: as if St. Paul's most ardent desire were to be *found* in Christ, hidden in His sacred wounds, whenever he might be *sought for* by the justice of God to be brought to punishment.

not having mine own righteousness,

i.e. which I acquired for myself, and which after all is

---

[g] Hom. i. 6, in 1 Cor.

only a fictitious righteousness. These words explain what it is ' to be found in Christ.'

"The righteousness which is of the Law was called the righteousness of man, because it was wrought by men's hands, that is to say, by circumcision, and the offering of gifts. This righteousness the Apostle rejected, and refused to have it any more [b]."

St. Chrysostom remarks, "If he who had righteousness ran to this other righteousness, because his own was nothing, how much rather ought they, who have it not, to turn to Him. Well said he, 'not having mine own righteousness,' not that which I gained by labour and toil, but that which I found from grace. For since it was likely they would say that the righteousness which comes from toil is the greater, he shews that it is dung in comparison with the other."

which is of the law,

i. e. which one may acquire for himself by a careful observance of all the precepts of the Law. See verse 6 ; and see also Rom. iv. 2, and x. 3, where this is called ἰδία δικαιοσύνη.

but that which is through the faith of Christ,

As opposed to righteousness which may be achieved by the works of the Law. This is the only true righteousness, "for whoso believeth on Him shall not have his own righteousness, which is of the Law, though it be a good Law, but shall fulfil this Law by a righteousness not his own, but given of God [i]."

Bishop Wilson explains the words 'the faith of Christ' as "revealed by Him, and performed by His assistance," and then goes on to say, "The unbelieving Jews conceited that they merited reward by observing the law of Moses ; that sin was to be expiated by legal sacrifices ; that these legal observances were their righteousness ; and that justification and life were on this account a due debt; and lastly, that

---

[b] Haymo.   [i] St. Augustine, Serm. cxix. 10, in Nov. Test.

the Gentiles were incapable of justification, unless they became proselytes to their law."

the righteousness which is of God by faith:

τὴν ἐκ Θεοῦ δικαιοσύνην ἐπὶ τῇ πίστει. For the expression 'righteousness of God,' see Rom. iii. 21. Ἐπὶ τῇ πίστει may be translated *super fidem*, in the sense in which ἐπὶ is used in Eph. ii. 20, and the meaning will be, 'the righteousness I say which is from God as its Author, and which is *founded* on faith.'

Observe here, our 'righteousness' is said to be *of* or *from* God, and *through* Christ conveying it to us as by a channel, viz. the union of the Humanity with the fount of good—the Divinity—and this *from God* as its Author, or efficient cause; *through Christ* as meriting it for us. St. Chrysostom connects 'by faith' with the next verse.

St. Augustine[k] shews that true righteousness is God's, and not our own: "For it is a commendation of grace," he says. "that none of us think his righteousness his own. For this is the righteousness of God, which God hath given thee to possess."

10. That I may know Him,

i. e. Christ in His Person and office. St. Paul desires to know three things, not speculatively, but practically, viz. (1) Christ, (2) "the power of His Resurrection," (3) "the fellowship of His sufferings." 'That I may *know* Him,' not with that knowledge which is *cognoscitiva*, but which is *directiva vitæ*. A natural man may have a knowledge of Christ; i. e. by hearsay, just as a blind man may of a beautiful landscape. But to 'know' Christ in the sense in which St. Paul uses the words, contains within itself everything necessary to salvation. "Not a bare knowledge," says Bishop Wilson, "but such as may produce a conformity in me to Him in all things." See Commentary on Ephesians, p. 265.

---

[k] In Ps. cxliii. 5.

and the power of His resurrection,

Not so much the power by which Christ raised *Himself* from the dead, as that by which He raises *us*. See 1 Pet. i. 3, 4, "Blessed be the God and Father of our Lord Jesus Christ, which according to His abundant mercy hath begotten us again unto a lively hope by the resurrection of Jesus Christ from the dead," &c. We must not forget that it is the Resurrection of Christ which assures us of our own [1]: "Knowing that He which raised up the Lord Jesus shall raise up us also by Jesus." See remarks on Eph. i. 19, 20; see also Col. ii. 12. The 'power of Christ's resurrection' is in us the resurrection from a threefold death; (1) from death eternal, (2) from the death of the body, (3) from spiritual death; which last is the quickening of the new man by the power of the Spirit of Christ. See Rom vi. 4; Eph. ii. 10.

St. Augustine says [m], "It is something great to know 'the power of Christ's Resurrection.'" And again [n], "The greatness of the Power of the Lord as He was made Man, in the virtue of the Resurrection doth appear. Think ye that this is the great thing, that He raised His own Flesh again? Did He call this 'the power of His Resurrection?' Shall there not be a resurrection of ourselves, too, at the end of the world? Shall not this our 'corruptible body,' too, 'put on incorruption, and this mortal put on immortality? As He rose again from the dead, shall it not be so with us too, even in a more wonderful manner, so to say? For His Flesh saw not corruption, ours is restored from ashes."

and the fellowship of His sufferings,

Compare 1 Pet. iv. 13. "To know I may become a partner in His afflictions and Passion [o]," so that I may cheerfully suffer for Him when called-upon to do so. The Apostle prays that he may have a share in the sufferings of Christ. He is not content with gazing on them as something endured *for* him; but the ardour of his love leads him to desire to

---

[1] 2 Cor. iv. 14. [m] Hom. cxix. 12, in Nov. Test.
[n] In Ps. lxvi. 6. [o] Gagneius.

have them reproduced in himself, so that he may become an actual *partaker* in them. See Col. i. 24, "Who now rejoice in my sufferings for you, and *fill up that which is behind of the afflictions of Christ in my flesh.*" And yet how many Christians long to reign with Christ in His glory, who shrink from suffering with Him in His humiliation! Happy they who seek after this 'fellowship,' (1) by dying to sin [p], and (2) by boldly bearing their Cross after Him [q].

being made conformable unto His death;

συμμορφούμενος τῷ θανάτῳ αὐτοῦ—"configuratus morti Ejus." See 1 Cor. xv. 31. Συμμορφούμενος is the *present* participle, and implies that the work is still progressing; being effected by the 'fellowship of Christ's sufferings,' of which he has already spoken; for to be afflicted for the sake of Christ is to be conformed to His death. "Die," says a holy Father, "that thou mayest live; be buried that thou mayest rise again; for when thou shalt have been buried, and risen again, then shall be true, 'We lift up our hearts.'"

"O how great is the dignity of sufferings," exclaims St. Chrysostom, *in loc.* "We believe that we are made 'conformable to His death' through sufferings! For as in Baptism we were 'buried in the likeness of His death,' thus here we are made conformable to His death. There did he rightly say, 'In the likeness of His death,' for there we died not entirely, we died not in the flesh, to the body, but to sin. Since then a death is spoken of, and a death; but He indeed died in the body, whilst we died to sin, and there the Man died which He assumed Who was in the flesh, but here the man of sin; for this cause he saith there, 'in the likeness of His death,' but here, no longer in the likeness of His death, but *to His very death*. For Paul in his persecutions no longer died to sin, but in his very body. Wherefore he endured the same death."

11. If by any means

εἴ πως; for a precisely similar use of the expression, see

---

[p] Rom. vi. 5, 8.   [q] Rom. viii. 17; 2 Tim. ii. 11, 12; 1 Pet. iv. 13.

Rom. xi. 14. The use of this word implies either (1) a *doubt* on the part of St. Paul about his *own final salvation*, shewing that it is quite possible so to fall from grace given as altogether to fail of attaining to eternal life, (see 1 Cor. ix. 27, and x. 12,) a mode of interpretation which conveys a most salutary warning to those boastful Christians who love to talk about the indefectibility of grace, and the consequent certainty of their salvation[r]; or (2) that what he was speaking of was a matter of *exceeding difficulty*, demanding constant labour and watchfulness; or (3) it may be understood, as Zanchius appears to have taken it, as conveying an *ardent wish* on the part of the Apostle. Either mode of interpretation gives a very good sense.

I might attain

καταντήσω. This word properly means *ad rem aliquam pertingere*; and it occurs in the same sense in Acts xxvi. 7, (εἰς ἣν τὸ δωδεκάφυλον ἡμῶν ἐλπίζει καταντῆσαι,) "unto which promise our twelve tribes hope *to come.*" The idea is, of course, *reaching the goal.* See 1 Cor. xiv. 36; Eph. iv. 13.

unto the resurrection of the dead.

Theophylact observes that the word used here for 'resurrection' is not ἀνάστασις, (which is most commonly found,) but ἐξανάστασις, i. e. something *higher* than a resurrection,—a selection *out of* those who have risen, (ἐξ); and no doubt the Apostle purposely used this word (and indeed *coined* it, since it occurs only in this place) to signify the resurrection of the *just* to eternal glory[s]. It is obvious that he must have been thinking of the 'better resurrection[t],' since there is *another* in which Judas and Pilate and Caiaphas and the rest of the wicked will have a share. Hooker says[u], "Our general consolation departing this life is the hope of that glorious and blessed resurrection which the Apostle St. Paul nameth ἐξανάστασιν, to note that as all men should have

---

[r] " Vis in timore securum esse ? Securitatem time."—*St. Bernard.*
[s] 1 Thess. iv. 15—17.   [t] Heb. xi. 35.   [u] Ecc. Pol., v. 68.

their ἀνάστασιν, and be raised again from the dead, so the just *shall be taken up and exalted above the rest*, whom the power of God doth but raise and not exalt."

This word ἐξανάστασις may also very properly be understood of the life of a baptized Christian here on earth, which should be like our Blessed Lord's *risen life.*

Observe '*of the dead*,' (τῶν νεκρῶν,) 'dead *bodies.*' The *body* is to partake in the ἐξανάστασις, whether to holiness in this life, or glory in the life to come.

12. Not as though I had already attained,

οὐχ ὅτι ἤδη ἔλαβον. Λαμβάνειν in its agonistical usage signifies receiving the reward that is due to the conqueror; and so it is used of the runner who has *finished* his course and gained the prize, although he has not yet actually *received* it. And in this way it is taken here, (as a kind of correction or explanation of the Apostle's previous words, lest any one should charge him with arrogance,) Not that I have *finished* my course, or that the crown is so absolutely awarded to me that I can speak with certainty of it, as having it in my own keeping; that which it is best for me to do is to use all diligence that I fail not of it through excess of confidence, or sluggishness.

After 'attained' we must understand (1) 'the prize,' (βραβεῖον,) i. e. of a glorious resurrection to life eternal; or (2) the height of Christian perfection in this world. The former sense is most in accordance with the context.

either were already perfect:

" As far as that wisdom is concerned which is vouchsafed to mortals, the blessed Apostle was the wisest of all men; but in relation to that perfection which the saints will receive after the general resurrection, he was not completely perfect; for now we see through a glass darkly, but then face to face, and then shall we see God as He is ʸ."

It is to be observed that the word 'perfect' (τετελείωμαι)

ʸ Haymo.

in this verse is also an agonistical term, and signifies being crowned or receiving the reward. Gregory Nyssen, speaking of the martyrs, uses the phrase τελείωσις ἀθλητοῦ, in the same sense as κατάρτισις in 2 Cor. xiii. 9, τοῦτο δὲ καὶ εὐχόμεθα, τὴν ὑμῶν κατάρτισιν. Eusebius also [x] uses the word τελειοῦσθαι for undergoing martyrdom. For the meaning of the word τέλειος see Commentary on the Ephesians, p. 248.

The use of the words 'attained' and 'perfect' is striking, and suggestive of a deep spiritual lesson; for if the Apostle spoke in so humble a way of himself, much more should all other Christians do so. See Commentary on the Ephesians, p. 247.

Thorndike [y] points out that Christian perfection is not perfectly attainable in this life. "The reason," he says, "is manifest, because it is not morally possible that the work of it should not be interrupted by original concupiscence; the mortification whereof, which proceeds by degrees, is that perfection which a Christian arriveth at, whatsoever he aim at. Notwithstanding the law of Christianity, which the Gospel preacheth, supposing this concupiscence; and providing a right of re-establishment into God's grace for all that, being cast down, shall return by repentance; manifest it is, that, though we are not saved by fulfilling the original rule of that righteousness to which the creation of our nature on God's behalf obligeth us, yet by undertaking and pursuing that perfection, which the profession of Christianity importeth; provided that we persevere in pursuing it unto the end, though sometimes this pursuit consist in turning from those sins by which we had started aside."

but I follow after,

διώκω, "persequor;" i.e. 'I am following after with an earnest desire to reach;' another agonistical word. Wordsworth [z] says that the use of this expression was suggested to the Apostle by the proximity of the Circus Maximus, which

---

[x] Eccl. Hist., vii. 15.   [y] Of the Covenant of Grace, xxxii. 41.
[z] Greek Test.

lay in the valley, on the south-western side of the Palatine Hill, on which he was confined. "Doubtless he there often heard the loud and enthusiastic shouts of the multitude cheering on their favourite charioteers, and applauding the successful efforts of the victors in the course, which stirred so strongly the passions of the Roman people in the age of Nero, who himself entered the lists of competitors for the prize. St. Paul derives his imagery and language from that exciting spectacle. He, too, is a charioteer. He presses eagerly onward to the mark. He also has a prize to gain— the palm-branch of victory from the hand of Christ." The meaning then is, "My life is still one of contest, I am still far from the end, I am still distant from the prize; still I run, still I pursue. And he said not 'I run,' but 'I pursue,' and rightly so. For we know with what eagerness a man pursues. He sees no one, he thrusts aside with great violence all who would interrupt his pursuit. He collects together his mind, and sight, and strength, and soul, and body, looking to nothing else but the prize [a]."

Speaking of perseverance, St. Cyprian [b] says, "It is little to have been able to attain anything, it is more to be able to keep what you have attained. Just as both the faith itself and saving birth, not received merely, but guarded, giveth life. Neither does the attainment of itself, but its being worked out to completion, keep a man unto God."

Cornelius à Lapide has a very interesting quotation from the *Vitæ Patr.* in illustration of the meaning of the word διώκω. Speaking of a Religious, he says, "He ought to look at dogs who hunt after hares; and as one of the pack, when he sees the hare, follows it, but the rest, only seeing the dog running, for a time run with him, but afterwards, growing weary, turn back again, while the dog alone who saw the hare follows until he catches it, and is not hindered from the pursuit either by the example of those who turn back, or by rough places in the ground, or woods, or thorns, but is pierced with prickles, and rests not until he seizes the hare; so also the Religious, or one who seeks the Lord Jesus, directs

---

[a] St. Chrysostom, in loc.   [b] Ep. xiii. 2.

his way to the Cross without ceasing, passing by all obstacles which meet him until he arrives at the Crucified."

if that I may apprehend that

"He is not speaking here of the prize of eternal life, which, in verse 14, he calls 'the prize of the high calling of God in Christ Jesus,' but of the perfection of knowledge to which, in this life, we must always aspire[c]."

The expression 'if that' (εἰ καί) does not imply *doubt*, but rather *affirmation*, and means 'so that.'

for which also I am apprehended of Christ Jesus.

"I was, he saith, of the number of the lost, I gasped for breath, I was nigh dead, God apprehended me. For He pursued us, when we fled from Him, with all speed. By this he points out all those things; for the words 'I am apprehended' shew the earnestness of Him Who wishes to apprehend us, our great aversion to Him, our wandering, our flight from Him[d]."

"This let me receive," says St. Augustine[e], "as the prize of my running the race! There will be a certain resting-place to terminate my course; and in the resting-place there will be a country, and no pilgrimage, no dissension, no temptation."

The same Father[f] points out that if we consider our attainments sufficient we make no progress:—"However we shall have lived here, however we shall have profited here, let no one say it is sufficient for me, I am a just man. He that shall have so said hath stopped on the way, he knoweth not how to attain to the end. Where he hath said 'it is sufficient,' there hath he stuck fast. Observe the Apostle, to whom there was no sufficiency; see in what manner he willeth himself to be aided, until he may attain . . . . He then runneth on, thou hast stuck fast. He speaketh of himself as not yet perfected, and dost thou already boast of perfection?"

---

[c] Estius.   [d] St. Chrysostom, in loc.   [e] In Ps. xxxix. 8.
[f] In Ps. lxx. 8.

The word 'apprehended' is still used in an agonistical sense, and being now applied to Christ it signifies most beautifully that Christ, as in a race, contends and strives, and that for no other object than to obtain *a sinner as His reward*, and when He converts and brings such an one to repentance He conceives Himself to have attained the prize; and so we are, as it were, the crown that is gained and worn by Him. Haymo says on this place: "All the elect, predestinated to eternal life, are 'apprehended' in the Passion of the Lord, because by that were redeemed not only those who after His Resurrection were to be saved and purged by Baptism, but likewise all the just who lived before His Advent. But some one may say, If I was 'apprehended' in His Passion, that is redeemed, and purged in Baptism, why have I not now at the present time perfection of faith, wisdom, and righteousness? To whom we must reply, You have polluted the renovation of Baptism by evil living, and you will not be able to attain that perfection until, being again cleansed by penance, you come to Him who cleansed you in Baptism."

With the latter part of this verse compare John vi. 44, "No man can come to Me, except the Father which hath sent Me draw him." Compare also xv. 16. Consistently with this St. Chrysostom says [g], "First we are apprehended, and afterwards we know; first we are known, and then we apprehend; first we are called, and then we obey." And St. Augustine [h]: "His righteousness hath prevented me, let mine follow Him. And then shall mine follow, if it be not mine."

In reference to the phrase ἐφ' ᾧ καὶ κατελήφθην see an article in Arnold's "Theological Critic," vol. i. p. 501, where the writer suggests a meaning to the phrase ἐφ' ᾧ, which occurs in four places—Rom. v. 12; 2 Cor. v. 4; Phil. iii. 12, (this passage,) and iv. 10. The meaning proposed is, 'so that,' 'upon the concession or supposition that.' The strict meaning of ἐπὶ with dative is *condition:* οἱ δὲ ἔφασαν ἀποδώσειν, ἐφ' ᾧ μὴ καίειν τὰς κώμας, 'on *condition that*

---

[g] Hom. i. 1, in Tit.   [h] Hom. cxix. 16, in Nov. Test.

he would not burn the villages[i];' τοὺς φυγάδας δὲ αὐτῶν κατιέναι ἐπὶ τοῖς ἡμίσεσι τῶν πότε ὄντων ὅτε ἔφυγον, 'on the terms of having half what they possessed when they were banished[k].' (See Viger, Greek Idioms, *sub voce*.) Understand therefore in this passage, 'I pursue, if that I may *fully* lay hold (this is the sense of κατὰ in καταλάβω) *yet so that* I have myself been fully laid hold of by Christ.' And so again in iv. 10: 'I rejoiced that you have bloomed again as to your care for me; *yet so that* ye *had* been caring for me, but wanted opportunity of shewing it.'

Clemens Alex. makes use of this passage against the Gnostics, who, as their name implies, boasted that they were the depositaries of all true knowledge, and that they possessed it in *perfection*.

13. Brethren, I count not myself to have apprehended:

i. e. to have secured my eternal happiness. He repeats emphatically what he has already said, specially directing his admonitions to the Philippians that they may learn to follow his humility; q. d. 'Be not deceived in me; I know myself better than you do. If I know not what is wanting to me, I know not what is present.' The pronoun 'I' is of course highly emphatic.

These words are intended to put us on our guard against carelessness about our spiritual state, to which we are all by nature liable; for, as St. Chrysostom says, "If Paul had not as yet apprehended, and is not confident about the resurrection and things to come, hardly should they be so, who have not even succeeded in the smallest proportion with him."

This sentence has sometimes been understood, "for I have not yet reached the goal;" i. e. I am not at present to die for Christ; see chap. i. 25. The former interpretation is the best.

but this one thing I do,

or, 'care for;' q. d. I am solely engaged on this one

---

[i] Xen. Anab. iv.   [k] Arr. Exp. Al. ii. 1.

thing, viz. 'reaching forth,' &c. This is the business of my whole life.

forgetting those things which are behind,

He continues the figure of runners in a course, who, forgetful of what is behind them, are entirely bent on what lies before. "This thing only I consider, that I may in truth advance; thus, too, we should act, we should forget our successes, and throw them behind us, for the runner reckons not up how many circuits he hath finished, but how many are left. We, too, should reckon up, not how far we are advanced in virtue, but how much remains for us. For what doth that which is finished profit us, when that which is deficient is not added [m]?"

There is great force in the word 'forgetting.' He did not merely say I do not look back, or reckon, or esteem, but I 'forget;' and this "to make us more zealous, for we then become eager when we apply all diligence to what is left, when we give to oblivion everything else [n]." Haymo explains the 'things behind' to be "all temporal and transitory things, such as estates, riches, and the interests of the present life generally. And these things are said to be 'behind,' since when we are removed from this life by the death of the flesh, we shall leave all things behind us." But this is probably a wrong interpretation. The meaning is evidently the same as "Nil actum reputans si quid superesset agendum."

and reaching forth unto those things which are before,

$\dot{\epsilon}\pi\epsilon\kappa\tau\epsilon\iota\nu\acute{o}\mu\epsilon\nu os$, a word of great force. "Before we arrive," says St. Chrysostom, "we strive to obtain. For he reacheth forth who endeavours to outstrip his feet, though running with the rest of his body, stretching himself forward, and reaching out his hands, that he may accomplish somewhat more of his course . . ." And again, he says with

---

[m] St. Chrysostom.   [n] Ibid.

great happiness of expression, "He wished not to *take* but to *snatch* the prize."

'Those things which are before,' will of course refer to the rewards which are laid up in heaven for all Christ's faithful people; and the whole verse thus contains an earnest exhortation to *perseverance* in the "race which is set before us." The baptized are the runners, the course is the period of life, the goal is perfection, and the prize the everlasting crown. Respecting this course it may truly be affirmed, "Si dixisti satis, periisti;" for satiety in religious matters is a most dangerous disease, and is the next step to a fall. St. Jerome exhorting to perseverance, says, "Righteousness will not profit a man from the day in which he ceases to be righteous." And St. Cyril[o], after warning Christians not to be enticed again to the service of the devil, continues, "Hast thou not heard the old history which tells us of Lot and his daughters? was not he himself saved with his daughters because he gained the mountain, while his wife became a pillar of salt, set up as a beacon for ever, as the memorial of her depraved will and her turning back? Take heed therefore to thyself, and turn not again to 'what is behind,' going back after having put thine hand to the plough, to the salt savour of this life's doings; but escape to the mountain, to Jesus Christ, that Stone hewn without hands[p], which has filled the world."

St. Cyprian[q] also quotes the case of Lot's wife, and says, "Let us not regard the things behind, whither the devil recalls, but the things before, whither Christ calls. Let us raise our eyes to heaven, that the earth seduce us not by its delights and allurements." And so also St. Augustine[r]: "Therefore if thou too art walking, if thou art stretching thyself out, if thou art thinking of the things which are to come, forget the past, do not look back upon them, lest thou remain where thou hast looked back. Remember Lot's wife."

The same Father[s] points out the analogy between the deliverance and trials of the Israelites and those of Christians:

[o] Lect. xix. 8.   [p] Dan. ii. 35, 45.   [q] Ep. xi. 9.
[r] Hom. cxix. 17, in Nov. Test.   [s] In Ps. lxxiii. 5.

"The people of Israel under the domination of Pharaoh and the Egyptians is the Christian people before believing already predestined for God, and as yet serving demons, and the devil the chief of them: behold the people under the yoke of the Egyptians is this people doing service to their sins. For not except through our sins is the devil able to have dominion. The people are delivered from the Egyptians through Moses: the people are delivered from the past life of sins through our Lord Jesus Christ. The one people doth pass through the Red Sea; the other through Baptism. There die in the Red Sea all the enemies of that people, there die in Baptism all our sins. Observe, brethren; after that Red Sea not forthwith is the land given, nor, as though foes are no more, do they triumph securely, but there remaineth the desert's solitude, there remain foes lying in wait in the way: so also after Baptism there remaineth the Christian life amid temptations. In that desert they sighed for the promised land: for what else do Christians sigh now that they have been washed in Baptism? Do they now by any means reign with Christ? We have not yet come to our land of promise, though that will not fail us, for there will not fail the hymns of David. This thing, however, let all believers hear, let them know where they are: in a desert they are, for the land they sigh. Dead are the foes in Baptism, but they follow behind. What is they follow behind? Before our face we have things future, behind our back things past: all past sins have been effaced in Baptism; those whereby now we are tried do follow us not behind, but lie in wait in the way. Whence the Apostle, while yet set in the way of this desert, saith, 'the things which are behind forgetting, unto those things which are before reaching out, with earnestness I follow unto the palm of the high calling of God;' as though he were saying, unto the land of the high promise of God. And there now, brethren, whatever that people suffered in the desert, and whatever God bestowed upon them, whatever those scourges were, whatever the gifts, they are intimations of those things which we, walking in Christ in the wilderness of this life, seeking the land, both receive for consolation, and suffer for probation."

14. I press toward the mark

κατὰ σκοπόν, "juxta præfixum signum;" for σκοπός signifies a *target* for archers to shoot at [t], but here, to preserve uniformity of metaphor, it must be taken to signify the *goal*. St. Augustine [u], however, translates these words, "secundum intentionem," which the Oxford Translators render "upon the strain I follow on unto the prize," &c.

The constant remembrance of the σκοπός, towards which all Christians are hastening, will be found to be the best preservative against sin, and encouragement to virtue, especially in contrast to the aimless life which the Apostle speaks of 1 Cor. ix. 26. " Whatsoever thou takest in hand, remember *the end*, and thou shalt never do amiss [x]," are words to be associated with every undertaking of a Christian man. Cornelius à Lapide also gives the following admirable advice: " In the morning when thou risest reflect with St. Anthony, To-day I have begun to run, to-day I have begun to serve God, and to-day perhaps I shall also finish. I will so live therefore as if about to die this day ; I will so run as if I were to finish my course to-day ; and so I will run swiftly, since the time of running is short, and a long way remains before I reach heaven."

for the prize of the high calling of God

βραβεῖον signifies the reward or prize which is set forth for the winner. See 1 Cor. ix. 24.

It is not to be supposed that St. Paul uses the expressions 'mark' and 'prize' to signify the same thing. The 'mark' is the *perfection* of which he said, " Not as though I were already perfect," and the 'prize' the crown of everlasting happiness and glory, for the obtaining of which he says he is running, having his eyes constantly fixed on the 'mark' of perfection which is set before him.

'The high calling of God' means the exalted honour to which we are called by God, and the expression as it occurs here is peculiarly significant, since the judges at the Games (βραβευταί) were accustomed to take their

---

[t] Job xvi. 12 ; Lam. iii. 12. [u] Hom. iv. in 1 Joh. [x] Ecclus. vii. 36.

places on raised seats, and to call the victors to them to receive the prize.

in Christ Jesus.

The meaning is, that God proposes this prize to us through the merits of Christ, and that we are called up on 'high' through Him alone. Compare Ephesians ii. 4—7.

St. Augustine[y], speaking of the longing after heavenly things which the faithful should ever feel, says: "The whole life of a good Christian is an holy desire. Now what thou longest for thou dost not yet see; howbeit by longing thou art made capable, so that when that is come which thou mayest see, thou shalt be filled. For just as if thou wouldest fill a bag, and knowest how great the thing is that shall be given, thou stretchest the opening of the sack, or the skin, or whatever else it may be; thou knowest how much thou wouldest put in, and seest that the bag is narrow; by stretching thou makest it capable of holding more; so God by deferring our hope stretches our desire, by the desiring stretches the mind, by stretching makes it more capacious. Let us desire therefore, my brethren, for we shall be filled."

15. Let us therefore, as many as be perfect,

It is obvious that the word 'perfect,' (τέλειοι,) is here used in a restricted sense, and relates only to a *comparative* degree of perfection, since the Apostle says of himself, ver. 12, "Not as though I had already attained, either were *already perfect.*"

St. Athanasius[z] says of St. Paul, "In relation to all that is future and perfect, the things known by him here were in part; but with respect to those things which were committed and entrusted to him by the Lord, he was perfect."

'Perfect,' then, must be understood to refer to the 'spiritual' as opposed to the 'carnal' and 'babes in Christ' in 1 Cor. iii. 1. See also Gal. vi. 1; Heb. v. 12—14; and Commentary on Ephesians, p. 248.

---

[y] Hom. iv. 6, in 1 Joh.   [z] Fest. Ep. xi.

St. Augustine[a] says on this place, "Perfect and not perfect; perfect travellers, not yet perfect possessors. And that you may know that he speaks of perfect travellers, (they who are now walking in the way are perfect travellers,) that you may know that he spoke of travellers, not inhabitants, not possessors, hear what follows, ' Let as many of us,' " &c.

Bp. Andrewes[b] asks : "Why, is there any perfection in this life ? There is ; else, how should the Apostle's exhortation there, (Heb. vi. 1,) or his blessing here, (Heb. xiii. 20, 21,) take place ? I wot well absolute, complete, consummate perfection, in this life, there is none ; it is agreed of all hands, none may be out of it. *Non puto me comprehendisse*, saith St. Paul ; ' I count not myself to have attained.' No more must we, not ' attained.' What then ? ' But this I do,' saith he, and so must we : ' I forget that which is behind, and endeavour myself, and make forward still, to that which is before.' Which is the perfection of travellers, of wayfaring men ; the farther onward on their journey, the nearer their journey's end, the more perfect ; which is the perfection of this life, for this life is a journey. Now good works are as so many steps onward. The Apostle calls them so, ' the steps of the faith of our father Abraham[c],' who went that way, and we to follow him in it. And the more of them we do, the more steps do we make ; the further still shall we find ourselves to depart from iniquity, the nearer still to approach unto God in the land of the living ; whither to attain, is the total, or *consummatum est* of our perfection."

But it is much more probable that St. Paul used the word τέλειοι in its technical sense taken from the language of the Eleusinian mysteries, and intended to designate those who, having been perfected in the Christian doctrine, have been admitted to the Sacrament of the Lord's Supper. This reading is the more probable since it was afterwards adopted as the language of the Church ; ἐπὶ τὸ τέλειον ἐλθεῖν signified to come to the Lord's Supper[d]. Hence

---

[a] Hom. cxix. 18, in Nov. Test. [b] Serm. xviii. On the Resurrection.
[c] Rom. iv. 12. [d] Concil. Ancyran., can. 4, 5, 6.

those who were admitted were called τέλειοι or τελειού-
μενοι [e]. St. Chrysostom uses the equivalent technicality,
μεμυημένοι, which is also used by St. Paul, Phil. iv. 12, ἐν
πᾶσι μεμύημαι. The verse, therefore, probably means, 'Let
as many as have received all the means of grace which the
Church has to bestow, be like-minded with her in the manner I have described.'

be thus minded:

Compare what he says about σοφία ἐν τοῖς τελείοις in
1 Cor. ii. 6.

and if in anything ye be otherwise minded,

i. e. if ye think otherwise concerning what I have been
saying, viz. about *perfection*, imagining that ye have already
attained to it, and that there is no further room for exertion
on your part.

God shall reveal even this unto you.

i. e. shall in His own time shew you your error. Hence
we gather that different measures of knowledge and holiness
are given to the saints at different times, since we are at
best but narrow-mouthed vessels, and cannot receive all at
once. See John xiii. 36.

Wordsworth [f] explains the passage somewhat differently.
He says, "Provided ye entertain this mind which I have
declared concerning the true *foundation* of the faith, I say
if *ye hold any opinion* concerning anything else *in a different
light* from what is right, God will reveal that other thing to
you in its *true* light."

The Venerable Bede thought that the expression 'otherwise minded' referred to some departure from Catholic practice. "Let each faithful man," he says, "carry out his faith
in deed, and study to abound in the Christian graces, and then
if he has any other opinion which is contrary to the faith,
God will reveal it to him, on account of the good works that
he has, so that he may correct it; as He did in the case of
Cyprian, Bishop of Carthage, who used to give one immer-

---

[e] Bingh., vol. i. p. 26.   [f] Greek Testament.

sion only to the baptized, doing this in ignorance. But because he was earnestly given to good works, and acted according to his understanding, he merited to receive a revelation from the Lord, to the effect that he should give trine-immersion to the baptized."

Abp. Bramhall [g] uses this verse to shew that there may be "some errors in disputable points," and that "some abuses are mere excesses without guilt, rather blemishes than sins; and for these alone no man ought to separate himself from a Christian society, or abandon a true Church for trivial dissensions. Our duty in such a case is to pray and persuade, without troubling the peace of the Church, and to leave the rest to God."

16. Nevertheless, whereto we have already attained,

πλὴν εἰς ὃ ἐφθάσαμεν. Φθάνειν here is *pervenire*. Compare Matt. xii. 28; Luke xi. 20; Rom. ix. 31; 2 Cor. x. 14.

There is great force in the word as used here, (it being an agonistic expression relating to those who are first in the race,) and means 'we have come beforehand.' Now the Philippians seem to have been 'beforehand' in regularly *organizing their Church;* they had the three orders, the offertory; and *perhaps*, (if κατατομὴ may be pressed a little in its meaning) *formalism* had begun to shew itself, an error which is scarcely possible to exist in an unorganized ecclesiastical body.

Observe, St. Paul says, "*We* have attained," (ἐφθάσαμεν,) completely identifying himself with them. In speaking of *errors* in doctrine and discipline he would of course use the second person.

The word 'nevertheless' (πλήν) with which St. Paul introduces this verse must also be observed. He had been speaking to those who had not as yet attained Christian perfection, and had promised that God should reveal this to them; but lest, while the revelation was delayed, they should turn aside from the oneness of the rule of faith, he immediately adds 'nevertheless,' &c. [h]

[g] Disc. iii. 5, against Romanists. [h] Caietan.

St. Augustine[i] extends this promise to all the faithful: "If whereunto we have attained, therein we walk, not only what we know not and ought to know, but also if in anything we be otherwise minded, that also shall God reveal unto us. Now we have attained unto the way of faith; this let us most perseveringly hold; the same shall bring us to the chamber of the King in Whom are laid up all the treasures of wisdom and knowledge."

let us walk by the same rule, let us mind the same thing.

τῷ αὐτῷ στοιχεῖν κανόνι, τὸ αὐτὸ φρονεῖν. These infinitives are to be taken as imperatives by a very common Attic usage. See Rom. xii. 15, χαίρειν μετὰ χαιρόντων, καὶ κλαίειν μετὰ κλαιόντων. For the expression στοιχεῖν κανόνι see Gal. vi. 16. Κανών has been interpreted to mean the white line that marked out the course within which the runners were to keep; but its more regular meanings are (1) the cross-bar of the shield, (2) a scribe's ruler, (3) a carpenter's measure, (4) part of a loom. The idea seems to be that of *accurate measurement*—to walk one after another without swerving from the right line.

The English Version misses the force of the word. It means 'to walk in a line, or row,' as well-trained soldiers do. And this gives a very beautiful sense here, being most highly suggestive of the *order* and precision which should be maintained among Christians as regards faith and discipline. Cornelius à Lapide well remarks, "Fides est quasi linea et regula rectissima, quam si vel modicum inflectas aberras à vero, et falsitatem incurris. Veritas enim consistit in puncto, in indivisibili; talis est norma credendi et vivendi quam nobis præscribit fides et lex Christi."

A part of the oath of Athenian citizens was μὴ ἐγκαταλιπεῖν τὸν παραστάτην ᾧ στοιχοίη, 'not to desert him by whose side he ought to stand in battle.'

St. Augustine[k], speaking of "the same rule," says, "The lame man gets on better *in* the way, than the swift-footed out of the way."

---

[i] Hom. liii. 7, in Joh.   [k] Hom. cxix. 18, in Nov. Test.

It is plain from this verse that the illumination which the Apostle has just been speaking of ("God shall reveal," &c.) is not *unconditional*, but will be vouchsafed to those only who have diligently used the grace already given for their own and others' good. See Matt. xiii. 12.

Dean Trench[1] says, "Augustine (or Cæsarius, as the Benedictine editors affirm) has an admirable discourse on the manner in which gifts multiply through being imparted, and diminish through being withholden. It is throughout an application of the story of the widow[m], whose two sons Elisha redeemed from bondage by multiplying the oil which she had in her single vessel so long as she provided other vessels into which to pour it, but which, when she had no more, at once stopped: "Et ait Scriptura stetisse oleum, posteaquam ubi poneret non invenit. Sic, dilectissimi fratres, tamdiu caritas augetur, quamdiu tribuitur. Et ideo etiam ex industriâ debemus vasa quærere, ubi oleum possumus infundere, quia probavimus quod dum aliis infundimus plus habemus. Vasa caritatis homines sunt."

17. Brethren, be followers together of me,

συμμιμηταί, "cöimitatores." He uses the simple word μιμηταί 1 Cor. iv. 16, xi. 1, Eph. v. 1, 1 Thess. i. 6, but here he employs the more expressive word συμμιμηταί, the force of which is probably 'be fellow-imitators with me;' that is, imitate Christ as you see me imitating Him. Haymo explains the Apostle's meaning to be, "If you are unable to imitate and follow Christ, at least imitate me His disciple in faith, in work, in doctrine; that as I believe, work, and teach, so ye also may believe, work, and teach.

and mark them which walk

The word σκοπεῖτε ('mark') is here taken in a good sense, and means, according to St. Ambrose, *considerate*, 'observe,' so as to *imitate;* while in Rom. xvi. 17, it means observe, so as to *avoid*, σκοπεῖν τοὺς τὰς διχοστασίας καὶ τὰ σκάνδαλα ποιοῦντας.

---

[1] Notes on Parables, p. 279. [m] 2 Kings iv. 1—7.

For the use of the word 'walk,' see Commentary on the Ephesians, pp. 109, 136, 216, 258, 294, 318.

so as ye have us for an ensample.

καθὼς ἔχετε τύπον ἡμᾶς—" sicut habetis formam nos ;" i. e. as long as ye have us for your pattern. Τύπος has the same sense Acts vii. 44. Others interpret "formam nostram ;" i. e. "formam doctrinæ nostræ." It is to be observed that he does not say προτότυπον, for that would refer to Christ, but τύπον.

The word 'us' must be understood as referring to himself, St. Timothy, Epaphroditus, Silvanus, and others who had been chiefly engaged in preaching the Gospel at Philippi.

18. He furnishes a reason for the precept of verse 17.

(For many walk,

i. e. "longe aliter quam ego." The meaning is, there are many who outwardly are Christians and who preach the Cross, but who have never learnt its fundamental doctrine of *self-denial*; for it is of the *self-indulgent*, a large class in every Church, that the Apostle is about to speak.

'Walk ;' the word used here is περιπατεῖν, not στοιχεῖν, as above ; as much as if he had said that these persons of whom he is about to speak, although *outwardly* walking *orderly* as Christians, (στοιχεῖν,) yet *inwardly* are walking after their own lusts, (περιπατεῖν). The change of words is highly expressive. But if this view (which undoubtedly is a pleasing one) should be thought to press the meaning of περιπατεῖν too far, it may be distinguished from στοιχεῖν thus :—στοιχεῖν, the *orderly* progress of the *whole* community of the Church, viewed in its corporate character ; περιπατεῖν, the daily walk of each *individual* member of the Church, whether in or out of order.

St. Chrysostom says, "There were some who made a pretence of Christianity, yet lived in ease and luxury. This is contrary to the Cross ; wherefore he thus spoke."

of whom I have told you often, and now tell you even weeping,

Lorinus remarks with great force on the word 'weeping,'

"Non tam atramento quam lachrymis chartas inficiebat Paulus," for truly he was a man of many tears, and might well have said,—

> "Tu quibus ista legis incertum est lector ocellis,
> Ipse quidem siccis scribere non potui."

Haymo says that "the love of the Apostle is to be imitated, who was wont to weep even over the 'enemies of the Cross of Christ,' as Samuel did over his enemy Saul, and as the same Apostle elsewhere did over the Corinthians, who after fornication did no penance."

that they are the enemies of the Cross of Christ:

As thinking only of this life and its interests and pleasures, living without *self-denial*, which is specially signified by the word 'cross,' and rapidly tending towards Antinomianism ; "so that if they say they are of Christ, still they are enemies of the Cross. For did they love the Cross, they would strive to lead a life befitting the Cross. Was not thy Master hung upon the tree? Imitate Him in some other way, if thou canst not in His own. Crucify thyself, though no one crucify thee. Learn how great is the power of the Cross. How many goods it hath attained and doth still : how it is the safety of our life. Through it all things are done. Baptism is through the Cross, for we must receive that seal. The laying on of hands is through the Cross. If we are in the way, if we are at home, wherever we are, the Cross is a great good, the armour of salvation, a shield which cannot be beaten down, a weapon to oppose the devil ; thou bearest the Cross when thou art at enmity with him, not simply when thou sealest thyself by it, but when thou sufferest the things belonging to the Cross. Christ thought fit to call our sufferings by the name of the Cross. As when He saith, 'Except a man take up his Cross and follow Me,' i. e. except he be prepared to die [u]."

This phrase is adopted by St. Polycarp in his Epistle to the Philippians, c. 12.

---

[u] St. Chrysostom, in loc.

19. Whose end is destruction,

'End,' in the way of wages [o]. The expression is probably borrowed from Numb. xxiv. 20. He is speaking of *eternal* destruction, and not merely of punishment in this world; since David testifies [p], "I myself have seen the ungodly in great power: and flourishing like a green bay-tree." The word 'end,' then, must be taken to denote their death, and 'destruction' that which follows after it.

whose God is their belly,

See Rom. xvi. 18; not that they actually call their belly by the name of God; yet, inasmuch as they are wholly under the dominion of their appetites and desires, and think mainly, if not exclusively, of them, their belly becomes their all in all, and so their god, since that is our god to which we give our chief service. See Eph. v. 5.

It is a well-known saying of Luther's, that "every one of us has by nature a Pope in his belly."

Thorndike [q] says that the Christian "making the will of God the ground, and His glory and service the intent, of all his doings, renounces all respect to the pleasure, or profit, or honour, or greatness of this world, so far as it is not the means to serve God; acknowledging that, when he declines from this resolution, he makes his belly his God, or his riches his idol, as St. Paul saith; or rather the devil, that offers him some little part of that which our Lord refused in gross, the god whom he worships."

Haymo refers these words to those false brethren who were preaching Christ for worldly ends [r], and remarks very happily, "'Whose God is their belly,' that is to say, of those who preach for the express purpose of *filling their belly*."

Compare with this verse Matt. vi. 24, where St. Chrysostom says our Lord "calls mammon a 'master,' not because of its own nature, but on account of the wretchedness of them that bow themselves beneath it. So also St. Paul calls

---

[o] Rom. vi. 21; 2 Cor. xi. 15; Gal. vi. 8.   [p] Ps. xxxvii. 36.
[q] Just Weights and Measures, chap. xxiii. 3.   [r] Chap. i. 16.

the belly a 'God,' not from the dignity of such a mistress, but from the wretchedness of them that are enslaved."

and whose glory is in their shame,

i. e. who boast of things that they ought to be ashamed of, "Who rejoice to do evil, and delight in the frowardness of the wicked[s]."

Pythagoras well remarked to a certain person who said he should prefer being reckoned among women than philosophers, "Sows had rather roll in mud than in clear streams."

ἐν τῇ αἰσχύνῃ αὐτῶν is translated by St. Ambrose[t] and by St. Augustine[u] *in pudendis eorum*, referring the words to the Judaizing teachers who gloried chiefly in circumcision, and making the sense to be "et quorum gloriatio est in eo membro quod pudendum est et abscondendum." It is perhaps enough to say of this interpretation that it does violence to the Greek, (as the word αἰσχύνη is never used in this sense,) and is exceedingly unnatural.

who mind earthly things.)

οἱ τὰ ἐπίγεια φρονοῦντες. See James iii. 15. Although φρονεῖν is more usually applied to the understanding, yet it is sometimes used of the affections also. See Col. iii. 2, τὰ ἄνω φρονεῖτε, μὴ τὰ ἐπὶ τῆς γῆς. See also Rom. viii. 5, οἱ γὰρ κατὰ σάρκα ὄντες, τὰ τῆς σαρκὸς φρονοῦσιν· οἱ δὲ κατὰ πνεῦμα, τὰ τοῦ πνεύματος. The meaning is, their affections do not rise above the earth where all their hopes and interests lie.

In Aristotelian philosophy the word φρόνησις signifies *the intellect as applied to morals*. We might call it 'moral wisdom,' and possibly the word φρονεῖν may have something of this sense with St. Paul in this place,—'who direct their affections and intellect alike towards earthly objects,' 'who employ heart and mind upon earthly things." Even the heathen philosophy could tell us to raise our views higher than the earth; in Aristotle's words, ἐφ' ὅσον ἐνδέχεται ἀθανατίζειν, 'to play the immortal as far as may be.'

---

[s] Prov. ii. 14. [t] Lib. i. de Cain et Abel, c. 5.
[u] Serm. xv. de verbis Apostoli, c. 1.

20. For our conversation is in heaven;

In contrast with τὰ ἐπίγεια φρονοῦντες which precedes, and the connexion is, But we are not such, for our conversation instead of being on the earth, is in heaven, and thus is fulfilled the prophecy of Daniel ii. 44, "And in the days of these kings shall the God of heaven set up a kingdom which shall never be destroyed: and the kingdom shall not be left to other people, but it shall break in pieces and consume all these kingdoms, and it shall stand for ever."

'Conversation,' πολίτευμα: see chap. i. 27. This word would answer to the Roman *municipium*, i.e. the condition of those who dwelling *out of the* city have yet the *jus civitatis Romanæ*. There was, however, this difference between them and those who dwelt in the city, that these last alone could be chosen to fill any office in it. Thus the Christian while on earth is συμπολίτης τῶν ἁγίων[v], and not ξένος or πάροικος[x]; i.e. he is a *free man*, or *municeps*, of heaven, though while on earth in an inferior condition to those who have their *domicilium in urbe*, viz. the saints in heaven, who are alone capable of reigning with God.

The force of the word 'is' (ὑπάρχει) must be noticed, as denoting something *present*. Christ, our Head, is there now; and we are reigning there in Him. See Eph. ii. 6—19. It also implies that if we hope to enjoy the rights of *full citizenship* with the saints in heaven, we must live as fellow-citizens with them *now*, since we shall never be in heaven *after* death, unless we have been there in affection *before*. "For ye are dead, *and your life is hid with Christ in God*[y]."

St. Athanasius[z] says, "That is the true life which a man lives in Christ; for although they are dead to the world, yet they dwell, as it were, in heaven, meditating on those things which are above, as he, (St. Paul,) who was a lover of such a habitation, said, While we walk on earth, our dwelling is in heaven."

So also St. Augustine[a]: "Already in longing we are there, already hope into that land, as it were an anchor, we have

[v] Eph. ii. 19. [x] Ibid. [y] Col. iii. 3.
[z] Fest. Ep. vii. [a] In Ps. lxv. 3.

sent before, lest in this sea being tossed we suffer shipwreck. In like manner, therefore, as of a ship which is at anchor we rightly say that already she is come to land, for still she rolleth, but to land in a manner she hath been brought safe in the teeth of winds, and in the teeth of storms; so against the temptations of this sojourning, our hope being grounded in that city Jerusalem causeth us not to be carried away upon rocks."

St. Gregory [b] remarks, in illustration of this passage, "As the house of our exterior life is the building which the body lives in, so the house of our thought is anything whatever that the mind is centred in by affection. For everything that we love, we, as it were, make our dwelling-place by reposing in it. Whence Paul, because he had fixed his heart in things above, being still upon earth indeed, yet a stranger to earth, said, 'Our conversation is in heaven.'"

And again [c]: "Let us behold the Eagle building itself the nest of hope in high places. He says, 'Our conversation is in heaven,' and again, 'Who hath raised us up together, and hath made us sit together in heavenly places.' He has his rest in high places, because in truth he fixes his thought on things above. He wishes not to degrade his mind to the lowest objects, he wishes not by the baseness of human conversation to dwell on things below. Paul was perhaps then confined in prison when he was witnessing that he was sitting together with Christ in heavenly places. But he was there, where he had already fixed his ardent mind, not there, where the sluggish flesh was still necessarily detaining him."

Tertullian [d] says, "But thou art a stranger in this world, a citizen of Jerusalem which is above. 'Our citizenship is in heaven.' Thou hast thine own enrolment, thine own solemn days. Thou hast no concern with the rejoicings of the world; yea, thou oughtest to do the contrary; for 'the world shall rejoice and ye shall lament.'"

Bp. Andrewes [e] says, "For the things contained in heaven, as they are heavenly, so we desire that we living on earth

---

[b] Moral. viii. 74.   [c] Moral. xxxi. 95.   [d] De Cor. 13.
[e] Serm. on Lord's Prayer.

may have 'our conversation in heaven;' that earthly man, to whom God said *Terra es*, may by this means be made heavenly."

from whence also we look for

'From whence;' i. e. from heaven, where we believe Christ to be in His true human Body. " Where Christ sitteth on the right hand of God[f]."

the Saviour, the Lord Jesus Christ :

i. e. waiting for the day when He will come to reward every man according to his works [g]. It is well worthy of remark, that in speaking of the second Advent of our Lord St. Paul uses the word 'Saviour,' rather than 'Judge,' being a title full of the richest comfort to all the faithful, pointing, as it does, to the redemption of the *body* which will then take place.

21. Who shall change our vile body,

ὃς μετασχηματίσει τὸ σῶμα τῆς ταπεινώσεως ἡμῶν— "Transfigurabit corpus humilitatis nostræ conformale corpori gloriæ suæ[h]." Bernard à Piconius well explains the expression : " Id est, in aliam figuram accidentalem commutabit : ex passibili, corruptibili, et terreno, faciens impassibile, incorruptibile, æternum." It would be heresy to suppose, as some have done, that the glorified bodies of the saints will have different figures from those which they now have. The bodies will be the same, but the condition and qualities will be different. See 1 Cor. xv. 42—44. At the Transfiguration of our Blessed Lord—which ancient doctors have called the Sacrament of the Resurrection, when the flesh shall be revived —no change of substance passed upon Him. He laid aside nothing of His true and natural body, but only withdrew the veil which concealed its supernal glory. And so will it be with the faithful at the resurrection ; their natural bodies will remain, but will be penetrated even to their inmost recesses with the glory of the eternal Godhead.

---

[f] Col. iii. 1.   [g] 1 Thess. iv. 16.   [h] Tertullian, de Resurr. Carn. 55.

'Our vile body' very inadequately translates τὸ σῶμα τῆς ταπεινώσεως ἡμῶν; it should be, 'the body of our humiliation.' A beautiful sense is thus obtained,—the *body* is the material in which our 'humiliation' has place, and is shewn by its suffering and degradation. But Christ Himself once had such a ταπείνωσις, (though free from *sin* which forms an important element in our humiliation,) and has passed through it to His glory, and He will hereafter so change us as to be like Him.

"What?" asks St. Chrysostom, *in loc.*, "shall this our body be fashioned like unto Him, Who sitteth at the Right Hand of the Father, to Him Who is worshipped by the angels, before Whom do stand the incorporeal powers, to Him Who is above all rule, and power, and might?"

that it may be fashioned like unto His glorious body,

Σύμμορφον τῷ σώματι τῆς δόξης αὐτοῦ [1]; literally, 'the body of His glory,' (as opposed to the body of our humiliation,) since it is in His Body, as its object, in which Christ's glory has place and is displayed.

Four glimpses of this glory have been vouchsafed to men: (1) in Moses' face, (2) in Christ's transfiguration, (3) in Stephen's countenance, (4) in the vision which St. Paul had of Christ—for that he really saw Him see 1 Cor. ix. 1.

It is to be observed here what a high value is put upon the resurrection and redemption of the *body;* as if this were the chief thing which Christians waited for [k]. Wherever the doctrine of the Incarnation is rightly apprehended, there will be no difficulty in perceiving the dignity that belongs to the body, as being actually a *part of Christ.* See chap. i. 1.

according to the working

κατὰ τὴν ἐνέργειαν. Ἐνέργεια signifies 'efficacy,' or 'efficacious operation.' See remarks on chap. ii. 12.

---

[1] 1 Cor. xv. 48; 2 Tim. ii. 12.   [k] Rom. viii. 23; Eph. v. 23.

whereby He is able even to subdue all things unto Himself.

Lest any one should suppose that what has been said is too hard, the Apostle gives the *cause* of the wonderful transformation he has just mentioned, viz. the *power of Christ*, whereby He is able to subdue all things to Himself, and therefore corruption and death [1].

St. Chrysostom, *in loc.*, says, "For tell me, which requireth the greater power, to subject demons, and Angels, and Archangels, and Cherubim, and Seraphim, or to make the body incorruptible and immortal? The latter certainly rather than the former; He shewed forth the greater works of His power that you might believe these too."

It is well worthy of remark that St. Paul here ascribes to the Son that which in other places is said to belong to the Father, (for ἐνέργεια is used of the Father Eph. i. 19,) thereby proving, against the Arians and others, that the power of the Father and the Son is the same, and so also their Essence and Divinity.

Hemmingius, writing to condole with Noviomagus on the death of his daughter, well says of this passage: "Believe me there is no such remedy for present affliction as the earnest belief in these words, and devout meditation on the resurrection." And so also St. Chrysostom, *in loc.*: "These our hopes are sufficient to raise up even the most sluggish and indolent."

The following beautiful passage, founded on this verse, occurs in the exposition of Bernard à Piconius: "Eodem ac Apostoli insignitus sum honore, cœlorum sum civis, domesticus Dei: cur ergo, ut talpa, hæreo terræ, mente et corde inclusus in terrâ? Sursum cor, o anima mea! mentem erige, suspice cœlum, hæc est patria tua, domusque æterna: ad hanc anhela, ibi conversare, donec veniat Salvator, qui te ab hujus exsilii miseriis eripiat, suâque gloriâ donet in patriâ."

---

[1] 1 Cor. xv. 25, 26.

SUMMARY OF CHAPTER IV.

HE first of all, in the tenderest terms, exhorts the Philippians to perseverance, ver. 1;
And then two women of their number, who were at variance, to unanimity, vers. 2, 3.
He next proceeds to encourage them to the manifestation of spiritual joy, ver. 4;
To cultivate moderation, ver. 5;
To be constant in prayer and thanksgiving, ver. 6;
And to the practice of everything that is praiseworthy, vers. 8, 9.
He next speaks with approval both of their past and present liberality towards him, vers. 10, 14, 15, 16;
And shews that he accepts it chiefly for their sake, since he himself knows how to bear poverty, vers. 11, 13, 17.
He then assures them of the continuance of God's favour, ver. 19;
And after some general salutations, vers. 21, 22,
Concludes the Epistle with his benediction, ver. 23.

CHAP. IV.

VER. 1. Therefore,

ὥστε—"cum tanta nobis proposita sint præmia [m];" i.e. since we have our citizenship in heaven, and look for such a Saviour, and expect such a change. Compare 1 Cor. xv. 58.

my brethren

In the faith of Christ.

dearly beloved and longed for,

ἐπιπόθητοι, 'longed for', "exoptati—multum desiderati;" see chap. i. 8. The preposition ἐπί very much intensifies the force of the word.

---

[m] Polus.

my joy and crown,

"Inasmuch as on your account it is that I rejoice at the present time, and hereafter shall be crowned[n]." Observe how affectionately the Apostle speaks of them! Compare 1 Thess. ii. 20. The word 'joy' is more significant than the preceding 'longed for,' since, as Aretius says, "πόθος lies concealed in the inmost recesses of the mind, so that it does not at once break forth; but χαρά ('joy') pours itself out in external signs, in the countenance, voice, gesture," &c.

The difference between 'joy' and 'crown' is the difference between this world and the world to come; it is as if St. Paul should say, "Ye, whose faith and love are my works, are a ground of happiness to me here, and will be so hereafter. The Apostle does not speak of this in the light of recompense or wages for work done, but it is a beautiful and not at all an antichristian idea that the very works which we have done on earth for Christ's sake, however little they may in themselves be worthy of reward, will form the gems that adorn our heavenly crown. Of course the word 'crown' in this passage must be taken in the sense in which our Lord uses the word 'reward' in Matt. x. 41, 42; in this sense our works may be said to 'follow us.'

There is something very encouraging in this verse for ministers in the midst of those manifold trials and disappointments which are inseparable from their vocation. Not only is it true that "when the chief Shepherd shall appear, they shall receive a crown of glory that fadeth not away[o]," but *those very souls* over which they have sorrowed, and which they have won to Christ with many prayers and tears, will form their everlasting crown; for if children are said to be the crown of their natural parents[p], much more will this be the case in reference to that spiritual offspring of which faithful ministers "travail in birth again until Christ be formed[q]" in them.

so

Either, 'as you have already stood firm,' or, 'as I have been describing.'

---

[n] Sedulius. [o] 1 Pet. v. 4. [p] Prov. xvii. 6. [q] Gal. iv. 19.

stand fast

στήκετε; i. e. against all the assaults of heretical teachers. The word denotes a high state of preparation against attack. See remarks on Eph. vi. 11.

A very good sense will be obtained from the use of the simple word 'stand,' (without the addition of 'fast,' as in the English Version,) as if the righteous man were like *a cube*, which in spite of any turn of fortune stands upright and firm.

in the Lord,

As the element wherein alone true stedfastness consists. See 1 Cor. xv. 1; 2 Cor. i. 24; 1 Pet. v. 12.

my dearly beloved.

He repeats these words to shew the intensity of his affection. The language of this verse may well be described as heart-melting; an admirable pattern for ministers to copy, who must be prepared to plead hard for Christ, if they would speak to any purpose. Compare Philem. 8, 9.

2. I beseech Euodias, and beseech Syntyche,

It should be *Euodia*. These were two *women*, as appears from the following verse, where αὐταῖς and αἵτινες are used respecting them. Theodoret, Theophylact, and Anselm say that they were persons of consequence among the Christians of Philippi, (Deaconesses probably, like Phœbe of Cenchrea,) who by their zeal had contributed much to the spread of the Gospel, by instructing the young, and performing those numerous other works of love which fall to the lot of a sister of charity. For a full account of the office of 'widows,' 'Deaconesses,' &c., in the primitive Church, see Bingham, bk. ii. c. 22; also Cave, Prim. Christ., part i. c. 8. It appears that some cause of disagreement had arisen between these two women, and the Apostle takes this opportunity of exhorting them to unanimity.

that they be of the same mind

i. e. preserve the bond of Christian love, so essential to the proper development of the faith, and without which labours and sacrifices are valueless.

in the Lord.

i. e. "with that concord, the bond of which is the Lord[r]," since all concord *out of the Lord* is easily broken and comes to nought. The expression may also mean (as Rosenmüller takes it) 'in things pertaining to the Lord,' i. e. the doctrine of Christ.

It is certain that the disagreement between these women, whatever it was, must have been sufficiently *public* to be productive of scandal to the Church, or the Apostle would not have alluded to it in a letter which was in a measure the common property of all, but would rather have spoken of it in private. The earnestness of his appeal finds its counterpart in the language of St. Augustine, who in relation to the differences that had unhappily sprung up between SS. Jerome and Ruffinus, said:—"Oh that I could but once find you together; I would fall down at your feet with much love and many tears; I would beseech you for yourselves and one another, and for weak Christians who are offended thereat, that you would not suffer these dissensions to spread."

Hemmingius on this place takes occasion to point out that the duty of a pious pastor is not merely to care for the flock as *a whole,* but also to seek for the salvation of *individual* sheep. "For he does not fulfil his office who teaches, exhorts, and threatens only *in public,* unless in *private* also he admonishes each, where and when he perceives it to be necessary."

3. And

καὶ; there is another reading, ναί.

I intreat thee also,

i. e. no less than those women whose names I have mentioned. For ἐρωτῶ in this sense, see John xiv. 16, xvi. 26, xvii. 9; 1 Thess. iv. 1, and v. 12; 2 Thess. ii. 1.

---

[r] Beza.

true yokefellow,

σύζυγε γνήσιε. Some have supposed that St. Paul is here addressing his wife. So Clemens Alexandrinus [s] and Eusebius [t]. St. Chrysostom mentions this supposition, but only to reject it. His words are, " Some say Paul here entreats his own wife; but it is not so, but some other woman, or the husband of some one of them." He also mentions that some understood the word 'yokefellow' (Syzygus) as a *proper name*, but abstains from pronouncing a decided opinion on the point. It is difficult, however, to see on what grounds people persist in applying these words to a *woman* at all, unless the explanation of Aretius is considered satisfactory, "Nam muliebris causa mulieri optimè videtur commendari." Such an application appears to be arbitrary, and to justify it the Greek should be γνησία σύζυγε, instead of the masculine γνήσιε σύζυγε. It is of course not *impossible* that these words might refer to a woman, but the use of them in this sense would involve an Atticism such as we should hardly expect to find in this place. Estius thinks that the term 'yokefellow' refers to the brother or husband of Euodias or Syntyche, or, perhaps, to the keeper of the prison who was converted by St. Paul [u]. Caietan maintains that the Apostle is speaking of his wife, and gives as his reason, "Nam dictio interpretata compar congruissimè interpretatur conjux; quoniam significat sub codem jugo." But why not under the *yoke of Christ* as well as of wedlock? It is not impossible that SS. Barnabas, or Silas, or Timothy may be alluded to under this appellation; more especially as St. Paul applies the term γνησίως in a very marked way in chap. ii. 20. Or, it may have been the colleague of Epaphroditus who was absent. Or, why may not Epaphroditus himself be intended, since he would be present at Philippi when this Epistle was read [v]?

---

[s] Strom. iii.
[t] Lib. iii. c. 30.
[u] Acts xvi. 29—33.
[v] Haymo seems to understand Γνήσιε as a *proper* name, and says, " Germanus comes erat ipsius in fide, in officio preaicatienis, et tamen dives; ideoque præcepit ut ipse qui abundabat opibus, vel etiam in predicatione adjuvaret illas." This interpretation proceeds on the assumption that it was of *material* assistance that the Apostle spoke, which does violence to the general spirit of the context.

It is, however, not a little remarkable that St. Paul should have seen fit to conceal the name, as if to tell us that the individual, whoever he or she may have been, was not to look for praise in this world, but from Him who seeth in secret and rewardeth openly.

help those women

"These women seem to me to be the chief of the Church which was there, and he commendeth them to some notable man whom he calls his 'yokefellow,' to whom perchance he was wont to commend them, as to an assistant, and fellow-soldier, and brother, and companion, as he doth in the Epistle to the Romans, when he saith, 'I commend unto you Phœbe our sister, which is a servant of the Church which is at Cenchrea [x].' "

The expression 'those women' refers of course to Euodias and Syntyche, and the special commendation of the Apostle shews how much may be done by self-denying women who are zealous for the cause of Christ. The word 'help' ($συλ$-$λαμβάνου$, *suscipe eas*) probably means, Assist their infirmities, and reconcile them to one another [y].

which laboured with me in the Gospel,

$αἵτινες$, *utpote quæ*, 'seeing that they.' The English Version entirely misses the force of this. The Gospel at Philippi was first received by *women* [z]; and these two, who are specially mentioned, must have been of the number of those who, having believed, laboured among their own sex for the spread of the faith.

'Laboured with me,' $συνήθλησάν$ $μοι$, i. e. "Quæ mecum *athleticè* decertarunt pro Evangelio [a]." It is not to be supposed that they did this by preaching, but by sharing the trials and difficulties that St. Paul there endured, with masculine spirit.

Hemmingius says, "This is a remarkable passage, shewing that it is the privilege of *women* as well as *men* to strive together for the Gospel, by defending and propagating it."

---

[x] St. Chrysostom, in loc.
[y] "Tu una cum aliis adesto illis ut idem sentiant."—*Zanchius*.
[z] Acts xvi. 13.   [a] Cornelius à Lap.

The use of the preposition σύν in the words συλλαμ-βάνου and συνήθλησαν must be observed, as if the Apostle had said, 'help them who helped me [b].'

with Clement also,

i. e. they rendered assistance to Clement also, who was in peril with St. Paul at Philippi [c]. This is generally supposed to be the Clement, surnamed 'Romanus,' who was a philosopher, but afterwards became the disciple of SS. Peter and Paul, and, having been Bishop of Rome, suffered martyrdom by being thrown into the sea. For a further account of him see Euseb., Hist. Eccl., v. 6.

St. Chrysostom [d] speaks of Clement as having been one of St. Paul's associates.

and with other my fellow-labourers,

Lest any of St. Paul's 'fellow-labourers' should take it amiss that the name of Clement only was mentioned in this Epistle, he puts them in mind of a higher and an enduring record of their names and actions, viz. 'the book of life.'

Thorndike [e] says that these "fellow-labourers" were companions of the Apostles, who "were both their disciples in the doctrine, and their coadjutors in the work of the Gospel. These, or some of these—which sometimes gave personal attendance upon the Apostles, not moving in their office but at their disposing—became afterwards settled by them upon particular Churches, which they found they could not attend so well themselves, for the government of those which were converted, and the conversion of those which were not."

whose names are in the book of life.

The expression 'book of life' refers to the well-known custom of the registering the names of citizens in a book kept for the purpose, and from which the names of criminals, and fugitives, and infamous persons were struck out,

---

[b] Estius.
[c] " Quæ mecum et cum Clemente et cæteris cooperariis meis certaverunt in Evangelio."—Caietan.
[d] Preface to Hom. in 1 Tim.
[e] Of Religious Assemblies, iv. 7.

(see Rev. iii. 5). The 'book of life,' then, is the register of all faithful people, (just as 'the book of the living^f' is the record of the number of men who live in the world,) from which the names of those are expunged that cease to continue such. The Divine Intelligence, then, by a figure adapted to the comprehension of men, is called '*the book* of life,' as containing the names of all who are predestinated to eternal salvation^g. This and similar expressions, however, must not be understood as signifying the election of any to eternal life in such a way that it is impossible for them to fail of it, but, as St. Basil^h says, "As men are written in this book when they are converted from vice to virtue; so may they be blotted out of it when they backslide from virtue to vice." The righteous, then, as long as they remain such, have a certain right to eternal life. But they may lose this, as Demas did, who in the Epistle to Philemonⁱ is honoured with the same title of συνεργός as occurs in this verse, and yet in another place the Apostle complains^j, "Demas hath forsaken me." It is this 'book of life' of which our Blessed Lord spoke when He said, "Rejoice that your names are written in heaven^k;" i. e. in 'the book of life,' or memory of God. This expression is first used by Moses^l, but the idea belonging to it was not unknown to the ancients, for we find Homer saying of Ulysses, τοὔνομα ἐν Διὸς αὐλῇ.

4. Rejoice in the Lord alway:

See chap. iii. 1. The Apostle repeats the exhortation to joy, since the Philippians had endured great afflictions for the sake of the Gospel, and would be likely to be downcast at the present aspect of affairs.

'In the Lord.' In saying this he speaks of a deep unutterable joy which no change of external circumstances can affect; for God being unchangeable, the joy which is in Him must be unchangeable also. So that the Apostle does not

---

^f Ps. lxix. 29; see also Ezek. xiii. 9.
^g " Per librum vitæ tam hoc loco quam Apo. 20 metaphoricè significatur notitia Dei, quâ firmiter in mente retinet eos quos ad vitam prædestinavit æternam."—*Estius*.
^h In Isa. iv. 3.
ⁱ Ver. 24.
^j 2 Tim. iv. 10.
^k Luke x. 20.
^l Exod. xxxii. 32; see also Dan. xii. 1.

bid them rejoice because they are rich, or noble, or wise, but because they are Christians, and as such have Christ as their Lord, Who has redeemed them from the power of death, has enriched them with His grace, and has called them to His kingdom of glory. See 1 Cor. i. 30.

"Rejoice," says St. Anselm, "not in the world, but in the Lord; for as no man can serve two masters, so no one can rejoice both in the world and in the Lord, for these two joys are contrary one to the other."

The force of the word 'alway [m]' must not be forgotten, shewing, as it does, that even in trials and afflictions the Christian finds matter for holy joy. See Acts iv. 41; James i. 2.

and again I say, Rejoice.

The repetition is highly emphatic. It is not enough for a heart that is really joyful in the Lord to express its gladness once. Bp. Andrewes[n] says, "If it be *gaudete in Domino*, nay then, *iterum dico gaudete*, saith the Apostle. Then to it again and again; double it, and treble it, and spare not. Good leave have you."

There is a most beautiful passage in St. Augustine's Confessions[o], where, speaking of the joy of penitents, he says, "Let them be turned and seek Thee; and behold Thou art there in their heart, in the heart of those that confess to Thee, and cast themselves upon Thee, and weep in Thy bosom, after all their rugged ways. Then dost Thou gently wipe away their tears, and they weep the more, and joy in weeping; even for that Thou, Lord—not man of flesh and blood, but—Thou, Lord, Who madest them, remakest and comfortest them."

And again[p], the same Father, discoursing on these words, asks: "What is rejoicing in the world? Rejoicing in iniquity, rejoicing in filthiness, rejoicing in what disgraces and deforms. In all these doth the world rejoice. What, then, is this world, and what the rejoicing of the world?

---

[m] "Tam in prosperis quàm in adversis."—*Sedulius.*
[n] Serm. v. of the Conspiracy of the Gowries.
[o] v. 3.   [p] Serm. cxxi. 4, in Nov. Test.

I say, brethren, with all the brevity I can, as the Lord helpeth me, in haste, and briefly I say, the joy of the world is unpunished wickedness. Let men live in luxuriousness, in fornication, in the trifles of the Spectacles, let them wallow in drunkenness, pollute themselves with filthiness, and suffer no evil,—and see the rejoicing of the world. Those evils which I have enumerated, let not famine chastise, nor the fear of war, nor any fear, nor any disease, nor any adversities; but let their all be in abundance of substance, in the peace of the flesh, in the security of an evil mind, lo, see the rejoicing of the world. But God thinketh not as man; the thought of God is one, that of man another. It is of great mercy not to leave wickedness unpunished; and He vouchsafeth now to chasten with the scourge, that He may not be compelled to condemn to hell at the last."

St. Chrysostom [q] says, "The joy he is speaking of is what springs from tears, (i. e. shed on account of sin). For as men's joy for the world's sake hath a sorrow in the same lot with it, even so godly tears are a germ of perpetual and unfading joy."

And again [r]: "He who rejoices in the Lord cannot be deprived of the pleasure by anything that may happen. For all other things in which we rejoice are mutable, liable to become fugitive, and subject to variation. And not only does this grievous circumstance attend them, but, moreover, while they remain they do not afford us a pleasure sufficient to repel and conceal the sadness that comes upon us from other quarters. But the fear of God contains both these requisites. It is firm, and immoveable, and sheds so much gladness that we can admit no sense of other evils."

The whole of this homily should be read as bearing upon this text.

5. **Let your moderation be known unto all men.**

τὸ ἐπιεικές ('moderation') = ἐπιείκεια, (see Acts xxiv. 4; 2 Cor. x. 1); the adjective being by a very common idiom

---

[q] Hom. vi. 8, in Matt.   [r] Hom. xviii. 6, in Stat.

used for the substantive. This word is frequently brought into contrast with δίκαιος, in the sense of 'not insisting on strict justice, making fair allowance ˢ.' Then, by an easy transition it comes to mean 'forbearance,' 'moderation.' It is used in the sense of 'gentle,' Tit. iii. 2 : μηδένα βλασφημεῖν, ἀμάχους εἶναι, ἐπιεικεῖς, κ.τ.λ. It is obvious that the word 'moderation' (as English Version) very insufficiently gives the meaning of the original, which refers to an accumulation of virtues, rather than any one quality. Polus truly says that this word is not to be restricted to the Aristotelian sense, but that it signifies what the Latins call *bonitas*, partly yielding much of one's right, and partly seeking occasion of doing good to others. Trench ᵗ has the following excellent remarks on this subject. He says ἐπιείκεια " means properly that moderation which recognises the impossibility cleaving to formal law, of anticipating and providing for all those cases that will emerge, and present themselves to it for its decision ; which, with this, recognises the danger that ever waits upon the assertion of *legal* rights, lest they should be pushed into *moral* wrongs, lest the *summum jus* should in practice prove the *summa injuria* ; which, therefore, urges not its own rights to the uttermost, but going back in part or the whole from these, rectifies and redresses the injustices of justice. . . . The archetype and pattern of this grace is to be found in God. All His goings back from the strictness of His rights as against men ; all His allowing of their imperfect righteousness, and giving of a value to that which, rigorously estimated, would have none ; all His refusals to exact extreme penalties ᵘ ; all His remembering whereof we are made, and measuring His dealings with us thereby ; all these we may contemplate as ἐπιείκεια upon His part ; as it demands the same, one toward another, upon ours. The greatly forgiven servant in the parable ˣ had known the ἐπιείκεια of his lord and king ; the same, therefore, was justly expected from him."

The Apostle, then, requires that the ἐπιείκεια of Christians

ˢ Arist., Eth. Nic., 5. 14.
ᵗ Synonyms of the New Testament, p. 182, and following.
ᵘ Wisd. xii. 18 ; 2 Macc. x. 4 ; Ps. lxxxv. 5.
ˣ Matt. xviii. 23.

should be "known unto all men." To the faithful, that they may be stimulated to become imitators of so admirable an example; to unbelievers, "that whereas they speak against you as evil-doers, they may by your good works which they shall behold glorify God in the day of visitation y."

The Lord is at hand.

ὁ Κύριος ἐγγύς. This may mean, (1) the Lord is at hand for judgment, when the time of retribution will have come, and full and ample justice will be done [z]; or, (2) the Lord is at hand to help you in all trials and difficulties [a]: "The Lord is nigh unto all them that call upon Him." So Sedulius, who says, "Scit quod opus sit vobis antequam petatis Eum." Both interpretations give a good sense, but it seems probable, upon the whole, that this expression ought to be regarded as a sort of formula, or watch-word, used to strengthen any warning given to Christians, by reminding them of a future judgment. Just so *Maran-atha*, 'our Lord cometh,' in 1 Cor. xvi. 22, added to *Anathema*, signifying that he who loved not Christ must be accursed, since God was no longer far off in mystery, but had shewn Himself in love, because 'our Lord has come,' or 'is coming.'

St. Augustine [b] says, in reference to our Lord's continual presence with His people: "His Body is removed indeed from your eyes, but God is not separated from your hearts: see Him going up, believe on Him absent, hope for Him coming; but yet through His secret mercy feel Him present."

Bernard à Piconius has the following beautiful reflections on this verse:—

"'The Lord is at hand:' in a short time I shall relinquish everything; why then do I love earthly things and cleave to them?

"'The Lord is at hand:' in a short time I must give an account of all I have; why then do I keep what is beyond my needs?

---

y 1 Pet. ii. 12.   z Rom. xiii. 11; Heb. x. 37.
a Ps. cxlv. 18.   b In Ps. xlvii. 7.

"'The Lord is at hand:' lo! the Saviour comes with His rewards; why then do I lose patience in tribulations?

"'The Lord is at hand,' to render to every one according to his work; why then do I envy the happiness and joy of worldly men?

"'The Lord is at hand,' and, therefore, let our modesty, moderation, gentleness of disposition, and orderliness of life be known to all men.

"Let them see gentleness in our actions, words, and steps, as becomes those who are disciples of Christ, Whom we bear in our hearts.

"Let them see patience in our sufferings, as becomes those who are expecting an eternal crown as the reward of them.

"Let them see frugality in our use of worldly things, as becomes those who will be judged for whatever they use superfluously."

6. Be careful for nothing;

μηδὲν μεριμνᾶτε; 'distress yourselves for nothing;' see Matt. vi. 25. Christians are to cast their burden upon the Lord, knowing that as He is able, so is He also willing to take upon Himself all their cares and distresses: "Casting all your care upon Him, for He careth for you[c]." Compare also Ps. lv. 23; Prov. xvi. 3; Luke xii. 22.

The Apostle does not here forbid anxiety about our *spiritual*, but about our *carnal* state; not diligence and zeal in performing the proper duties of our calling, but anxiety of mind respecting the issue of our labours and of affairs generally, which arises from distrust in the providence and promise of God.

but in everything by prayer and supplication

This is the best, and indeed the only, remedy against care. See Ps. xxxiv. 4—6. There is a beautiful contrast between 'everything' in this clause, and 'nothing' in the former one. The meaning is, whatever your necessities may be,

---

[c] 1 Pet. v. 7.

be not disquieted with anxious care, but turn to God. See Commentary on Ephesians, p. 330.

For the difference between 'prayer' ($\pi\rho o\sigma \epsilon v\chi\eta$) and 'supplication' ($\delta\epsilon\eta\sigma\iota s$), see chap. i. 4.

with thanksgiving

i. e. whatever the event may be, both for blessings and afflictions. A very important element in devotion; for how can any one pray aright for *future* blessings who is not grateful for *past*? In this respect Christians should be like Joseph's brethren, who "made ready the present against he came at noon," and stood with it in their hands. Compare Cant. iii. 6; and see Ps. xviii. 2, "I will call upon the Lord *which is worthy to be praised*," where the thanksgiving for *past* deliverance runs side by side with the prayer for *present* aid.

St. Chrysostom [d] says, "There is nothing so pleasing to God as for a man to be thankful."

And again [e]: "That which he exhorts others to do, saying, 'Let your requests be made known unto God,' the same also he used to do himself, teaching us to begin always from these words, and before all things to give thanks unto God. For nothing is so acceptable to God as that men should be thankful, both for themselves and for others; wherefore also he prefaces almost every Epistle with this."

So also St. Athanasius, who says [f], "The blessed Apostle, who gave thanks at all times, urges us in the same manner to draw near to God. And being desirous that we should never desist from such a purpose as this, he says, 'At all times give thanks; pray without ceasing.' For he knew that believers are strong while employed in thanksgiving; and that rejoicing they pass over the walls of the enemy, like those saints who said, 'Through Thee will we pierce through our enemies, and in my God I will leap over a wall.'"

let your requests be made known unto God.

i. e. let them be such as may be worthily offered to Him.

---

[d] Hom. xix. in Eph.   [e] Hom. ii. 1, in 1 Cor.   [f] Fest. Ep. iii.

In ver. 5 he had pointed out what he wished to be made known unto *men*, he now shews what should be made known to *God*.

Haymo understands the 'requests' of the faithful to be 'made known unto God' by the ministry of angels; and proceeds to enquire, "If, therefore, the Almighty knows all things, not merely past and present, but also future, and discerns not only works, but also thoughts, and is entire everywhere, what need is there that what we do should be told to Him by the ministry of angels? It is not because anything escapes His observation that they tell this to Him, according to the words of Solomon, 'Thou alone knowest the hearts of the sons of men,' but that they may fulfil their office and ministry, because they are messengers." There is something very beautiful in the idea embodied in the above extract. Compare Tobit xii. 15, "I am Raphael, one of the seven holy angels, which present the prayers of the Saints, and which go in and out before the glory of the Holy One."

Bernard à Piconius notes three conditions of prayer: "We must pray," he says, "with confidence, with perseverance, and with gratitude. With confidence of receiving; with gratitude for what we have received; with perseverance through Jesus Christ our Mediator."

7. And the peace of God,

The word 'and' connects this verse with what immediately goes before, q. d. 'if you do what I have said, *then* the peace,' &c. 'The peace of God' means "that peace which rests in God, and is wrought by Him in the soul, the counterpoise of all troubles and anxieties, (John xvi. 33)[g]." It is well called 'the peace of God,' since He alone can give it. "Quia in Seipso pacatus et quietissimus est Deus, Cujus natura est Pax[h]." So also St. Augustine, who in his well-known description of God's attributes[i], most beautifully pourtrays the rest which He has in Himself, "unchange-

---

[g] Alford.   [h] St. Anselm.   [i] Conf. i. 4.

able, yet all changing; never new, never old; all-renewing, and bringing age upon the proud, and they know it not; ever working, ever at rest; still gathering, yet nothing lacking; supporting, filling, and overspreading; creating, nourishing, and maturing; seeking, yet having all things."

The expression may also mean the peace which *we have in God*, by being reconciled to Him through the death of His Son. In Eph. ii. 14 Christ is described as "our Peace;" since it is through His most salutary Passion alone that we can obtain peace. Probably both interpretations are included in the expression.

It is to be observed that the Apostle in this place speaks of prayer as having a *virtutem pacativam*. See Job xxii. 21, "Acquaint now thyself with Him, and be at peace."

which passeth all understanding,

ἡ ὑπερέχουσα πάντα νοῦν. Νοῦς is the intelligent faculty, acting on and regulating matter. The meaning is, the nature and extent of this 'peace' cannot be expressed or understood. It is something which can only be *felt* in the inmost soul of believers, ("O *taste* and see how gracious the Lord is [k],") but will be fully realized hereafter [l]; for, as far as regards the present, St. Augustine truly says [m], "How much soever thou mayest reflect upon that peace, the mind is scarce able to conceive it while set amid the heaviness of the body."

Haymo well remarks, "It passeth all understanding, except the understanding of the Lord, because no angel, no man is able to fathom the mystery of the Passion of the Son of God, and of our reconciliation, and how great was the love which was in Him, Who, when He was God, for our sakes deigned to become man."

And so St. Augustine [n]: "So that in that he said 'all,' not even the understanding of the holy angels may be excepted,

---

[k] Ps. xxxiv. 8.
[l] Caietan says, "Nullæ siquidem vires creaturarum sufficiunt ad tranquillitatem etiam participandam divini ordinis, quo mens inhæret Deo charitate et omni studio."
[m] In Ps. cxxxii. 10.
[n] Enchir., 16.

but of God alone: for His peace surpasseth not His own understanding."

shall keep your hearts and minds

φρουρήσει, 'shall keep as with a garrison.' See 1 Pet. i. 5. This word is highly emphatic, and gives us a most beautiful idea of the care that God has for His people. Solomon's bed was not so well guarded with his threescore valiant men, all holding swords [o], as each faithful Christian is by the power of God without him, and the peace of God within him. This holy peace, like David's harp, chases away the evil spirit of anxiety and fear [p], and surrounds the sorrowing heart with profound repose. It is obvious, however, that this word is only to be understood *conditionally*.

'Your hearts;' i. e. your affections, lest they turn aside to what is evil.

'And minds;' your intellectual powers, lest they receive anything that is contrary to the faith.

through Christ Jesus.

Better, '*in* (ἐν) Christ Jesus;' shall keep us in Him, (i. e. in living union with His risen and ascended Humanity,) so that we may remain stedfast, and not fall from the faith.

Hemmingius says, "Let each one to whom piety and salvation is a matter of care, observe this text. The snares of the devil are great; but do thou oppose prayer to them, and thou shalt be safe. The world presses thee down; but do thou shake off the burden by prayer. Various and manifold stumblingblocks and difficulties are thrown in thy way in civil and ecclesiastical government; but do thou flee unto God in prayer as unto a most certain refuge, and thou shalt be safe, even against the gates of hell."

8. Finally, brethren,

τὸ λοιπόν, "quod reliquum est." See chap. iii. 1. "Id est, ad extremum omnium, ut omnia breviter comprehendam; vel de reliquo vitæ vestræ [q]."

---

[o] Cant. iii. 7, 8.   [p] 1 Sam. xvi. 23.   [q] Sedulius.

St. Chrysostom says, "it stands for 'I have said all.'"
"Before closing the Epistle the Apostle adds a general precept, embracing in a comprehensive way many points relating to morals and holy conversation q."

These are the words of one who loves to linger on his subject, and the exhortation throughout is exceedingly earnest, and well calculated to arouse the Philippians to the practice of virtue.

whatsoever things are true,

Understand, 'think upon.' 'True,' as excluding all hypocrisy and double dealing; no doubt also with a reference to the truths of the Gospel. Compare Hor. Ep. i. 1, 11. "Quid *verum* atque *decens* curo et rogo."

whatsoever things are honest,

σεμνά. St. Ambrose translates 'magnifica,' but it is probably 'pudica;' i. e. whatever is suited to the character of a grave and virtuous man, as excluding all lightness in conversation and manner. Diog. Laert. says of Socrates, αὐτάρκης ἦν καὶ σεμνός. And Caietan remarks, "*vera* spectant ad intellectum, *honesta* ad affectum."

whatsoever things are just,

Excluding the power or desire of doing injuries to one another. "Ad reddendum unicuique debitum præcipimur ut simus prompti r."

whatsoever things are pure,

ἁγνά, excluding all sins of the flesh. See 2 Cor. xi. 2; Tit. ii. 5. There is another reading, ἅγια.

whatsoever things are lovely,

προσφιλῆ, "quæ grata sunt omnibus." Excluding all asperity of manner, and enjoining a gentle and conciliatory disposition. Sedulius, however, seems to take this in the sense of pleasing *to God*.

---

q Estius.   r Caietan.

whatsoever things are of good report;

εὔφημα, "quæ bonam famam nos faciunt habere." Excluding all words and actions that may in any way tend to bring the name of Christian into ill-repute. See above, ver. 5, " Let your moderation," &c.

St. Augustine [a] cites this passage to shew that good report is to be preserved for the sake of others : " Wherefore whosoever guards his life from charges of shameful and evil deeds does good to himself; but whosoever guards his character too is merciful towards others. For unto ourselves our own life is necessary, unto others, our character; and certainly even what we mercifully minister unto others for their health, abounds also to our own profit."

if there be any virtue,

εἴ τις, equivalent to ὅσα, " whatever is virtuous, whatever is praiseworthy." He varies his mode of expression because there is no *regular* word for 'virtuous' derived from ἀρετή.

St. Paul is here speaking of virtue as opposed to vice, and his meaning is that they should exercise themselves diligently in every branch of virtue.

and if there be any praise,

Metonymy for anything *deserving* of praise. Not that he wishes them to seek for praise, but to do deeds *worthy of praise*. We gather hence that nothing which is *really deserving of praise* is forbidden, but that whatever is truly praiseworthy is consonant with the Christian religion. Our praise is not necessarily of men (see Rom. ii. 29), but to render the applause of men worth anything it must be awarded not on *worldly*, but on divine principles. E.g. We must be praised, not because we have been successful, or adroit, but because we have been successful by keeping the faith, doing our duty, and seeking God's honour and glory. This praise *ought* to be desired ; for it is the ἔπαινος ἐκ τοῦ Θεοῦ.

think on these things.

i. e. Meditate on, so as to practise them. " His delight is

---

[a] De bono Viduitatis, 22.

in the law of the Lord: and in His law will he exercise himself day and night[t]."

"Seest thou," says St. Chrysostom, "that he desires to banish every evil imagination from our souls; for evil actions spring from thoughts?"

9. *Those things which ye have both learned, and received, and heard, and seen in me,*

Again the Apostle proposes himself as an example. See iii. 17; see also 1 Cor. iv. 16 and xi. 1; 1 Thess. i. 6.

The word 'learned' (ἐμάθετε) signifies elementary instruction; 'received' (παρελάβετε) more accurate teaching; 'heard' (ἠκούσατε) refers to familiar discourses; 'seen' (εἴδετε) to St. Paul's actions; for, as Hemmingius well says, "The life of a pastor ought to be a mirror of his teaching."

Bernard à Piconius understands the words thus: what ye have 'learned,' from my teaching; what ye have 'received' from my writing; what ye have 'heard' concerning me in my absence; what ye have 'seen' in me when present.

do :

He had just said 'think on these things,' and he now further enjoins that they should be carried into practice [u].

"Not only *say* them, but *do* them also [v]."

and the God of peace

i. e. God, Who is the Father of Peace; viz. of our Lord Jesus Christ, Who is 'our Peace [x];' or God, Who is the Lover of Peace [y].

Observe, it is not merely the 'peace of God,' as in verse 7, but 'the God of Peace.'

Bp. Andrewes [z], speaking of God's titles, says, "All the Old Testament through you shall observe God's great title is 'the Lord of Hosts [a],' which in the New you shall never read; but ever since He rose from the dead it is, instead of it, the 'God of peace.' It is not amiss for us, this change.

---

[t] Ps. i. 2.
[u] "Mens imprimis requiritur, secundo externa facta."—*Zanchius*.
[v] St. Chrysostom.
[x] Eph. ii. 14.
[y] Rom. xv. 33.
[z] Serm. xviii. Of the Resurrection.
[a] 1 Sam. i. 11; Isa. i. 24; Jer. xlvi. 18; Hab. ii. 13; Mal. i. 14.

For if the Lord of Hosts come to be at peace with us, His Hosts shall be all for us, which were against us, while it was no peace. So as make but God 'the God of peace,' and more needs not. For His peace will command His power straight."

It is well known that St. Augustine finds a mysterious meaning in the word peace (*pax*), which, he says, consisting of three letters, denotes the Trinity, from Whom comes all true peace.

shall be with you.

i. e. shall help and defend you.

10. But I rejoiced in the Lord greatly,

He now passes on to giving of thanks; not, however, without a slight admixture of expostulation, as Estius thinks, for the contributions of the Philippians having ceased for a time. It is obvious that the Apostle's rejoicing is founded not so much on the gift itself, as on the readiness and zeal they had shewn in sending.

'I rejoiced in the Lord greatly [b];' "not with worldly rejoicing, nor with the joy of this life, but 'in the Lord.' Not because I had refreshment, but because ye advanced; for this is my refreshment. Wherefore he saith 'greatly;' since this joy was not corporeal, nor on account of his own refreshment, but because of their advancement [c]."

Rosenmüller translates ἐν Κυρίῳ, " propter Christum, doctrinæ Christi causa."

that now at the last your care of me hath flourished again ;

ὅτι ἤδη ποτὲ ἀνεθάλετε τὸ ὑπὲρ ἐμοῦ φρονεῖν. The words ἤδη ποτὲ (*jam aliquando*) seem to imply that some considerable time had elapsed : " Quasi dicat post longam intermissionem [d]."

'Flourished again,' (ἀνεθάλετε) 'your care concerning me has revived;' a metaphor taken from trees and plants,

---

[b] " In principio Epistolæ inter alia proposuit gaudium proprium de Philippensibus : modo illud in specie tractat super charitate Philippensium erga ipsum Paulum demonstrata factis."— *Caietan.*

[c] St. Chrysostom.

[d] Aretius.

which become dry and barren in winter, (see Isa. vi. 13,) but blossom again in spring. Perhaps 'your care concerning me *came into leaf again,*' would be the nearest translation that could be given; but we need not suppose, with Bengel, that *it was actually spring-time* when the contributions arrived!

St. Chrysostom says, "Hath flourished again, as trees which have shot forth, then dried up, and again shot forth. Hence he sheweth that they who had formerly borne flowers had withered, and after withering again budded forth. So that the words 'flourished again' have both rebuke and praise. For it is no small thing that he who hath withered should flourish again."

So also St. Augustine [a], "These Philippians had now dried up with a long weariness, and withered as it were as to bearing this fruit of a good work; and he rejoiceth for them that they 'flourished again,' not for himself, that they supplied his wants. Therefore subjoins he, ' not that I speak in respect of want,' &c." See also the same Father in Ps. l. 11.

Haymo accounts for this expression thus: "At the beginning of the preaching of the Apostle, when the Philippians believed, they shewed him the greatest kindness, joyfully ministering to him such things as were needful; but when they had begun to suffer persecution at the hands of their unbelieving fellow-citizens, they ceased from this supply, for they were not able, situated as they were in the midst of sedition and persecution, to fulfil their office of love, as they had done in a time of tranquillity. But when peace was restored to them, they returned to their former manner of life, and began to minister to the Apostle and other saints such things as were needful. Wherefore he rejoices over them," &c.

wherein ye were also careful, but ye lacked opportunity.

ἐφ' ᾧ καὶ ἐφρονεῖτε, ἠκαιρεῖσθε δέ; implying that even when the Philippians did not send pecuniary assistance they bore the Apostle in their minds. On ἐφ' ᾧ, see chap. iii. 12.

---

[a] Conf. xiii. 26.

They did not lack the *will* to help but the *opportunity*, (ἠκαιρεῖσθε). This word probably means, not only that they had no opportunity of sending, but that they had nothing to send, and possibly also had no fitting messenger. It is plain that this sentence is introduced to mitigate any apparent severity that might lie in the use of such a word as ἀνεθάλετε. St. Chrysostom enquires, " What meaneth ' lacked opportunity?' It came not, saith he, of indolence, but of necessity. Ye had it not in your hands, nor were in abundance. This is the meaning of ' ye lacked opportunity.' Thus most men speak when the things of this life do not flow in to them abundantly, and are in short supply."

11. Not that I speak in respect of want:

καθ' ὑστέρησιν. This may be rendered *propter*, or *secundum penuriam*; i. e. not regarding the want which I am suffering, as if I was bent on my own interest; and the full meaning will be, that the joy which the Apostle has just been speaking of did not arise from the relief which their contributions had afforded him, but from the love which was shewn by their sending. Perhaps ὑστέρησις in this place might be rendered ' neglect,' and then the meaning will be, ' I do not now speak because ye neglected me.' Arctius takes ὑστέρησις, ' slowness,' (from ὑστερίζειν, ' to come late'), and then the sense will be, ' I do not complain of your slowness in sending.' This agrees very well with what immediately follows.

for I have learned,

i. e. in Christ's school, since nature can teach no such lesson. "This is an object of discipline," says St. Chrysostom, "and exercise, and care, for it is not easy of attainment, but very difficult and full of toil."

in whatsoever state I am, therewith to be content.

αὐτάρκης; "Id est sibi sufficiens, suâ sorte et re contentus, adeo ut nihil appetens nihil indigeat, sed potius pro suâ sorte se suaque aliis communicat et liberaliter effundat[f]."

---

[f] Cornelius à Lap.

Caietan well remarks, "I have learnt to be sufficient for the things which I have, although the things which I have are not sufficient for me."

The virtue of αὐτάρκεια is mentioned in 2 Cor. ix. 8, and 1 Tim. vi. 6, and is a most important one for a Christian to cultivate. Socrates used to say that that man was most like the gods who wanted the fewest possible things, since the gods want nothing at all.

St. Augustine[g] exclaims in reference to St. Paul's description of himself in this verse, "Behold a soldier of the heavenly camp, not the dust which we are."

12. I know both how to be abased, and I know how to abound:

The antithesis between 'abased' (ταπεινοῦσθαι) and 'abound' (περισσεύειν) must be observed. The English Version scarcely recognises this sufficiently. Ταπεινοῦσθαι should be translated so as to convey the idea of *suffering want*, in opposition to περισσεύειν, *being in abundance*, and the meaning will be, 'I know how to bear poverty with patience, and plenty with moderation.' St. Chrysostom shews the difficulties of either condition: "For as want inclines us to do many evil things, so too doth plenty. For many ofttimes coming into plenty have become indolent, and have not known how to bear their good fortune. Many men have taken it as an occasion of no longer working. But Paul did not so, for what he received he consumed on others, and emptied himself for them. This is to know how to make good use of what we have. He was in no wise relaxed, nor did he exult at his abundance; Paul was the same in want and in plenty, he was neither oppressed on the one hand, nor rendered a boaster on the other."

everywhere and in all things

i. e. whatever happens, I am prepared to meet it with equanimity. He repeats the previous sentiment, but with more particularity. Wordsworth translates ἐν παντὶ in each thing, taken singly; ἐν πᾶσι in all, taken collectively.

---

[g] Conf. x. 31.

I am instructed

μεμύημαι, ("I am instructed,")—a most significant word, used in reference to the Greek mysteries, which, however, the Apostle does not hesitate to transfer to a better use. As, therefore, the word μυστήριον, as well as μεμύημαι, is admitted into the number of Christian forms of expression, does it not seem likely that the opinions of those are sound who consider the heathen mysteries to have been really the rites of a *purer faith*, and to have consisted in the instruction of the μύσται in the patriarchal revelation? Some have supposed that Socrates' offence was in revealing the mysteries in his purer teaching, and that he was made away with *really* for violating his engagement as one initiated, and teaching the public the true religion he had sworn to conceal from them. The word τέλειοι in ch. iii. 15 may be taken in the same sense, for it was used to signify not perfect men, but men perfectly instructed in the mysteries.

The Apostle means that what he has just been speaking of is not with him mere *theoretical* learning, since he has been *practically initiated* into it. And a high and holy state it is to be thus 'initiated.' For as none but the strongest and healthiest bodies can bear sudden alternations of heat and cold, so none but those who are practised in Christian discipline, and whose hearts are fashioned by God[h], will be able to preserve calmness amidst the changes and chances of life.

both to be full and to be hungry,

St. Bernard very beautifully remarks, "A great and rare virtue it is to remain hungry at a feast, to endure cold while surrounded by garments, to be lowly in the midst of honours. Hannibal knew how to suffer hunger and want; but he knew not how to be full and to have abundance, for the allurements of Capua enervated him who had hitherto been unconquered, and laid him open to the Romans to be vanquished, invincible though he had been."

[h] Ps. xxxiii. 14.

both to abound and to suffer need.

St. Augustine [k], speaking of earthly goods, says : "Nor doth any use them well save he who hath power also not to use them. Many, indeed, with more ease practise abstinence, so as not to use, than practise temperance, so as to use well. But no one can wisely use them, save he who can also continently not use them. Forsooth, to suffer want is the part of any men soever, but to *know* to suffer want is the part of great men. So also to abound, who cannot? But to know also to abound, is not, save of those whom abundance corrupts not."

Bp. Andrewes [l] remarks on this passage, "How admirably did the Apostle follow the example of *obedience* furnished by his Blessed Master—'Not My will but Thine be done!' And also that obedience manifested in the holy Angels, who at God's command are ready not only to ascend, but also to descend [m], to shew that they are content not only to appear in heavenly glory, which is their nature, but also to be abased, according to the Apostle's rule, 'I can abound, and I can want.'"

See also St. Francis de Sales' "Devout Life," part i. c. 2.

13. Having said before 'I know,' and 'I have learned,' lest this perchance should sound like boasting, the Apostle hastens to ascribe all to *Christ*, the Source of all strength.

I can do all things through Christ which strengtheneth me.

It is to be observed that the expression πάντα ἰσχύω means a great deal more than 'I can *do* all things :' it is 'I *can* all things,' a form of expression which modern English has unhappily lost, implying the capacity not only of *doing*, but also of suffering, understanding, caring for, &c.

'All things,' without limitation, so manifold in its gifts and operations is divine grace! The complete way in which St. Paul ascribes everything to Christ is still further seen

---

[k] De Bono Conjugali, 21.   [l] Serm. on Lord's Prayer.   [m] Gen. xxviii. 12.

from the use of the compound word ἐνδυναμοῦντι instead of the simple δυναμοῦντι, the preposition ἐν being highly emphatic. It has been truly said, "Great were the merits of Paul; but that they were in him the grace of God had effected." See 1 Cor. xv. 10; 2 Cor. iii. 5. What a soul-stirring passage, then, is this! It tells the faithful Christian that he is a conqueror, yea, much more than a conqueror, having power given him over *all* things; so that nothing is impossible to him. Compare 1 Cor. iii. 21—23.

14. Notwithstanding ye have well done, that ye did communicate with my affliction.

A protest against Solifidianism. The meaning is, 'Great as Christ's power is in me, still you were right in ministering to my wants.' This verse is a good motto for charitable institutions. God will indeed provide for His own, and accomplish His work; but men must labour, as if the work depended entirely on themselves.

It is probable, also, that the Apostle added these words lest the Philippians should suppose that he despised their gift. Although he was disciplined to bear any turn of fortune with equanimity, yet he rejoiced at the arrival of their present supply on *their* account, because it made them partakers of his reward. And so he does not say 'ye gave,' but 'ye communicated (συγκοινωνήσαντες) with my affliction,' (see i. 7,) implying that as they sent their contributions to mitigate the rigour of his captivity, so did they become sharers in the recompense which would follow upon it [n].

St. Augustine [o] says, "Hereat he rejoiceth, hereon feedeth; because they had well done, not because his strait was eased."

Hemmingius remarks here, "Observe that the Apostle defines liberality towards ministers to be a *good work*; whence it follows that they *do ill* who contribute nothing to the support of the ministry."

---

[n] Bengel remarks on the word συγκοινωνήσαντες, "Composito verbo innuitur etiam alios alio modo fuisse κοινωνήσαντες."
[o] Conf. xiii. 26.

15. **Now ye Philippians know also,**

And therefore are able to testify.

that in the beginning of the Gospel,

i. e. of the preaching of the Gospel among you; shewing that they must have acted *spontaneously*, having no others to set them an example. Hitherto the Apostle has simply commended the liberality of the Philippians; he now does the same by comparing them with others.

Wordsworth [p] says that "this mention of the kindness of the Philippians at the *beginning* of his Apostolic ministry is more striking, as a record of his thankful remembrance of them, because it is made in this Epistle, almost at the end of his ministry."

when I departed from Macedonia,

He is speaking of his first departure from Macedonia, respecting which see Acts xvii. and xviii., for that he was a second time in Macedonia appears from Acts xx. 1.

It is to be observed that 'departed from Macedonia' hardly expresses the force of ἐξῆλθον ἀπὸ Μακεδονίας. St. Paul was *compelled* to leave Macedonia on account of a persecution stirred up against him by the Jews [q]. The phrase then would rather have the meaning of having been *driven out* of Macedonia, and would thus contain very great praise of the Philippians, since even under such unfavourable circumstances they did not desert him.

no Church communicated with me as concerning giving and receiving,

εἰς λόγον δόσεως καὶ λήψεως—"in rationem dationis et acceptionis;" or, "ad rationem expensorum et acceptorum." The Apostle introduces a familiar illustration, taken from the way in which accounts are kept by merchants. There is always a debtor and a creditor side. Though it might perhaps appear that the 'giving' was all on the side of the

---

[p] Greek Test.   [q] Acts xvii. 5—10.

Philippians, and the 'receiving' all on the side of St. Paul, yet it was not really so, since in return for their contributions they became partakers of his grace.

but ye only.

This shews that the Philippians were the only Christians in Macedonia who at that time had opened such an account with him—the λόγον δόσεως referring to the necessaries of life, the λόγον λήψεως to spiritual gifts imparted by the Apostle. St. Chrysostom says, "Behold how they communicated, by giving carnal things and receiving spiritual. For as they who sell and buy communicate with each other, by mutually giving what they have, (and this is communication,) so, too, is it here. For there is not anything more profitable than this trade and traffic. It is performed on the earth, but it is completed in heaven. They who buy are on the earth, but they buy and agree about heavenly things, whilst they lay down an earthly price."

Some have supposed that St. Paul carried about with him an account-book, in which he put down on one side the various sums supplied by the Church for the necessities of himself and companions, and other pious uses, and on the other the amount actually expended; the object of this being to shew the Church that the money entrusted to him had been properly used: but there is no necessity to force this present passage to such a meaning.

St. Augustine[r], speaking of mutual good offices, says, "Bodily works of mercy may be joined with spiritual works of preaching, and peace may result from giving and receiving. For the Apostle, who hath declared that this alms-giving is a balance of giving and receiving, saith, 'If we have sown unto you spiritual things, is it a great thing if we shall reap your carnal things?' And concerning the same thing he elsewhere saith, 'He that had gathered much had nothing over, and he that had gathered little had no lack.' Why had he nothing over who had much? Because what he had over he gave to the needy. And what meaneth,

---

[r] In Ps. cxxii. 9.

'he that had gathered little had no lack?' Because he received from the other's abundance, that there might be equality, as he saith."

Bp. Andrewes* makes use of this verse to shew that because "Gifts are rather *commendata quam data*, because there is λόγος δόσεως, seeing God will come and take account of the talents, we must neither wastefully misspend them nor have them without profit. *Ut crescit donum, sic crescat ratio donati.*"

16. For even in Thessalonica ye sent once and again unto my necessity.

St. Chrysostom remarks on this verse, "Here again is great praise, that he when dwelling in the metropolis should be nourished by a little city."

There evidently must have been some good reason why St. Paul preferred to receive contributions from Philippi rather than be supported by the Christians of Thessalonica, during his sojourn in that city. It may have been that they were inclined to *avarice*, and so would have considered it burdensome to supply what was needful for the Apostle. But whatever the true reason may have been, we find St. Paul, in his Epistles to the Thessalonians, specially dwelling on the fact that he had not been chargeable unto any of them; and this certainly looks as if a spirit of grudging had manifested itself among them. See 1 Thess. ii. 9, and 2 Thess. iii. 8. Be this as it may, he here recites the remembrance of the aid he received from Philippi with gratitude.

The 'necessity' he speaks of were the things required for his daily support. A caution to ministers, surely, not to take from their people more than is enough to supply their needs.

17. Not because I desire a gift:

οὐχ ὅτι ἐπιζητῶ τὸ δόμα; better, perhaps, 'not that I want *a repetition of the gift* for myself.' He had said

---

* Serm. ii. on Preparation to Prayer.

before, (ver. 11,) "not that I speak in respect of want." The meaning is, he is not writing from *selfish* motives. Unless he had added this, illnatured persons might have misinterpreted his praise of the Philippians' liberality.

but I desire fruit that may abound to your account.

He returns to the figure of account-keeping, (see ver. 15); and the meaning is, if I wish to receive anything from you it is that your future recompense may be increased, and that further *interest* may be added 'to your account;' i. e. with God, Who keeps an accurate reckoning of all that is laid out in His service.

St. Augustine[t], shewing that alms given to the righteous procures treasure in heaven, says: "See what thou art buying, when thou mayest buy, at what price. For thou art buying the kingdom of heaven; and there is no time for buying except in this life. Remark, also, at how low a price thou buyest. Its value to thee is that of all that thou canst ever possess."

St. Gregory[u] takes occasion to point out from this place that 'good preachers' are not actuated by desire of gain, since "it is not for the sake of the means of living that preaching is rendered, but for the sake of preaching that the means of living are accepted. And as often as what is wanted is bestowed on those that preach by those that hear them, they are not used to take delight in the benefit of the good things, but in the reward of those bestowing them."

So also St. Augustine[x]: "I have learned of Thee, my God, to distinguish betwixt a 'gift' and 'fruit.' A 'gift' is the thing itself which he gives that imparts these necessaries unto us, as money, meat, drink, clothing, shelter, help; but the 'fruit' is the good and right will of the giver."

And here it may be remarked in passing, that we trace in St. Paul the character which, as we should say, belonged to a *perfect gentleman*. He is on all occasions courteous, courageous, and spirited, and here, as elsewhere also, liberal in money matters, (see 1 Cor. ix. 12—18; 2 Cor. xi. 9, &c.);

[t] In Ps. ciii. 12.   [u] Moral., xix. 22.   [x] Conf., xiii. 26.

shrinking from anything like avarice, or from what is very significantly called 'dirty conduct.' Add to this character of the gentleman that he was probably well to do in the world before his conversion, and well educated, since he quotes classical authors, writes very fair Greek, and expresses himself logically.

18. But I have all, and abound:

'I have,' ἀπέχω, probably *receptum habeo*. There is a notion contained in this word of receiving in the sense of produce from a farm, or wages for work done. Compare Matt. vi. 2 and 5. By using this word rather than the simple ἔχω the Apostle probably intended to hint that, after all, whatever they sent was not so much a matter of favour, as a recompense for his labour in having imparted to them spiritual gifts. The English Version misses the delicate sense of this.

'And abound,'—"satis superque habeo." He adds this, as well to shew that they need not send a further supply, as that they had already contributed munificently.

Haymo, evidently referring this to the ἀντάρκεια of the Apostle, remarks, "Ille omnia habet qui nullo indiget, qui præter necessaria nihil requirit."

I am full,

either of 'joy,' 2 Tim. i. 4, or 'comfort,' 2 Cor. vii. 4.

having received from Epaphroditus the things which were sent from you,

τὰ παρ' ὑμῶν. They had sent money, or clothes, and other things which might be useful to him in his imprisonment. Johnson [y] says, on the authority of St. Irenæus, that "what St. Paul received was some considerable part of what the people had offered at the altar."

an odour of a sweet smell,

By far the highest commendation of the gift sent by the Philippians. The expression occurs in Gen. viii. 21. Ham-

---

[y] Unbloody Sacrifice, chap. ii. sect. iv.

mond says, "There were two altars in the temple of the Jews, θυμιατήριον, 'the altar of incense,' within the temple, and θυσιαστήριον, 'the altar of sacrifice,' without in the court. On these two were offered all things that were offered to God; and under these two heads of 'incense' and 'burnt offering' are almsdeeds, or works of charity, here set down, as being the prime things now under the Gospel to obtain God's favour and acceptance." See Commentary on Ephesians, p. 295.

a sacrifice acceptable, well-pleasing to God.

The expression 'acceptable sacrifice[z]' (θυσίαν δεκτήν) as applied to *alms* is very remarkable; not, as Estius remarks, that they have the proper nature of a sacrifice offered to God, but that they are received by Him just as if they were a sacrifice offered to His honour. See Heb. xiii. 16.

Bp. Andrewes [a] shews how the revival of the liberality of the Philippians was connected with our Lord's Resurrection: "St. Paul doth call the bounteous supplying of his wants from the Philippians θυσίαν δεκτήν, 'a sacrifice right acceptable and pleasing to God,' and ὀσμὴν εὐωδίας, 'a most delightful sweet savour.' And that you may still see he looks to the Resurrection, he saith, the Philippians had lain dead and dry a great while, as in winter trees do use. But when that work of bounty came from them, they did ἀναθάλλειν, that is, shoot forth, wax fresh, grow green again, as now at this season plants do. That so the very virtue of Christ's Resurrection did shew forth itself in them; so fitting nature's resurrection-time, the time of bringing things as it were from the dead again, with this of Christ. Which time is therefore the most pleasing time, the time of the greatest pleasure of all times of the year."

19. St. Chrysostom remarks here, "Behold how he blesseth them, as poor men do."

---

[z] "Observanda est hoc loco anthropopathia. Deus enim se hujusmodi locutionibus ad rudis populi captum accommodat. Ut enim homini bonus odor est gratus, et fœtor displicet, ita obedientia quævis ex fide præstita dicitur hostia accepta, et odor suavitatis Deo; contra vero quicquid non est ex fide, fœtor est et displicet Deo. Est igitur hæc figura metalepsis."—*Hemmingius.*

[a] Serm. xviii. of the Resurrection.

But my God shall supply all your need

i. e. as you have ministered to *my* necessities, so will God, in answer to my prayer, and in requital of your love, supply *your* wants, as He did the widow's vessels with oil [b]. For if He made great promises to those who supported Levites, how much more to those who have supported Apostles? St. Chrysostom is careful to point out here that St. Paul did not promise or desire that God should "make them *rich*, and to abound greatly; but what said he? 'Supply all your need,' so that ye may not be in want, but have things for your necessities. Since Christ, too, when He gave us a form of prayer, inserted also this in the prayer, when He taught us to say, 'Give us this day our daily bread.'" See also Matt. vi. 25—34.

There are other readings, of χάριν, 'grace,' and also χαράν, 'joy,' instead of χρείαν, 'need;' either gives a good sense. Estius enquires, "Why did the Apostle say '*my* God,' and not '*our* God,' when in the next verse he says 'God and *our* Father?' Because he was speaking of the kindness which had been shewn towards him being repaid; as if he had said, Although I who am poor am unable to return a similar act of kindness, yet *my* God, Whom I serve, can do that, since He is all-Rich."

according to His riches

It is easy to Him to repay you, and He will do it quickly. But lest their minds should be occupied with thoughts of a recompence in *this world*, he immediately adds,

in glory by Christ Jesus.

What the nature of that reward will be we can but faintly guess at now, for "eye hath not seen, nor ear heard, neither have entered into the heart of man, the things which God hath prepared for them that love Him [c]."

---

[b] 2 Kings iv. 3.   [c] 1 Cor. ii. 9.

20. Now unto God and our Father be glory for ever and ever. Amen.

i. e. to the Holy Trinity, which is One God. The conjunction 'and' here is exegetical, not copulative.

He concludes the Epistle by ascribing glory to God, (with special reference of course to the gift which he has received,) through Whom alone good works can be done, and to Whom all praise is to be offered. Compare Rom. xvi. 27.

This doxology naturally flows from the *joy* which pervades the Epistle.

21. Salute every saint in Christ Jesus.

i. e. convey my words of salutation to all the faithful that are among you, saying how I invoke upon them all those blessings of which Christ is the Author[d].

For the meaning of the word 'saint' see chap. i. 1.

Hemmingius well says that if we are desirous to retain this title we must devote ourselves without ceasing to holiness and innocence.

The brethren which are with me greet you.

As distinguished from 'all the saints' in the next verse. These 'brethren' were no doubt St. Paul's special attendants, as Aristarchus, Epaphras, Demas, Timotheus, Linus, &c.

22. All the saints salute you,

i. e. all who are at Rome; in other words, the whole Roman Church.

chiefly they that are of Cæsar's household.

No doubt St. Paul makes special mention of this that the Philippians might be comforted on hearing that there were Christians even in the palace of Nero, ("for what was this but that God reigned as King even in the midst of the very regions of hell[e],") and so might understand that devotion is suitable to all sorts of vocations and professions. St. Francis de Sales[f] says on this subject, "It is an error, or rather a he-

---

[d] Estius.   [e] Beza.   [f] Devout Life, part i. c. 3.

resy, to endeavour to banish a devout life from the companies of soldiers, the shops of tradesmen, the courts of princes, or the affairs of married people. It is true that devotion merely contemplative, monastical, and religious, cannot be exercised in these vocations; but besides these three sorts of devotion there are divers others proper to make those perfect who live in secular conditions. Abraham, Isaac and Jacob, David, Job, Tobias, Sarah, Rebecca and Judith bear witness of this in the Old Testament; and in the New, St. Joseph, Lydia, and St. Crispin were perfectly devout in their shops; St. Anne, St. Martha, St. Monica, Acquila, Priscilla, in their families; Cornelius, St. Sebastian, St. Maurice, in the wars; Constantine, Helena, St. Louis, St. Anne, and St. Edward on their thrones. Nay, it has happened, that many have lost perfection in solitude, (which notwithstanding is so much to be desired for perfection,) and have preserved it in company, which seems so little favourable to perfection. Lot (says St. Gregory) who was so chaste in the city defiled himself in solitude. Wheresoever we are, we may, and ought to aspire to a perfect life."

Some understand the expression 'they of Cæsar's household' of relations of the Emperor himself; others refer it to Seneca the philosopher, and Lucan the poet, whom they suppose to have embraced Christianity; while others think that the domestic servants (freedmen) or slaves of the imperial family are meant. St. Chrysostom says that St. Paul "elevated and strengthened them (the Philippians), by shewing that his preaching had reached even to the king's household. For if those who were in the palace despised all things for the sake of the King of Heaven, far more ought they to do this. And this, too, was a proof of the love of Paul, that he had told many things of them, and said great things of them, whence he had led those who were in the palace, and who had never seen them, to desire to salute them."

† Wordsworth [g] remarks very appropriately on this place, "The Gospel was first preached to the poor [h], and God chose the weak things of this world [i], and the Apostle had shewn

---

[g] Greek Test.   [h] Matt. xi. 5.   [i] 1 Cor. i. 26—28.

his Christian tenderness for the large and despised class to which Onesimus belonged, by his letter to Philemon [k]. Now Christianity has found its way into the household of Cæsar. At length, after it had been persecuted by the Cæsars, it won Emperors to Christ. Thus the mustard-seed of the Gospel grew, and stretched forth its branches, and overshadowed the world[l]."

23. The grace of our Lord Jesus Christ be with you all. Amen.

The Apostolic benediction. The Epistle begins (i. 2) and ends with 'grace,' a word that contains the sum of all that is conferred upon us by Christ. See Commentary on Ephesians, p. 123[m].

Conybeare well remarks that this Epistle "gives an unusual amount of information concerning the personal situation of its writer. But nothing in it is more suggestive than St. Paul's allusion to the Prætorian guards, and to the converts he has gained in the household of Nero. He tells us that throughout the Prætorian quarters he was well known as a prisoner for the cause of Christ[n], and he sends special salutations to the Philippian Church from the Christians in the Imperial household. These notices bring before us very vividly the moral contrasts by which the Apostle was surrounded. The soldier to whom he was chained to-day might have been in Nero's body-guard yesterday; his comrade who next relieved guard upon the prisoner might have been one of the executioners of Octavia, and might have carried her head to Poppæa a few weeks before. Such were the ordinary employments of the fierce and blood-stained veterans who were daily present, like wolves in the midst of sheep, at the meetings of the Christian brotherhood. If there were any of these soldiers not utterly hardened by a life of cruelty, their hearts must surely have

---

[k] Philem. 16.
[l] Matt. xiii. 31; Luke xiii. 19.
[m] "Deus unus cor nostrum implere potest et beare: gratia, Dei emanatio ac quasi vicaria, illud nunc impleat et incipiat beare, donec gloria penitus repleat et accumulet, reddatque in æternum felix et beatum."—*Bernard à Piconius.*
[n] Chap. i. 13.

been touched by the character of their prisoner, brought as they were into so close a contact with him. They must have been at least astonished to see a man, under such circumstances, so utterly careless of selfish interests, and devoting himself with an energy so unaccountable to the teaching of others. Strange indeed to their ears, fresh from the brutality of a Roman barrack, must have been the sound of Christian exhortation, of prayers, and of hymns; stranger still, perhaps, the tender love which bound the converts to their teacher and to one another, and shewed itself in every look and tone."

LAUS SIT DEO.

A Prayer of St. Augustine, which he was wont to use after his Sermons and Lectures.

"TURN we to the Lord God, the Father Almighty, and with pure hearts offer to Him, so far as our meanness can, great and true thanks, with all our hearts praying His exceeding kindness, that of His good pleasure He would deign to hear our prayers, that by His power He would drive out the enemy from our deeds and thoughts, that He would increase our faith, guide our understandings, give us spiritual thoughts, and lead us to His bliss, through Jesus Christ His Son our Lord, Who liveth and reigneth with Him, in the Unity of the Holy Spirit, one God, for ever and ever. Amen."

A LITERAL TRANSLATION OF THE GOTHIC VERSION OF THE EPISTLE TO THE PHILIPPIANS.

CHAP. I.

The MS. is imperfect to the middle of verse 14.

¹⁴ . . . . . of the brethren in the Lord, taking courage by my bonds, dare more to declare the word of God fearlessly: ¹⁵ some truly of envy and strife, ¹⁶ but some of good will, preach Christ; ¹⁷ and some in love, knowing that I am appointed for the truth of the Gospel. ¹⁶ But those who preach Christ out of strife, *do it* not sincerely, supposing that they raise up afflictions in my bonds. ¹⁸ And what? all the while, in all ways, whether in pretence or in truth, Christ is preached; and in this I rejoice, yes, and will rejoice: ¹⁹ for I know that this results in salvation for me through your prayer and the supply of the Spirit of Christ Jesus, ²⁰ according to my expectation and hope, that in nothing I become ashamed, but in all confidence, as continually, *so* also now Christ is magnified in my body whether through life or through death. ²¹ Now to me to live is Christ, and to die gain: ²² but if to live in the body, this is to me the fruit of work, then what I should wish, I know not; ²³ but *am* straitened indeed by the two, (or, [*am*] *divided by the two*) having a desire to be released, and to be with Christ, (it is much better): ²⁴ but to be in the body is more needful for you. ²⁵ And this I know certainly, that I shall be and shall remain with you all, to your progress and the joy of your faith, that your boasting may abound in Christ Jesus by me through my coming again to you. ²⁷ Only have your conversation worthy of the Gospel of Christ, that whether I come and visit you or from elsewhere hear of you, *I may learn* that ye stand in one spirit, one soul, together labouring

for the faith of the Gospel, [28] and in nothing terrified by the adversaries, which is to them a betokening of perdition, but to you of salvation, and that from God. [29] To you it is given, for Christ, not only to believe in Him, but also to suffer for Him, [30] having the same strife which ye see in me, and now hear of in me.

CHAP. II.

[1] If now *there be* aught of consolations in Christ, if aught of soothings of love, if aught of communions of the spirit, if aught of mildnesses and of pityings, [2] fill ye up my joy, that ye may think the same thing, having the same love, with the same soul, with the same mind. [3] *Let* nothing *be done* according to strife or vain exaltation; but in all humility of mind one esteeming another superior to himself. [4] Not considering each one his own *good*, but also each one that of others. [5] Let this also be thought among you, which also was in Christ Jesus: [6] Who being in God's form, did not reckon it robbery that He should be like [a] God: [7] but emptied Himself, taking the appearance of a servant, being made in the likeness of men: [8] and being found in fashion as a man, humbled Himself, becoming obedient to the Father, and . . . . [22] that as a child with a father, he has served with me in the Gospel. [23] Him now I hope to send, after I see what is my state, soon. [24] Now I trust in the Lord that also I myself am coming quickly: [25] but I considered it needful to send to you Epaphroditus, my brother, and fellow worker, and comrade, but your apostle and minister of my need. [26] For he was yearning after you all, and sorrowful because ye heard him to be sick: [27] and he was sick too, near to death; but God had mercy on him; and not only him, but also me, that I might not have grief upon grief. [28] Now I sent him more carefully, that seeing him ye may afterwards rejoice, and I may be more glad,

---

[a] *Galeiks* = Greek συνομοίως. The word only means 'like together,' although it is the origin of the modern German *gleich*. The word for 'equal' would be *ibn*, which *galeiks* cannot mean.

remembering your state. ²⁹ Receive him now in the Lord with all joy; and hold such men precious: ³⁰ for in the work of Christ he was near even to death, neglecting his own soul, that he might fill up your short-coming as regards my ministry.

CHAP. III.

¹ Further, (lit. *this other thing,*) my brethren, rejoice in the Lord: to write these same things to you, to me indeed is not a trouble, but to you is safety. ² Look to the dogs, look to the evil workers, look to the concision ᵇ. ³ But we are the circumcision, we who serve the Spirit of God, and boast in Christ Jesus, and we do not trust in the body. ⁴ And indeed I, having confidence even in the flesh, if any other thinks to trust in the flesh, I more: ⁵ circumcised the eighth day, from the race of Israel, of the tribe of Benjamin, a Hebrew of Hebrews; according to the law, a Pharisee; ⁶ according to zeal, racking the Church; according to the righteousness which is in the law, being blameless. ⁷ But what was gain to me, that I reckoned for Christ's sake to be loss: ⁸ and indeed I deem all to be loss for the excellence of the knowledge of Jesus Christ my Lord, in Whom I have suffered loss in everything, and deem all to be dirt, that I may have Christ for gain, ⁹ and may be found in Him, not having my own righteousness, that from the law, but through the faith of Jesus Christ, which is from God, a righteousness by faith, ¹⁰ to know Him, and the might of His resurrection, and the fellowship of His sufferings, I was laden with His death; ¹¹ that in some way I may arrive at the resurrection from the dead: ¹² not that I have already received, or am already deemed righteous; but I follow, that I may lay hold *of that* in which I was laid hold of by Christ. ¹³ Brethren, I do not indeed think myself to be laying hold; ¹⁴ but one *thing I do,* indeed, forgetting the *things* behind, but

---

ᵇ *Gamaitano*, a literal translation of κατατομὴ, or rather συντομὴ, *concisio*. Circumcision is *limait*.

stretching myself out to those which are before, I follow, according to the mark, after the prize of the upward calling of God in Christ Jesus. [15] Now let so many of us as are perfect think this; and if ye think anything differently, God reveals this also to you. [16] But indeed,—to which we have attained,—let us think the same, let us mind the same, to walk by the same rule. [17] Brethren, become my imitators, and observe for yourselves those who walk so as ye have us *for* an example. [18] For many walk, of whom I often said to you, and now even weeping say, *that they are* the enemies of the cross of Christ; [19] whose end is perdition; their god is the belly, and *their* glory in their shame, who mind earthly *things*. [20] But our habitation is in heaven, whence also we wait for a Saviour, the Lord Jesus Christ, [21] Who changes the body of our humiliation to *one* conformed to the body of His glory, according to *His* work: for He can even subdue all things to Himself.

CHAP. IV.

[1] Therefore, now my loved and desired brethren, my joy and crown, so stand in the Lord. [2] I pray Eodia, and pray Syntyke, to mind the same in the Lord. [3] Yea, I pray thee also, chosen yoke-fellow [c], help the women who laboured with me in the Gospel, with Clement and others my fellow-workers, whose names are in the books of life. [4] Now therefore rejoice in the Lord continually; again I say, rejoice. [5] Let your self-restraint [d] be known to all men. The Lord is near. [6] Be not anxious in anything, but in all prayer and supplication with thanksgivings let your prayers be made known to God: [7] and may the peace of God, which is above all understanding, keep fast your hearts and bodies in Christ Jesus. [8] Further, brethren, whatever is true, whatever is honourable, whatever is righteous, whatever is holy, whatever is lovely, whatever is well-spoken of, if *there be* aught of virtues, if aught of praises,

---

[c] *Valiso gajuko*—feminine; the masc. would be *valisa gajuka*.
[d] *Anaviljei*, against-willing, = self-command or self-restraint.

think of this. ⁹ What also ye have learnt, and received, and heard, and seen in me, that do; and the God of peace be with you. ¹⁰ But I rejoiced in the Lord greatly, for already ye have somewhat advanced in thinking of me; on which also ye thought, but were hindered. ¹¹ Not that I speak in respect of need, for I have learnt to be content *with the state* in which I am. I know both *how* to humble myself, and I know *how* to have abundance; ¹² in every *place* and in all *things* I am used both to be full and hungry, and to have abundance and to suffer need. ¹³ I can *do* everything in Him Who strengthens me, Christ. ¹⁴ But indeed ye did well, *in* communicating with my affliction. ¹⁵ Now ye Philippians also know that in the beginning of the Gospel, when I came out from Macedonia, not one of the Churches communicated with me in the way of giving and receiving, except you only. ¹⁶ For even in Thessalonica both once and twice ye sent a supply to me. ¹⁷ Not that I seek a gift, but I seek . . . . . .ᶜ

ᶜ The rest is wanting in MS.

INDEX

OF

TEXTS EXPLAINED OR REFERRED TO IN THIS VOLUME.

CHAP.	VER.	PAGE
GENESIS.		
i.	14.	97
—	16.	97
viii.	21.	192
xxviii.	12.	186
xxxi.	50.	15
EXODUS.		
i.	12.	21
iii.	14.	69
xix.	6.	3
xx.	4.	85
xxix.	40, 41.	101
xxxii.	32.	168
xxxv.	33.	88
NUMBERS.		
xi.	29.	30
xxiv.	20.	154
DEUTERONOMY.		
iv.	17, 18.	85
vii.	6.	3
xxiii.	18.	120
xxxii.	20.	96
1 SAMUEL.		
i.	11.	180
ix.	2.	96
xvi.	23.	177
xxiv.	4—22.	64
2 SAMUEL.		
xxiv.	14.	41
2 KINGS.		
iv.	1—7.	151
—	3.	193
NEHEMIAH.		
vii.	2.	108
JOB.		
xvi.	12.	145
—	19.	15
xxii.	21.	176

CHAP.	VER.	PAGE
PSALMS.		
i.	2.	180
—	6.	12
ii.	11.	89
iii.	6.	50
xviii.	2.	174
xxxiii.	14.	185
xxxiv.	1.	7
—	4—6.	173
—	8.	176
—	22.	34
xxxvii.	36.	154
xlii.	1.	15
lv.	23.	173
lxix.	29.	168
lxxvi.	10.	21
lxxxv.	5.	171
xcvi.	11.	85
cxxxiii.	1.	59
cxlv.	18.	172
PROVERBS.		
ii.	14.	155
viii.	10.	18
xvi.	3.	173
xvii.	3.	18
—	6.	162
CANTICLES.		
iii.	6.	174
—	7, 8.	177
ISAIAH.		
i.	24.	180
vi.	13.	181
xxix.	13.	122
xlii.	1.	75
xlv.	23.	86
lxiv.	6.	129
JEREMIAH.		
xlvi.	18.	180
LAMENTATIONS.		
iii.	12.	115

CHAP.	EZEKIEL. VER.	PAGE	CHAP.	VER.	PAGE
xiii.	9.	168	xi.	29.	65
xxxiv.	23.	75	xii.	28.	149
xxxviii.	20.	85	xiii.	12.	151
			—	31.	197
			xv.	23.	79
	DANIEL.		—	26.	120
ii.	35.	143	xvi.	24.	129
—	44.	156	xviii.	16.	2
—	45.	143	—	23.	171
iv.	27.	20	—	32.	56
ix.	26.	71	xx.	26, 27.	2
xii.	1.	168	xxiii.	3.	30
—	3.	99	xxv.	21.	92
			—	23.	92
	HOSEA.		—	34.	92
ii.	15.	37	—	35.	20, 92
			—	36.	114
	JONAH.			ST. MARK.	
iv.	5.	109	vii.	36.	43
	HABAKKUK.				
ii.	13.	180		ST. LUKE.	
			i.	6.	95, 126
	ZECHARIAH.		—	46.	35
iii.	8.	75	—	58.	35
			ii.	14.	94
	MALACHI.		—	34.	28
i.	14.	180	iv.	13.	51
			x.	20.	168
	TOBIT.		xi.	20.	149
xii.	15.	175	—	28.	128
			xii.	22.	173
	WISDOM.		—	50.	41
xii.	18.	171	—	56.	18
xiii.	2.	98	xiii.	19.	197
			xiv.	19.	18
	ECCLESIASTICUS.		xviii.	13.	6
vii.	36.	145	xxi.	13.	31
xviii.	7.	98	xxiv.	26.	80
	2 MACCABEES.			ST. JOHN.	
x.	4.	171	i.	4.	36
xiv.	8.	106	—	14.	72, 77, 80
			—	20.	69
	ST. MATTHEW.		ii.	17.	125
v.	14.	98	iii.	29.	58
—	16.	20	iv.	24.	122
—	34.	16	v.	18.	69
—	37.	16	vi.	38.	78
vi.	2.	192	—	44.	140
—	5.	192	vii.	3—5.	64
—	24.	154	x.	17.	80
—	25.	173	—	18.	78
—	25—34.	194	—	30.	69
vii.	6.	120	xi.	19.	56
viii.	20.	71	xiii.	1—17.	75
x.	16.	95	—	36.	148
—	41.	9	xiv.	16.	164
—	41, 42.	162	—	31.	78
xi.	5.	196	xv.	5.	20, 130
—	26.	94	—	6.	20

CHAP.	VER.	PAGE	CHAP.	VER.	PAGE
xv.	16.	140	i.	9.	15
xvi.	23.	84	—	11.	46, 111
—	26.	164	—	13.	40
—	33.	175	ii.	8.	26
xvii.	9.	164	—	18.	18
xx.	28.	128	—	28.	121
xxi.	19.	36	—	29.	121, 179
			iii.	21.	132
	Acts.		—	27.	47
			—	30.	121
ii.	40.	96	iv.	2.	131
—	45.	111	—	9.	121
iii.	21.	11	—	11.	122
iv.	12.	84	—	12.	122, 147
—	19.	12	v.	1—5.	46
—	24.	85	—	4.	108
—	32.	49, 59	—	12.	140
—	34.	9	vi.	4.	133
—	35.	9, 111	—	5.	134
—	41.	169	—	8.	134
v.	17.	125	—	21.	154
—	41.	53	—	22.	20
vi.	3.	111	vii.	6.	122
vii.	44.	152	—	18.	88
viii.	4.	23	—	22.	122
ix.	5.	81	viii.	3.	76
x.	46.	35	—	5.	155
xii.	6.	41	—	11.	35
xiv.	11.	112	—	16.	96
xvi.	1—3.	108	—	17.	134
—	12.	4	—	23.	159
—	13.	166	—	29.	96
—	25.	53	ix.	1.	16, 113
—	29—33.	165	—	2.	113
xvii.	5—10.	188	—	3.	24, 41
—	14.	108	—	8.	96
xviii.	5.	41, 108	—	31.	149
xix.	17.	35	x.	2.	125
—	22.	108	—	3.	131
xx.	1.	188	xi.	1.	124
—	24.	101	—	14.	135
—	31.	103	xii.	2.	18
—	34.	111	—	3.	14
—	35.	101	—	13.	9
—	37.	103	—	15.	150
xxiii.	1.	48, 126	—	16.	58
—	6.	125	xiii.	11.	172
xxiv.	4.	170	—	13.	125
—	16.	19	xiv.	8.	36
xxvi.	5.	125	—	9.	85
—	7.	135	—	11.	86
xxvii.	23.	6	xv.	2, 3.	66
xxviii.	10.	111	—	5.	58, 59
—	16.	27	—	16.	102
—	17.	13	—	26.	9
—	30.	13, 27	—	30, 31.	33
—	31.	27	—	33.	180
			xvi.	17.	31, 151
	Romans.		—	18.	120, 154
i.	7.	5	—	19.	95
—	8.	6	—	27.	195

INDEX OF TEXTS.

	1 Corinthians.			Chap.	ver.	page
chap.	ver.	page		iv.	4.	67
i.	1.	2		—	12.	93
—	4.	6		—	14.	133
—	9.	8		—	16.	122
—	10.	49		—	17.	50, 92
—	21.	47		v.	3.	130
—	26—28.	196		—	4.	140
—	30.	169		—	8.	43
—	31.	20		—	20.	56
ii.	3.	90		vi.	12.	16
—	6.	148		—	16.	10
—	9.	194		vii.	3.	13
iii.	1.	146		—	4.	192
—	6.	101		—	13.	43
—	8.	100		—	15.	90
—	10.	14		viii.	2.	108
—	13.	18		—	4.	9
—	21—23.	187		—	5.	6
iv.	1.	114		—	8.	18
—	3.	11		—	9.	66, 71
—	16.	151, 180		ix.	2.	125
v.	6.	47		—	8.	184
—	8.	29		—	9.	20
vii.	39.	117		—	13.	9, 108
ix.	1.	159		x.	1.	170
—	12—18.	191		—	14.	149
—	16.	28		xi.	2.	178
—	24.	145		—	9.	191
—	26.	145		—	13.	120
—	27.	90, 135		—	15.	154
x.	12.	135		—	18.	123
—	24.	64, 106		—	21.	123
—	31.	117		—	22.	124, 125
—	32.	19		—	23.	41
xi.	1.	151, 180		—	23—28.	53
xii.	4.	57		—	29.	113
xiii.	5.	64		xii.	10.	24
—	7.	10		—	20.	26, 61
xiv.	36.	135		xiii.	3.	108
xv.	1.	163		—	5.	18, 43
—	9.	126		—	9.	137
—	10.	101, 186		—	11.	58, 116
—	24—28.	86				
—	25, 26.	160			Galatians.	
—	31.	134				
—	42—44.	158		i.	2.	2
—	48.	159		—	3.	5
—	58.	161		—	20.	16
xvi.	10.	108		ii.	2.	101
—	17.	115		—	9.	8, 121
—	18.	114		—	17.	130
				—	20.	39
	2 Corinthians.			iv.	19.	117, 162
i.	2.	5		—	28.	96
—	11.	33		v.	2, 3.	121
—	23.	15		—	20.	61, 125
—	24.	163		vi.	1.	146
ii.	4.	8		—	4.	18
—	9.	108		—	6.	9
iii.	2.	13		—	8.	92, 154
—	5.	186		—	13.	36

INDEX OF TEXTS.

CHAP.	VER.	PAGE	CHAP.	VER.	PAGE
vi.	16.	150	iii.	4.	37
—	17.	116	—	12.	16, 57
			v.	12.	110
EPHESIANS.					
i.	1.	3		**1 THESSALONIANS.**	
—	2.	5, 6	i.	6.	151, 180
—	4.	95, 96	ii.	5.	15
—	9.	94	—	9.	190
—	9, 10.	94	—	10.	15
—	13.	100	—	11.	56
—	16.	6	—	20.	162
—	19.	160	iii.	3.	28
—	19, 20.	133	iv.	1.	164
—	20, 21.	80	—	15—17.	135
—	21.	85	—	16.	158
ii.	2.	93	v.	5.	97
—	6—19.	156	—	12.	114, 164
—	8, 9.	9	—	14.	56
—	10.	133	—	16.	116
—	14.	176	—	17.	114
—	20.	132			
iii.	8.	3, 14		**2 THESSALONIANS.**	
—	12.	10	i.	8.	88
—	13.	117	ii.	1.	94, 164
—	17.	43	iii.	1.	116
—	18, 19.	18	—	8.	190
—	20.	17	—	14.	88
iv.	1.	22, 96			
—	2.	62		**1 TIMOTHY.**	
—	3.	49			
—	13.	135	i.	13, 14.	126
—	16.	33	—	15.	127
—	28.	111	iv.	10.	101
—	32.	16	v.	8.	65
v.	1.	96, 151	—	17.	101
—	2.	66	vi.	6.	184
—	5.	154	—	20.	18
—	8.	97			
—	10.	18		**2 TIMOTHY.**	
—	23.	159	i.	3.	126
—	27.	96	—	4.	111, 192
—	30.	3	—	15.	8
vi.	5.	90	ii.	3.	110
—	10.	116	—	1, 12.	134
—	11.	49, 163	—	12.	159
—	12.	90	iv.	6.	101
—	13, 14.	49	—	7.	101
—	18.	7	—	8.	12, 33
—	21.	21	—	10.	8, 168
			—	14.	50
COLOSSIANS.			—	16.	8
i.	7.	110			
—	9.	19		**TITUS.**	
—	15.	67	ii.	5.	178
—	22.	96	iii.	2.	171
—	24.	134			
—	29.	93		**PHILEMON.**	
ii.	12.	133		2.	110
iii.	1.	158		7.	16
—	2.	155		8, 9.	163
—	3.	156		12.	16

CHAP.	VER.	PAGE	CHAP.	VER.	PAGE
	13.	115	ii.	12.	172
	16.	196	iii.	22.	85
	20.	16	iv.	9.	95
	22.	33	—	13.	133, 134
	23.	110	v.	4.	162
	24.	168	—	6.	80
			—	7.	173
	HEBREWS.		—	12.	163
i.	3.	67			
ii.	9.	80		2 PETER.	
—	16.	76	i.	1.	2
v.	12—14.	146	ii.	7, 8.	96
vi.	1.	147	iii.	1.	19
viii.	5.	66	—	4.	96
x.	37.	172			
xi.	35.	135		1 JOHN.	
xii.	2.	80	iii.	17.	16
—	11.	20	iv.	13.	43
xiii.	14.	48	v.	4.	50
	16.	8, 193			
—	20, 21.	147		JUDE.	
				3.	49
	JAMES.			16.	95
i.	1.	2		24.	96
—	2.	169			
ii.	19.	85		REVELATION.	
iii.	14.	26, 125	i.	20.	111
—	15.	155	ii.	3.	101
—	16.	26, 61	—	10.	19
—	18.	20	—	13.	97
iv.	15.	104	iii.	5.	168
			v.	12.	80
	1 PETER.		—	13.	85
i.	3, 4.	133	vii.	14, 15.	92
—	5.	177	xii.	8.	130
—	7.	18	xiv.	5.	96
—	17.	89	xxii.	15.	120

INDEX.

N.B. The numbers mark the page.

Abstinence easier than temperance, 186.
Abundance has its own peculiar perils, 184; St. Paul an example of bearing it properly, 184.
'*Acceptable sacrifice*,' why this expression is applied to alms, 193.
Account-book, supposed to have been carried about by St. Paul, 189.
Accounts, an illustration taken from the way in which they are kept by merchants, 189, 191.
Actions, evil, arise from evil thoughts, 180.
Adjuration of St. Paul reconciled with our Lord's command, "Swear not at all," 16.
Admonitions of ministers must be private as well as public, 164.
Adoration of the Name of Jesus enjoined by the English Church, 84.
Adversaries, the way in which they are to be withstood shewn by the example of St. Paul, 54.
Affection makes a dwelling-place, 157; affection of St. Paul a pattern for ministers, 163.
Affliction, meaning of the word as applied to St. Paul, 27; over-ruled by God for the furtherance of the Gospel, 32; furnishes no real cause for alarm, 50; is the means of greater exaltation, 50; not merely a token of salvation, but also a cause, 50; furnishes ground for rejoicing, 169; a remedy for it, 160.
Alms-giving, its blessedness, 187, 189; the Philippians specially commended for it, 188; procures treasure in heaven, 191; is called an acceptable sacrifice, 193; likened to incense, and a burnt-offering, 193.
Altar, two in the Jewish temple, 193; St. Paul received a portion of the offerings made at the altar, 192.
Anathema, why followed by Maranatha, 172.
Angels, worship our Lord in His Name of Jesus, 81; are not startled at seeing a Man introduced into their realms, 81; their different orders, 85; why Bishops are called angels by St. John, 111; make known to God the prayers of the faithful, 175; their obedience, 186; cannot fathom the peace of God, 176.
Anthony, St, an admirable practice of, commended to Christians, 145.
Anxiety about worldly things discouraged, 173; arises from distrust of God's providence, 173; a remedy against it, 173.
Apostles, the, rejoiced in suffering, 53; the blessedness of ministering to their wants, 194.
Apostolic office designated by the term 'grace,' 14.
'*Apprehended*,' peculiar beauty of the word as applied to Christ, 140; those who have been so apprehended by Him may yet fall short of perfection, 140.
Approve, various senses of the word, 18.
Arians refuted, 160.
'*As*' denotes truth and identity, 77.
Assistance rendered to ministers, its high value and reward, 9.
'*Attained*,' meaning of the word, 149; its peculiar force as applied to the Philippians, 149; if we hold fast what we have attained, God will give us further revelations, 150.
Augustine, St., his deep reverence and love for our Lord's Name, 84; his excellent advice to preachers, 118; his earnest appeal to Jerome and Ruffinus, 164.

Baptism, makes people become actually a part of Christ, 3; typified by the Red Sea, 144; the way in which it was administered by St. Cyprian, 148.
Baptized, the, likened to runners in a race, 143.
Bede, Venerable, account of his last moments, 37, 38.
Behind, peculiar force of the word as applied to earthly things, 142.

'Being,' important doctrine involved in the use of the word, 69.
Belly, the, in what sense it becomes a god, 154, 155; Luther's saying respecting it, 154; the filling of it the object which false teachers have in view, 154.
Benjamin, why St. Paul is careful to mention his connection with that tribe, 125; its peculiar honours, 125.
Bernard, St., an anecdote of, 27, 28.
'*Beware*,' emphatic repetition of the word, 121.
Bishop, used as an interchangeable term with presbyter, 5; bishops should remember that those entrusted to their charge are sons, 108; why they are called angels by St. John, 111.
Blameless, in what sense Christians must be, 95; limitation of the word, 126; its peculiar propriety as applied to St. Paul, 126.
Boasting, St. Paul had grounds of, 123, 124; but entirely disclaimed by him, 186; the word 'thinketh' shews that there was no ground of boasting before God, 124.
Body, the, God must be glorified in it, 35; this the result of the Incarnation, 35; body and flesh distinguished, 36; will partake in the resurrection to glory, 136; and be redeemed from corruption, 158; will be the same at the resurrection, but its qualities will be different, 158; will be penetrated with the glory of God, 158; high value put upon its resurrection, 159; greater power shewn in its resurrection than in subduing demons, 160; is now subject to humiliation on account of sin, 159.
Boldness, shewn in the case of St.Paul, 34, 35.
Bonds, in what sense they were a confirmation of St. Paul's preaching, 13; they could not bind his love, 13; furthered the spread of the Gospel, 21, 22; gave confidence to weak brethren, 24.
'*Bonds in Christ*,' meaning of the expression, 22.
Book of life, a figure taken from the registers of citizens, 167; is applied to the Divine Intelligence, 168; does not imply that election to life is certain, 168; referred to by our Lord, 168; the idea not unknown to the ancients, 168.

Bowels, figurative sense of, 15, 16, 57; why coupled with 'mercies,' 57.
Bowing the knee, meaning of, 83, 84.
Brethren, why this title is used by St. Paul in addressing the Philippians, instead of children, 117, 118; the brethren of our Lord an example of vain-glory, 64.
Brethren in the Lord, force of the expression as applied to Christians, 24.
Brother, two-fold sense of the word, 110.

Cæsar's household, why special mention is made of, 195; who are included under the term, 196.
Calling, ('high calling of God,') peculiar force of the expression, 145; derived from the Games, 146.
Calmness, the difficulty of preserving it, 185; exhibited in a remarkable degree by St. Paul, 187.
Camerinus, the inscription on his tomb, 42.
Care about worldly things discouraged, 173; is founded on distrust of God, 173; a remedy against it, 173; the wonderful care of God for His people, 177.
Carelessness, a caution against, 141.
Carnal things may be used to buy heavenly things, 189; carnal circumcision contrasted with spiritual, 123; carnal claims not mentioned by St. Paul, 55.
Character, importance of keeping it unsullied, 179.
Charioteer, St. Paul very appropriately likens himself to one, 138.
Charitable institutions, a good motto for, 187.
Children of Israel, analogy between their trials and deliverance and that of Christians, 143, 144.
Christ, all in all to St. Paul, 41, 128; his sole object in life, 36, 37; who are 'in Christ,' 43; and 'with Christ,' 43, 45; the central Figure in all St. Paul's thoughts, 47; how Christians are *in* Him, 130; how the power of His Resurrection is displayed, 133; His sufferings an object of desire to St. Paul, 133, 134; we must be made conformable to His death, 134; how He is said to 'apprehend' sinners, 140; He must draw them before they can come, 140; His Divinity most strongly asserted, 67, 68, 69; His continual presence with His people, 172; why called 'our Peace,' 176; union with

INDEX. 215

Him necessary, 177; everything ascribed to Him, 186; meaning of winning Him, 129; how far He may be known by a natural man, 132.
Christian, in time of the Apostles a term of reproach, 3.
Christians, are actually a part of Christ, 3; why the early Christians sold their lands and goods, 9; why called 'brethren in the Lord,' 24; must not be terrified by persecutions, 50; are proved by God, 51; must never be satisfied with their spiritual condition, 139; are bound to comfort one another, 57; in what sense they must daily strive to shew forth Christ to the world, 66; their exalted dignity, 96; why they must be blameless and harmless, 96; they must shine as lights, 97; and must transmit light to others, 98; are like the sun, 98; like the stars, as shining in darkness, 98; and as not caring for earthly things, 98; likened to a nurse in making others partakers of grace, 99; must not live for themselves alone, 107; are the servants of God, 108; not forbidden to shew their grief, 113; are the true circumcision, 121; are circumcised in affections, 122; their worship distinguished from that of Jews, 122; are in Christ, 130; must not shrink from suffering, 134; their life must be like Christ's risen life, 136; must exercise humility, 141; must take example from runners, 142; warned against enticements of the world, 143; should ever be longing after heavenly things, 146; should joyfully look for death, 43, 103; likened to travellers, 147; must all walk by the same rule, 150; should be like well-drilled soldiers, 150; are free men of heaven, 156; and fellow-citizens of the Saints, 156; have no concern with the rejoicings of the world, 157; why their moderation must be known to all men, 171, 172; likened to a cube, 163; must be truthful in all their dealings, 178; must be free from levity in conversation and manner, 178; must keep themselves pure, 178; must be gentle, 178; must practise every kind of virtue, 179; in what sense they may seek for praise, 179; are delivered from a three-fold death, 133; are more than conquerors, 187; their reward not in this world, 194; how they are said to be 'found in

Christ,' 130; their mutual love strange to the heathen, 198.
Church, the, grows in persecutions, 21; is watered by the blood of martyrs, 52; must not be forsaken on account of trivial dissensions, 149; English Church commands a sign of adoration at the Name of Jesus, 84; three fold orders a note of the Church, 5; organization of the Church of Philippi, 5, 14, 149.
Church government, founded on the notion of paternity, 109.
Circumcision, a title applied to Christians, 121; its propriety shewn from their believing in the true Messiah, 122; is no longer to be found among the Jews, 121; why Christians are said to be the circumcision instead of to have it, 122; for what reasons St. Paul could appropriately contrast spiritual with carnal circumcision, 123; why it is so prominently referred to, 124.
Circus Maximus, a striking figure suggested to St. Paul by its proximity to his prison, 137, 138.
Citizen, full meaning of the word, 48; the faithful are citizens of heaven now, 156.
Clement, formerly a philosopher, afterwards Bishop of Rome, 167; was in peril with St. Paul at Philippi, 167; martyred by being thrown into the sea, 167.
Communicate, a word used of almsgiving, 187.
Companions of St. Paul specially mentioned, 195.
Concision, meaning of the word, 121.
Confession of two kinds, 6, 7.
Confessors, their constancy admired, 24.
Confidence in the flesh, wherein it consists, 123.
Conflict, a term appropriately applied to the sufferings of Christians, 53.
Conqueror, the Christian is more than a, 187.
Consolation, of what kind sought by St. Paul from the Philippians, 56; whence it may be sought on the death of friends, 38, 39, 43; a mutual consolation exists between those who suffer for Christ's sake, 56; great consolation for ministers in the midst of trials and disappointments, 162.
Contempt of earthly things illustrated, 128, 130.
Contention, meaning of the word, 26.

Contentment, difficult of attainment, 183; St. Paul an example of it, 183; a most important virtue to cultivate, 184.
Conversation (πολίτευμα), answers to the Roman *municipium*, 156.
Conversion, different way in which St. Paul speaks of himself before and after, 126, 127.
Converts to the faith even in the household of Nero, 197.
Cowardice, absence of it in St. Paul, 119.
Crispina, St., a story of, 52.
Crooked, a term rightly applied to the wicked, 96.
Cross, the, a testimony to the world, 22; its death that of the lowest shame, 79; a legend concerning the tree from which it was made, 79; who are the enemies of it, 153; its wonderful power, 153; Christians should make the sign of it, 153; all suffering rightly called by this name, 153.
Crown, sinners are the crown of Christ, 140; works done for Christ's sake will be our crown, 162; souls will be the crown of faithful ministers, 162.
Cube, a, Christians likened to, 163.
Cyprian, St., his method of baptizing, 148.

Danger, disregard of, shewn by Epaphroditus, 114, 115.
David, an example of lowliness of mind, 64.
'*Day of Christ*,' meaning of the expression, 11, 19, 100; contrasted with man's day, 12; a day of overwhelming grandeur and glory, 12.
Deacon, nature of the office, 5.
Deaconesses, their duties, 163.
Dead, the, to be remembered in our prayers, 38, 39; and specially at Holy Communion, 39.
Dead, the resurrection of the, peculiar force of the expression, 136.
Death, equally acceptable with life to St. Paul, 36; why death would be gain to him, 37; is a door of hope to the faithful, 37; likened to birth, 38; whence comfort is to be sought on the death of friends, 38, 39, 43; what sort of change it effects, 42; example of exultation at its approach, 42; only to be desired as uniting to Christ, 43; reasons why Christians should joyfully look for it, 43, 103; no repentance after it, 85; Christians are delivered from a three-fold death, 133; is signified by 'end,' 154.
Death of our Lord, the highest evidence of His obedience, 78; was one of the lowest shame, 79; how we must be made conformable to it, 134.
Depart, a term used instead of 'to die,' 42; St. Paul anxiously longed to, 43; three reasons why a Christian should desire to depart, 43.
Departed, the, not to be mourned for excessively, 44.
Devil, the, the nature of his devices, 51; his subtlety, 95; entices first by pleasurable things, 51; then by painful things, 51.
Devils acknowledge and adore the Name of Jesus, 85, 86.
Devotion, three different kinds of it mentioned, 196.
Devout life, suited to all vocations and professions, 195; shewn by examples, 196.
Die, to, an expression very seldom used of Christians, 42.
Dignity of Christians, 96.
Disputings, meaning of, 95; distinguished from murmurings, 95.
Dissensions furnish no reason why the Church should be forsaken, 149.
Dissenters, no justification for their teaching, 31.
Divinity of our Lord most strongly asserted, 67, 68, 69; shewn by His not fearing to descend from His rights, 70; strikingly witnessed to by Justin Martyr, 70; opinions of certain heretics in reference to it, 68, 69; Divinity of the Holy Ghost asserted, 122.
Dogs, Gentiles formerly called by that name, 119; applied by St. Paul to the Jews, 120; a term appropriately used of false teachers, 120; Christians may learn a lesson of perseverance from dogs, 138.
Doxology of this Epistle flows from joy, 195.
Dung, what is meant by the expression, 129; intended to denote extreme contempt, 129.

Eagle, an, St. Paul compared to, 157.
Earthly things, how people are said to mind, 155.
Eighth day, value of this kind of circumcision, 124.
Election to life may be forfeited by sin, 168.

Eleusinian mysteries, language borrowed from, 147.
Elisha restoring the dead child to life a type of our Lord's humiliation, 72, 73; his staff a type of the Law, 72, 73.
'*Emptied Himself*,' peculiar force of this expression as applied to our Lord, 71; an expression much dwelt on by the Fathers, 72, 73, 74; does not imply that He ceased to be God, 74, 76.
'*End*,' an expression to denote death, 154.
Enemies of the Cross, who are understood by the expression, 153; are wept over by St. Paul, 153.
Entreaty, its exceeding earnestness as used by St. Paul, 55.
Envy, shewn by false teachers at the reputation of St. Paul, 25; a remarkable saying of Socrates in reference to it, 27; shafts of envy turned into instruments of good, 30; envy shewn to another person passes on to Christ, 30; turns to the advantage of the faithful, 34.
Epaphroditus, the Bishop of Philippi, 5, 111; supposed to have been the same as Epaphras, 110; his five titles of commendation, 110; in what sense he was the messenger (ἀπόστολος) of the Philippians, 110, 111; the term minister (λειτουργός) as applied to him shews that he was discharging a public trust, 111; his heart was among his flock, 111; did not grieve for his own sufferings, 111; an example to ministers, 112; his sickness caused by attendance on St. Paul, 112; acted from love of God, 114; despised all danger, 114, 115; supplied the place of the Philippians, 115; supposed to be alluded to by the title 'true yoke-fellow,' 165.
Epistle, a lost one referred to, 118; Epistles of St. Paul written with many tears, 153.
Eucharist, Holy, the departed to be specially remembered at, 39; those admitted to it sometimes called 'perfect,' 147, 148.
Euodias, a woman of consequence at Philippi, 163, 164; helped the spread of the Gospel, 163; at variance with Syntyche, 163, 164; their dispute the cause of public scandal, 164; exhorted to union, 163, 164.
Evil-workers described, 120; distinguished from evil-doers, 120.

Exaltation of our Lord merited by His humiliation, 79, 87; why St. Paul dwells so strongly upon it, 79, 80; is beyond all height, 80; relates only to His Human Nature, 80; the intent of it, 83.
Example, an, limitation of the word as applied to any mere man, 152; St. Paul sets himself forth as, 180.
Expectation, meaning of, 33, 34.

Faith produces joy, 46; men are not merely the passive recipients of it, 52; is the foundation of righteousness, 132; gives life, not when it is merely received, but preserved, 138; must have its increase in love, 163, 164.
'*Faith of Christ*,' meaning of the expression, 131.
Faith, the, allows of no deviation from its strict rule, 150.
False doctrine, not to be received under pretence of love, 18.
False teachers, envious of St. Paul, 25; hoped to excite Nero's wrath against him, 26; preached for the sake of temporal advantages, 26, 27; and to fill their belly, 154; desired St. Paul's death in order to spoil the Church, 27; sought to procure a reputation for wisdom, 64; warnings against them, 116, 123; why they are fitly called 'dogs,' 120; not merely mentioned by name, but by epithets calculated to shew their real character, 121.
Fear, freedom from not to be acquired by our own natural powers, 51; is necessary for the attainment of Christian perfection, 90; strongly shewn in the case of St. Paul, 90; salutary fear distinguished from slavish, 90; prepares the way for the entrance of love, 91; is not inconsistent with true gladness, 91; is to be produced by constant remembrance of the presence of God, 91, 92; four different kinds of it distinguished by the Schoolmen, 91; arises from the consideration that it is God Who works in us, 93.
Fellow-imitators, force of the expression, 151.
Fellow-labourers, to whom the title is applied, 167.
Fellowship, all true to be found only in union with the Holy Spirit, 57.
'*Fellowship of the Gospel*,' how this expression is to be understood, 8, 9.

Fellow-soldier, a much stronger expression than fellow-labourer, 110.
Flesh, distinguished from body, 36; confidence in, wherein it consists, 123.
'*Flourished again,*' a figure taken from trees and plants, 181; expresses both rebuke and praise, 182.
Forget, emphatic use of the word, 142.
'*Form of God,*' what is meant by the expression, 67, 68; contrasted with 'form of a servant,' 68.
'*Form of man,*' Christ truly had this, 77.
Formalism, indications of in the Church at Philippi, 149.
Fortitude, wonderful example of shewn by the martyrs, 53, 54, 104.
Found, equivalent to ' to be,' 130; how the faithful are found in Christ, 130.
'*Fruit,*' distinguished from a 'gift,' 191.

Games, heathen, illustrations borrowed from, 49, 50, 67, 100, 135, 136, 137, 138, 140; very strongly stirred the passions of the Roman people, 138.
Gentiles called 'dogs' by way of reproach, 119, 120.
Gentleness of manner to be cultivated, 178.
Gift, a, distinguished from 'fruit,' 191.
Gifts, account must be rendered to God for, 190.
'*Given,*' how the word is applied to Christ, 80.
Gladiators, illustrations borrowed from, 50.
Gladness, true, not inconsistent with fear, 91.
Glory of God, the end of all things, 20; the great object of our Lord's work, 86; should be the all-absorbing thought of His followers, 86; the glory of the Father not separated from that of the Son, 86; must ever be aimed at by Christians, 107; four glimpses of God's glory have been seen by men, 159; will penetrate the human body at the resurrection, 158.
Glory, not sought by St. Paul, 100.
Gnostics, their heresies refuted, 141; their perversion of the word knowledge, 17.
God, the peculiar possession of His people, 6; why invoked as a witness by St. Paul, 15; His glory the end of all things, 20; His care for His people, 47, 177; makes all things work together for their good, 32; proves them by affliction, 51; His attributes most beautifully described by St. Augustine, 176; in what way the heart of man is kept by Him, 177; must be earnestly sought in prayer, 177; keeps an accurate account of all that is laid out in His service, 191; will supply all the needs of His people, 194; will repay their good actions, though not in this world, 194.
'*God of peace,*' meaning of the expression, 180; why this term is specially used in the New Testament, 180, 181.
Good-pleasure of God, wherein it consists, 94.
Gospel, the, how Christians are said to walk worthily in it, 48; spread by means of persecutions, 52; why called 'the 'Word of life,' 100; the preaching of it likened to labour, 101; and to a runner's course, 101; first received at Philippi by women, 166; the wonderful spread of it, 196, 197; furthered by St. Paul's bonds, 21, 22; and afflictions, 32.
Grace, not indefectible, 11; this shewn by the example of St. Paul, 135; continued to those who are desirous of retaining it, 11; distinction to be drawn between justifying grace and perseverance, 11; a term applied to suffering for the sake of Christ, 14; and to the Apostolic office, 14; the power of grace shewn in St. Paul, 37; must be imparted to one another, 99; if diligently used will be increased, 151; illustrated by the multiplying of the widow's oil, 151; its manifold gifts and operations, 186.
Gregory Nazianzen, his ground of rejoicing, 127.
Grief, not wholly forbidden to Christians, 113; but when excessive is an injury to Christ, 44.

Hannibal, subdued by the allurements of Capua, 185.
Harmless, meaning of the word as applied to Christians, 93.
Healing, the gift of, within what limits exercised in the Church, 112.
Heart, the, in what way it is kept by God, 177; St. Paul's overflowed with love, 7.
Heaven, Christians are citizens of,

156; are already there in expectation, 156, 157; Christ as Man is seated there, 158.
Heavenly things, should ever be ardently longed for, 146.
Hebrew of the Hebrews, meaning of the expression, 125.
Heresies, have a natural tendency to die away, 21; several grievous ones against the Nature and Person of our Lord overthrown, 67.
Heretics, no sanction for their preaching, 25, 29, 31; their opinions on the Divinity of our Lord, 68, 69; maintained that our Lord's obedience was a proof of His inferiority to the Father, 78; this opinion refuted, 78.
Hirelings, St. Paul in the midst of, 105.
Holiness is progressive, 11.
Holy Ghost, proceeds from Christ, as well as from the Father, 33; all true Christian fellowship in Him alone, 57; His Divinity asserted, 122.
Honest, comprehensive meaning of the word, 178.
Human Nature of our Lord not an 'accident,' 77; 'humbled' and 'exalted' spoken of it, and not of His Divinity, 80; is seated in heaven, 158; must be adored with the same degree of worship as His Divinity, 83.
Humiliation of our Lord described, 71; a theme on which the Fathers specially love to dwell, 72; used to exhort teachers to mildness and gentleness with their pupils, 72; typified by Elisha restoring the dead child to life, 72, 73; St. Jerome absorbed in the contemplation of it, 72; a voluntary act on His part, 75, 78; the depth of it described, 78; His death the most wonderful part of it, 79; merited His exaltation, 79, 87; relates only to His Human Nature, 80.
Humiliation, the body now subject to on account of sin, 159.
Humility, taught by St. Paul, 9, 66; and enforced by his personal example, 33, 35, 66, 137, 141; to be learnt from the example of our Lord, 66, 74, 87; His example contrasted with that of the wisest heathens, 66; this virtue must be exercised by Christians, 141.
Husbandmen, an example to ministers, 45.
Hymn of the most Holy Name of Jesus, 82, 83.

Jerome, St., absorbed in the contemplation of our Lord's humiliation, 72.
Jesus, the glory, power, and delights of the Name set forth, 81, 82; is worshipped by the angels, 81; Litany of the Name, 82; the hymn of it, 82, 83.
Jews, why called 'dogs,' 120; are no longer the true circumcision, 121.
If, the use of this word does not express doubt, 56, 139.
Ignatius Loyola, a rule of his, 64.
Ignatius, St., his eager des're for martyrdom, 38.
Illumination, the promise of it conditional, 150.
Impatience, shewn by excessive mourning for the dead, 44.
Imprisonment of St. Paul the means of spreading the Gospel, 23; he had no supernatural means of knowing how it would end, 36, 46, 48, 109; the mission of St. Timothy to Philippi delayed on account of it, 109.
Incarnation, the, its influence on the human body, 35.
Incense, alms likened to, 193.
Job, his praise consisted in being good among bad men, 96.
Joy, the sum and substance of this Epistle, 7, 117, 118; a necessary companion of love, 8; results from a living faith, 46; its fulness desired by St. Paul, 58; Christian joy distinguished from worldly, 114, 117; why continual exhortations to joy should be needed by the Philippians, 117, 118, 168; distinguished from longing, 161; 'joy in the Lord,' meaning of, 168; nothing can rob us of it, 170; true joy will not be content with expressing its gladness once, 169; springs from tears, 170; joy of penitents described, 169; in what worldly joy consists, 169, 170.
'Is' (ὑπάρχει,) force of the word as shewing the Christian's *present* citizenship in heaven, 156.
Israel, children of, analogy between their trials and deliverance and that of Christians, 143, 144.
Justin Martyr, a striking testimony of to the eternal Godhead of our Lord, 70, 71.

Knowledge, a word perverted by the Gnostics, 17; in what sense used by St. Paul, 18; how far a natural man may have knowledge of Christ, 132;

bare knowledge not sufficient for salvation, 132.

Labour, man rewarded according to, and not according to the fruit of it, 100; preaching of the Gospel likened to it, 101; remission from it must not be sought, 106.

Law, the, typified by the staff of Elisha, 72, 73; wherein its righteousness consisted, 126.

Legal rights may become moral wrongs, 171.

Levity in manner and conversation must be avoided, 178.

Libation, how the term is used by St. Paul in reference to himself, 101, 102.

Liberality in giving worldly things, how connected with our Lord's Resurrection, 193.

Life or death acceptable to St. Paul, 36; Christ the sole object of life to him, 36, 37; no reproach cast by him upon life, 39; uncertain whether to choose life or death, 40; why he chose life, 44; life of Christians must be like Christ's risen life, 136; faith preserved gives life, 138.

Life, book of; see *Book*.

Lights, in what sense Christians are to shine as, 97; they must transmit light to others, 98.

Likemindedness, meaning of the expression, 58, 105; must be accompanied with love, 59.

Likeness, in what sense our Lord was made in the likeness of men, 75, 76; how likeness to Him is to be effected, 134; meaning of 'in the likeness of His death,' 134.

Litany of the most Holy Name of Jesus, 82.

Longing, distinguished from love, 161; increases our power of receiving, 146; St. Paul's ardent longing for Christ, 128; his longing for the Philippians, 161.

Look, how Christians are to look on the things of others, 64; it does not imply that one's own business is to be neglected, 65.

Lord, the, is at hand, double explanation of the expression, 172; moral uses to be drawn from it, 172, 173.

Loss, peculiar force of the expression, 127; 'loss for Christ,' meaning of, 127; includes all possible things, 128.

Lot, his wife a caution against the enticements of the world, 143.

Love, among Christians, a fragment of Christ's love, 16; strange and unaccountable to the heathen, 198; the subject of the Apostle's prayer on behalf of the Philippians, 17; is a good of which there can be no satiety, 17; must ever be the ruling principle, 18; must be tempered with discretion, 18, 19; is called righteousness, 20; equivalent to 'good-will,' 28; shewn in a remarkable way by St. Paul, 41; how it should be shewn by ministers towards their flocks, 45; will prompt us to study the welfare of others, 64; is not fettered by bonds, 13; is shewn by offering consolation, 56; should ever be the most forcible argument, 57; objects to which it must be shewn, 59; how the love of another is to be obtained, 59; an entrance into the heart prepared for it by fear, 91; increases by being imparted, 151; illustrated by the multiplying of the widow's oil, 151; love of St. Paul to be imitated in weeping over the enemies of the Cross, 153; is essential to the development of the faith, 163, 164.

Lowliness of mind, does not consist in disparaging one's own gifts, but in a humble estimate of the way in which they are used, 62; the means of preserving it, 63; especially when in relation to a person guilty of notorious sin, 63; David an example of it, 64.

Luther, his excellent counsel to ministers, 27; a remarkable saying of his, 154.

Macedonia, St. Paul driven out from, 188.

'*Made*,' special force of the word as applied to our Lord, 75, 76.

Mammon, in what sense it is a master, 154.

Man, the nature of truly taken by our Lord, 75; this a voluntary act on His part, 75; His Manhood not an 'accident,' 77; different senses of the word as applied to Him, 77; He is as Man the object of adoration to all created things, 86.

Maranatha, why added to anathema, 172.

Mark, the, meaning of the word, 145; its constant remembrance a preservative against sin, 145; not to be confounded with the word 'prize,' 145.

Mark, to, used sometimes in a good, and sometimes in a bad sense, 151.
Martyrs, the triumph of, in their death, 42; the Church watered by their blood, 52; their wonderful fortitude under suffering, 53, 103; enter at once upon their reward, 103; are called 'perfect,' 137.
Merciful, the, specially rewarded, 20.
Messenger (ἀπόστολος), meaning of the word as applied to Epaphroditus, 110, 111.
Messiah, the, believed in by Christians, 122.
Micipsa, his testimony in favour of unity, 60.
Military affairs referred to, 41, 197.
Mind, the, necessity of its being under God's keeping, 177.
Minister (λειτουργός), this term as applied to Epaphroditus shews that he was discharging a public trust, 111.
Ministers need the prayers of their people, 33; should follow St. Paul's example of self-denial, 45; and the zeal of Epaphroditus, 112; a description of the love they should shew to their flock, 15; should take example from husbandmen and sailors, 45; must postpone all considerations for the good of their flock, 105; younger ministers should shew reverence to their elder brethren, 108; are to be esteemed for their works' sake, 114; insufficient respect shewn to them at the present day, 114; great consolation for them in the midst of trials and disappointments, 162; must plead hard for Christ, 163; must admonish in private, as well as in public, 161; their maintenance a good work, 187; must not take from their people more than enough to supply their wants, 190.
Moderation, meaning of the word, 170, 171; its archetype to be found in God, 171; why the moderation of Christians must be known to all men, 171, 172.
Mourning, excessive for the departed discouraged, 44; is an evidence of impatience, 44; and is an injury to Christ, 44.
Municipium, equivalent to conversation (πολίτευμα), 156.
Murmurings, meaning of, 95; distinguished from disputings, 95.
Mysteries, the, language borrowed from, 147, 185; may have consisted of the Patriarchal revelation, 185; Socrates supposed to have been put to death for revealing them to the public generally, 185.

Naked, sinners must come to Christ thus, 129.
Name of Jesus, what is signified by it, 81; is worshipped by angels, 81; its power and delights, 81, 82; why our Lord's Human Name is mentioned, 84; is adored by the faithful, 84; adoration of it enjoined by the English Church, 84; deep reverence shewn to it by St. Paul, 84; and by St. Augustine, 84; is acknowledged and adored by devils, 85; a most beautiful hymn in honour of it, 82, 83.
Nature of our Lord, certain heresies about it overthrown, 67.
Necessity means things required for daily support, 190.
Need, all of ours will be supplied by God, 194.
Nero, converts in his household, 197; St. Paul a champion of the faith before him, 28.
Nestorius, his heresy refuted, 66, 76.
Nurse, a, Christians likened to in making others partakers of grace, 99.

Oath, an, within what limits used by St. Paul, 16.
Obedience, all our Lord's actions as Man proceeded from, 78; His death the highest exemplification of it, 78; heretics have regarded it as a proof of His inferiority to the Father, 78; this opinion refuted, 78; His obedience a pattern to Christians, 87; followed by St. Paul, 186; exhibited by the Philippians, 87, 88; shewn by the angels, 186.
Offence, in what sense Christians are to be without, 19.
Offered, a sacrificial word appropriately applied to St. Paul, 102.
Offertory, a portion of it sent by Philippians to St. Paul, 192.
Oil, the widow's which multiplied, illustrative of Divine grace, 151.
Orders, threefold, a note of the Church, 5.
Organization of the Philippian Church, 5, 14, 149.

Pagan, origin of the word, 57.
Paternity, the right understanding of necessary to Church government, 109.

Patriarchal revelation, may have been the foundation of the heathen mysteries, 185.

Paul, St., an example of his humility, 2, 35; why he does not insist on his title of Apostle, 2. 3; he alone the author of this Epistle, 6; why he begins it with thanksgiving, 6; his heart overflowing with love, 7; the ground of his joy on behalf of the Philippians, 8; he incidentally teaches a lesson of humility, 9; his ardent love, 13, 15; it knew no bounds, 15; not founded on mercenary considerations, 15; his patience in suffering, 13; why his teaching would be sure to attract at Rome, 23; his great reputation excited envy, 25; he was a champion of the faith before Nero, 28; his only care that Christ should be preached, 28, 29; his great wisdom shewn, 29; his afflictions overruled for the furtherance of the Gospel, 32; seeks the prayers of the Philippians, 32; an example of boldness, 34, 35; unconscious of shame, 35; prepared for any turn of fortune, 36; a remarkable monument of grace, 37; entirely void of selfishness, 40, 58; postponed his own happiness to the welfare of his converts, 41; his ardent love for souls, 41; his trials and difficulties, 41; how said to be 'in a strait,' 41; an example of longing to depart this life, 43; his wonderful self-denial, 45; rejoiced in suffering, 53; a pattern of the way in which adversaries are to be withstood, 54; the exceeding earnestness of his entreaty, 55; does not mention carnal, but spiritual claims, 55; desires consolation from the Philippians, 56; desires the fulness of joy, 58; his deep love for our Lord's Name, 84; an example of holy fear, 90; not desirous of glory, 100; willing to seal his preaching with his blood, 101, 102; desires that his converts should share his glory, 103; his great self-denial in sending St. Timothy to the Philippians, 104; his mission a proof of excessive care, 104; he refers everything to Christ, 104; his desolate condition, 105; was in the midst of hirelings, 105; his deep love for St. Timothy, 108; his humility, 109; adapts his language to the capacity of his hearers, 113; never free from sorrow, 113; even in prison endeavours to revive the drooping spirits of the Philippians, 117; entirely free from cowardice, 119; why he speaks with such severity of false teachers, 121; why he could with great propriety contrast spiritual with carnal circumcision, 123; had grounds for boasting, 123; was duly circumcised, 124; why he specially mentions that he belonged to the tribe of Benjamin, 125; and that he was a Pharisee, 125; why he speaks of his zeal, 125; was righteous according to the Law, 126; in what sense he was blameless, 126; different way in which he speaks of himself before and after conversion, 126, 127; exhibits great vehemence, 128; why he despised all earthly things, 128; and voluntarily surrendered them, 128, 129; the ardour of his longing for Christ, 128; disallows his own righteousness, 130, 131; desires to have a share in the sufferings of Christ, 133, 134; not confident about his final salvation, 135, 136; likens himself to a runner, 136; and to a charioteer, 138; in what sense he was perfect, 136, 140; speaks of his spiritual state with humility, 137; unmindful of everything but the prize, 138; his eagerness to snatch it, 143; constantly kept perfection in view, 145; wrote his Epistles with many tears, 153; resembled Samuel in weeping over the enemies of God, 153; compared to an eagle, 157; though in prison, was seated in heavenly places, 157; his affection a pattern for ministers, 163; an example of continual thanksgiving, 174; his exceeding earnestness, 178; sets himself forward as an example, 180; special grounds for his thanksgiving, 181; an example of contentment, 183; and of bearing poverty and abundance, 184; practically initiated in the Christian mysteries, 185; followed the example of obedience set by Christ, 186; ascribed everything to Christ, 186; was driven out of Macedonia, 188; a summary of his character, 191.

Peace, flows from our sense of God's love and favour, 6; in what sense Christ is called 'our Peace,' 176; symbolism of the word *pax*, 181.

Peace of God, meaning of the expression, 175, 176; passes all under-

standing, 176; must be felt in the soul in order to be realized, 176; not even angels can fathom it, 176; surrounds the sorrowing heart with deep repose, 177.
Pelagian heresy respecting the will of man, 89.
Penitents, their joy described, 169.
Perfect, in what sense St. Paul was, 136; the technical usage of the word, 117; sometimes taken for receiving a crown, 137; also for undergoing martyrdom, 137; is a word of limited meaning, 146; sometimes means those who are admitted to the Holy Eucharist, 147, 148.
Perfection, not attainable in this life, 137; yet we must aspire to it, 139; like travellers, who hasten to the end of their journey, though they have not yet reached it, 147; must not be looked for as long as we are satisfied with our spiritual condition, 139; how we may fall short of it, 140; constantly kept in view by St. Paul, 145; is not to be acquired without fear, 90; is favoured by solitude, 196.
Persecution, beneficial to the Church, 21, 23, 32; this illustrated by a story from the writings of St. Athanasius, 24; exemption from it not desired by St. Paul, 34; furnishes no real cause for alarm, 50; is the means of procuring greater exaltation, 50; helps to propagate the faith, 52.
Perseverance, not certain, 10; is to be distinguished from justifying grace, 11; the necessity of it, 19; is the gift of God, 49; its difficulties shewn, 138; an exhortation to it, 143; we may learn a lesson in it from dogs, 138.
Pharaoh a type of the devil, 144.
Pharisee, why St. Paul mentions that he was one, 125.
Philippians, the, in what sense they were helpers of St. Paul, 14; their Church thoroughly organized, 5, 14, 149; were exposed to severe persecution, 54; were held in very high esteem by St. Paul for their spiritual eminence, 33; St. Paul expected to remain long with them at the termination of his imprisonment, 46; highly commended for their obedience, 87, 88; shewed their virtue even in St. Paul's absence, 88; sent money to him, 111; why they stood in special need of exhortations to joy, 117; why called 'brethren,' and not 'children,' by St. Paul, 117, 118; much longed for by him, 161; his joy and crown, 162; reason why their supply of the Apostle's wants ceased for a time, 182, 183; they constantly bore him in their mind, 182; how they became partakers in his reward, 187; did not desert him even under the most unfavourable circumstances, 188; why they contributed to his support, even when he was at Thessalonica, 190; how their liberality was connected with our Lord's Resurrection, 193.
Philippians, the Epistle to the, circumstances from which it arose, Introd. x.; no difference of opinion as to its authorship, Introd. x.; its date, Introd. xi.; why of special value to the Church, Introd. xi., xii.; not always appreciated as it ought to be, Introd. xii.; is the work of St. Paul alone, 2; the least official of all the Epistles, 3; addressed to the laity as well as to the clergy, 4; supposed by some to be addressed to all the Christians throughout Macedonia, 4; its whole burden is joy, 7, 117; was nearly the last written by St. Paul, 117, 121; gives an unusual amount of information concerning the personal situation of St. Paul, 197.
Prætorian guards referred to, 197.
Prætorium, meaning of the word as used in this Epistle, 22, 23.
Praise, the great peril of seeking it, 61; the way in which it is lawful to do so, 179; must be offered to God, 159.
Prayer, must be accompanied by thanksgiving, 6; its different divisions, 6, 7; must be offered by the people on behalf of their ministers, 33; is intimately connected with help that comes from God, 33; too much must not be left to the prayers of others, 34; must be offered for the dead, 38, 39; the prayers of the faithful are made known to God by the ministry of angels, 175; three necessary conditions of prayer noted, 175; has the power of causing peace, 176; is an effectual safeguard against all temptation, 177.
'Preach,' not used by St. Paul in the technical sense of the word, 25, 47.
Preachers, two different kinds of distinguished, 25; the motives that

actuate unfaithful preachers, 26, 27; and faithful ones, 28; what use is to be made of the bad, 30; are admonished constantly to repeat the same topic, 118; the reason of this, 118, 119; shewn from the analogy of physicians, 119; and from a well-known saying of Socrates, 119; faithful preachers not actuated by desire of gain, 191.

Presbyter (priest), used as an interchangeable term with bishop, 5.

Presence of Christ with His people is continual, 172; remembrance of presence of God will produce holy fear, 91, 92.

Poverty, thoroughly understood by St. Paul, 184; its peculiar perils, 184.

Power of God shewn in resurrection of the body more than in subduing demons, 160; power of the Cross, 153.

Pride, how to be corrected, 62, 63; our Lord became Man to cure it, 74.

Prize, means the crown of everlasting glory, 145; must not be confounded with the word 'mark,' 145.

Purity, to be cultivated, 178.

Pythagoras, a remarkable saying of his, 155.

Raphael, presents the prayers of the faithful before God, 175.

Red Sea, a type of Baptism, 144.

Rejoicing, in what sense the word is used by St. Paul, 47; ground of the rejoicing of Gregory Nazianzen, 127; in what worldly rejoicing consists, 169, 170; nothing can rob us of Christian rejoicing, 170; why the Philippians are specially encouraged to it, 169.

Repentance, none after death, 85.

Repetition of well-known truths urged upon preachers, 118; will have the effect of strengthening people in the faith, 119.

Resurrection of our Lord, assures us of our own, 133; delivers us from a threefold death, 133; in what sense our resurrection may be said to be more wonderful than Christ's, 133; how the liberality of the Philippians depended upon it, 193.

Resurrection (ἐξανάστασις), peculiar force of the word, 135, 136; high value put upon the resurrection of the body, 159.

Revelation, different measures of it, according to the varying capabilities of Christians, 148; God bestows it on those who diligently employ grace already given, 118; the promise of it conditional, 150; the patriarchal revelation may have been the foundation of the heathen mysteries, 185.

Reverence, to be shewn at the Name of Jesus, 84; must not be merely an internal feeling, 84, 85; to be shewn by younger ministers to their elder brethren, 108.

Reward of Christians must not be sought in this world, 194; martyrs enter upon their reward immediately after death, 103.

Righteousness, equivalent to exact fulfilment of the Law, 126; man's own is only fictitious, 130, 131; utterly repudiated by St. Paul, 131; wherein true righteousness consists, 131; two kinds of it distinguished, 20; comes to us *from* God and *through* Christ, 132; in what the righteousness of the Law consisted, 126; love is sometimes called by this name, 20.

'*Righteousness of God*,' meaning of the expression, 132.

'*Righteousness, the fruit of*,' explained, 20.

Robbery, in what sense the word is applied to our Lord, 69.

Rule, the use of this word shews that Christians must walk after one another without swerving, 150.

Runner, a, St. Paul likens himself to one, 136, 142; must reckon not how far he has already run, but how much still remains, 142; each of the baptized is a runner, 113; they should ever keep the remembrance of this before them, 145.

Sacrifice, a, St. Paul willing to make himself one, 102; how the term may be applied to Christians generally, 102; in what sense alms are a sacrifice, 193.

Sacrificial rites, a figure borrowed from, 101.

Sailors, an example to ministers, 45.

Saints, a term applied to Christians generally, 3; specially claimed by the Jews, 3; lives of the Saints not sufficiently studied, 25; permitted to have infirmities to prevent their undue exaltation, 112; the title obliges Christians to holiness, 195; the faithful are fellow-citizens of the Saints, 156.

Salvation, capable of bearing two

INDEX.   225

senses, 32; is not necessarily limited to *final* salvation, 89; St. Paul did not speak with certainty of his own, 135.

Saviour, why this term is used of our Lord in reference to His second Advent, 158.

Scholmen, the, distinguished four kinds of fear, 91.

Scipio, a story of, 60.

Self-denial, St. Paul an example of it, 45, 58; specially by sending St. Timothy to the Philippians, 104, 105.

Self-indulgent, the, a large class in the Church, 152; are enemies of the Cross, 153.

Selfishness to be avoided, 64; St. Cyprian's complaint about it, 65.

Self-seekers, their prevalence, 106; preach Christ only for temporal advantages, 107.

Semi-Pelagians refuted, 10.

Servant, our Lord predicted under that name, 75; He performed servants' work, 75; the faithful are the servants of God, 108.

Servant of Christ, a most distinguished title, 2; belongs peculiarly to ministers, 2.

'*Servant* of the servants of God,' a title borne by the popes, 2.

'*Served*,' peculiar force of the word as applied to St. Timothy, 108.

Service, its technical sense as used of the Philippians, 115; why this word is employed by St. Paul, 115.

Severity of St. Paul towards false teachers, 121.

Shame, a feeling unknown to St. Paul, 35; false and true shame distinguished, 35; the wicked glory in their shame, 155.

Sickness, recovery from is a mercy, 112.

Simon Magus, his blasphemous assertion, 69.

Sincere, in what sense Christians are to be, 19.

Sinners are mingled with the righteous to try them, 96; this shewn by the example of the sons of Noah, 97; the sons of Isaac, 97; the sons of Jacob, 97; and the twelve Apostles, 97; in what sense they are 'apprehended' by Christ, 140; they are His crown, 140.

Sleep, a term appropriately applied to death, 42.

Socrates, remarkable sayings of his, 27, 119; supposed to have been put to death for revealing the mysteries to the public generally, 185.

Soldiers, Roman, their employments described, 197; Christians should be like well-drilled soldiers, 150.

Solifidianism, a protest against, 187.

Solitude favourable to the acquirement of perfection, 196.

Sorcerers rebuked, 44.

Sorrow, not wholly forbidden to Christians, 113; St. Paul never free from it, 113.

Spirit, the, use of the word not necessarily restricted to the Holy Ghost, 49, 57.

Spirits, disembodied, not allowed to roam about at pleasure, 44.

Spiritual and carnal circumcision contrasted, 123; spiritual and not carnal claims mentioned by St. Paul, 55; his humility in speaking of his own spiritual state, 137; we must never be satisfied with our own, 139.

Stand, the word denotes a high state of preparation against attack, 163; a figure borrowed from a cube, 163; it is only possible to stand as long as we are in union with Christ, 177.

Stars, the faithful likened to, because they shine in darkness, 98.

Strait, in what sense St. Paul felt himself to be in one, 41; this expression illustrated by a reference to St. Cyprian, 42.

Strife, wherein it consists, 61.

Strive, in what sense Christians are bound to, 49; it must not be for trifles, 49.

Suffering, whence St. Paul derived comfort under it, 13, 14; is a distinguished mark of favour, 14; Christians must not shrink from it, 134; suffering for Christ occupies a position even above faith, 51; is grace, 14; is more wonderful than raising the dead, 52; it makes Christ our debtor, 52; should fill us with joy, 53; makes us acceptable to Christ, 54; fellowship in suffering begets mutual consolation, 56; is all summed up in the one word 'Cross,' 153; is appropriately likened to a conflict, 53; wonderful fortitude of the martyrs under it, 53, 103.

Sufferings of Christ, St. Paul desires to have a share in them, 133.

Sun, the, a type of Christians in its transmission of light, 98.

'Swear not at all,' our Lord's command reconciled with an adjuration of St. Paul, 16.

Syntyche, a woman of consequence at Philippi, 163; helped the spread of the Gospel, 163; at variance with Euodias, 163; their dispute created public scandal, 164; earnestly exhorted to union, 163, 164.

Teachers exhorted to mildness with their pupils by the example of our Lord's humiliation, 72.

Tears, St. Paul's Epistles written with, 153; true joy springs from them, 170.

Temperance harder than abstinence, 186.

Temptation must be looked for all our life long, 144; is to be overcome by the power of prayer, 177.

Thanksgiving, a necessary accompaniment of prayer, 6, 174; nothing more acceptable to God, 174; commended to us by the example of St. Paul, 174; his special reasons for it, 181; must never be discontinued, 174.

Thessalonica, why St. Paul during his sojourn there was supported by contributions from Philippi, 190.

'*Things behind*,' the expression means all temporal and transitory things, 142.

'*Things which are before*,' the rewards laid up in heaven, 143.

'*Thinketh*,' force of the word as used in reference to grounds of boasting, 124.

Timothy, St., was well known to the Philippians, 1; had no share in the composition of the Epistle, 1; may possibly have written it at the dictation of St. Paul, 2; why his name is mentioned in the salutation, 2; the object of his mission to Philippi, 104; delayed on account of St. Paul's imprisonment, 109; was a proof of excessive care on the part of the Apostle, 104; and of self-denial, 105; he was St. Paul's second self, 105; why he would be likely to take special care of the Philippians, 106; had exhibited many proofs of faith, 108; was much loved by St. Paul, 108; peculiar force of the word 'served' as applied to him, 108; an example to younger ministers to shew reverence to their elder brethren, 108.

'*Token*,' in what sense the word is used in this Epistle, 50.

Torches, a figure borrowed from the custom of carrying them in the streets, 99.

Transfiguration of our Lord, called the Sacrament of the Resurrection, 158; He did not then lay aside His natural Body, 158.

Travellers, the faithful are likened to, 147.

Tree, a, man redeemed by means of, 79; legend of the tree from which the Cross was made, 79.

Triumph of the martyrs, 42.

True, the use of the word excludes all double-dealing, 178.

Trust in God shewn by the example of St. Paul, 34, 109.

Truth, the, may be preached by those who yet do not preach with a true heart, 29.

Truthfulness must be strictly cultivated, 178.

Unity, an exhortation to, 49, 58, 59, 60; reason of St. Paul's earnestness in exhorting to it, 60; is a fruit of love, 59; is little realized in our days, 59; its benefits well known to the heathen, 59; much insisted on by Christian writers, 60; does not exist out of Christ, 164.

Vain-glory, wherein it consists, 61; exemplified in the case of the brethren of our Lord, 61.

'*Vile body*,' meaning of the expression, 159; an unsatisfactory translation of the original words, 159.

Virtue must be diligently practised in all its branches, 179.

Voluntary, our Lord's humiliation a voluntary act, 75, 78; the surrender of earthly things voluntary on the part of St. Paul, 128, 129.

Walk, meaning of the word, 152; why two different Greek words are used to express it, 152.

Weak brethren strengthened by St. Paul's bonds, 24.

Wicked, the, their efforts like winter torrents, 21; are well described by the word 'crooked,' 96; glory in their shame, 155; they may prosper in this world, but are destroyed at last, 154; wicked ministers do not destroy the truth of Christ, 30.

Widow's oil, the, its multiplying an illustration of Divine grace, 151.

Will of God, two different words used by the Greeks to express it, 94.

Will of man, must be worked upon

by God, 93; Pelagian heresy respecting it, 89.

Wisdom, St. Paul an example of it, 29; a reputation for it coveted by false teachers, 61.

Women may do much for the cause of Christ, 166; were the first to receive the Gospel at Philippi, 166.

Word, the, a title of the Gospel, 25; also called 'the Word of life,' 100.

Work, God's, does not exclude the agency of man, 10, 92, 95; He will continue it up to the Judgment-day, 12; it is efficacious, 92; and yet may be retarded by man, 92; God's work in us the reason why man should work with fear, 93; different ways in which He works, 93.

Work, to, how this expression is applied to God, 88; how man is said to work out his own salvation, 89; man cannot work by proxy, 89.

'*Work of Christ*,' meaning of the expression, 114.

Works, good, not merely signs of faith, 92; their true position in connection with man's salvation, 92; will be our crown, 162; will be rewarded, though not in this world, 194; can be done only in the strength of God, 195.

Works of mercy, properly called works of Christ, 114.

World, Christ must be shewn forth before it, 66; a warning against its enticements, 143; its rejoicings are nothing to Christians, 157; their reward is not to be sought in it, 194.

Worldly things fittingly described by the word 'behind,' 112; the true way of using them, 185, 186.

Worship of Christians, contrasted with that of the Jews, 122; the same worship to be paid to our Lord's Human Nature as to His Divine, 83.

Wrestling, a figure borrowed from, 49.

Yoke-fellow, to whom this title is supposed to be applied by St. Paul, 165; sometimes taken as a proper name (Syzygus), 165; reason why the name is suppressed, 166.

Zeal is used sometimes in a good and sometimes in a bad sense, 125; why St. Paul mentions his zeal, 125, 126; how it was shewed by him, 126, and by Epaphroditus, 112.

INDEX

OF

GREEK WORDS AND PHRASES.

ἀγαλλίαμα, 47.
ἄγγελος, 111.
ἅγιοι (οἱ), 3.
ἁγνά, 178.
ἁγνῶς (οὐχ), 26.
ἀγών, 53.
αἱρήσομαι (καὶ τί), 40.
αἴσθησις, 18.
αἵτινες 166.
ἀκέραιοι, 95.
ἀκέρατος, 95.
ἄμεμπτοι, 95.
ἀμώμητα, 96.
ἄμωμοι, 95.
ἀναγκαιότερον δι' ὑμᾶς, 44.
ἀναλῦσαι, 42.
ἀνάστασις, 135.
ἀνεθάλετε, 181, 183.
ἀπάθεια, 113.
ἀπέχω, 192.
ἀπίδω (ὡς ἂν), 109.
ἀποβήσεται. 31.
ἀπόδειξις, 50.
ἀποκαραδοκία, 33.
ἀπόστολος, 110.
ἀπρόσκοποι, 19.
ἁρπαγμός, 69.
αὐτάρκεια, 184, 192.
αὐτομολόγησις, 7.

βεβαιώσει τοῦ εὐαγγελίου, 14.
βλέπετε, 121.
βραβεῖον, 136, 145.
βραβευταί, 146.

γάρ, 15.
γνησίως, 106, 165.
γνοὺς τὰ περὶ ὑμῶν, 104.
γνῶσις, 17.
γογγυσμός, 95.

δέησις, 7, 174.
διὰ τὸ ὑπερέχον τῆς γνώσεως, 128.
διαφέροντα (τά), 18.
διό, 79.
διώκω, 138.
δοκιμάζειν, 18.
δοκιμή, 108.
δόξαν (εἰς), 86.
δύναμις, 88, 89.

ἑαυτὸν ἐκένωσε, 71.
ἐγγύς (ὁ Κύριος), 172.
ἐδούλευσε, 108.
εἰ, 39.
εἴδετε, 180.
εἰ καί, 139.
εἰλικρινεῖς, 19.
εἶναι ἴσα Θεῷ, 70.
εἴ πως, 134.
εἴτε ἀληθείᾳ, 29.
εἴ τις, 179.
εἰς λόγον δόσεως καὶ λήψεως, 188, 189.
ἐλπίζω, 104.
ἐμάθετε, 180.
ἐν, 177.
ἐναρξάμενος, 10.
ἔνδειξις, 50.
ἐνδυναμοῦντι, 187.
ἐνέργεια, 88, 159, 160.
ἐνεργεῖν, 88.
ἐνεργῶν (ὁ), 92.
ἐν ὅλῳ τῷ Πραιτωρίῳ, 22.
ἐν τῇ αἰσχύνῃ αὐτῶν, 155.
ἐξανάστασις, 135.
ἐξῆλθον ἀπὸ Μακεδονίας, 188.
ἕξις, 88.
ἐξομολογήσεται, 86.
ἐξομολόγησις, 6.
ἐπεκτεινόμενος, 142.
ἐπέχοντες, 99.
ἐπίγνωσις, 17, 18.
ἐπιείκεια, 170, 171.
ἐπιεικές (τὸ), 170.
ἐπιζητῶ τὸ δόμα, 190.
ἐπιμένειν ἐν τῇ σαρκί, 42.
ἐπὶ πάσῃ τῇ μνείᾳ ὑμῶν, 6.
ἐπιπόθητοι, 161.
ἐπιποθῶ, 15.
ἐπιποθῶν ἦν, 111.
ἐπιτελέσει, 10.
ἐπὶ τὸ τέλειον ἐλθεῖν, 147.
ἐπιχορηγία, 33.
ἐργάτας (τοὺς κακοὺς), 120.
ἐριθεία, 61.
ἐριθείας (ἐξ), 26.
ἐριθεύομαι, 61.
εὐαγγέλιον (εἰς τὸ), 8, 108.
εὐδοκία, 94.
εὑρίσκεσθαι, 77.
εὔφημα, 179.

ἐφ' ᾧ, 140, 182.
ἐχαρίσατο, 80.
ἐχαρίσθη, 14, 52.

ζῆλος, 125.
ζημία, 127.

ἡγοῦμαι, 128.
ἤδη ποτέ, 181.
ἠκαιρεῖσθε, 182.
ἠκούσατε, 180.
ἡμέρα, 11.

θέλημα, 94.
θυμιατήριον, 193.
θυσία, 101, 102.
θυσίαν δεκτήν, 193.
θυσιαστήριον, 193.

ἰσόψυχος, 105.

καθώς ἐστι δίκαιον, 12.
καί, 65.
καὶ ἐν σαρκί, 123.
καὶ τοῖς λοιποῖς πᾶσι, 23.
κανών, 150.
καρπὸς ἔργου, 40.
καταγγέλλω, 25.
καταντήσω, 135.
κατάρτισις, 137.
κατατέμνειν, 121.
κατατομή, 121, 149, 203.
κατ' ἐμέ (τὰ), 21.
κατεργάζεσθε, 88.
καύχημα, 47, 100.
καύχησις, 47.
κεῖμαι, 28.
κέρδη, 127.
κήρυγμα, 47.
κήρυξις, 47.
κηρύσσω, 25.
κοινωνίᾳ (ἐπὶ τῇ), 8.
κοινωνία πνεύματος, 57.
κύνας (τοὺς), 119.
Κυρίῳ (ἐν), 181.

λαμβάνειν, 136.
λειτουργία, 102, 115.
λειτουργός, 111.
λοιπόν (τὸ), 116, 177.
λοιποῦ (τοῦ), 116.

μεγαλυνθήσεται, 35.
μεμύημαι, 185.
μεμυημένοι, 148.
μετασχηματίσει, 158.
μηδὲν μεριμνᾶτε, 173.
μορφή, 67, 68.
μορφὴ δούλου, 68, 75.
μορφὴ Θεοῦ, 68.
μύσται, 185.
μυστήριον, 185.

νεκρῶν (τῶν), 136.
νοῦς, 176.

οἰκτιρμοί, 57.
οἱ πνεύματι Θεῷ λατρεύοντες, 122.
ὀκνηρόν, 119.
ὁμοίωμα, 76.
ὄνομα (τὸ), 81.
ὀνόματι (ἐν τῷ), 83.
ὀσμὴν εὐωδίας, 193.
οὐσία, 67, 68.

πάντα ἰσχύω, 186.
παντί (ἐν), 184.
παραβολευσάμενος, 115.
παραβουλευσάμενος, 115.
παράκλησις, 56.
παραμύθιον, 56.
παρ' ὑμῶν (τὰ), 192.
παρελάβετε, 180.
παρρησία, 34.
πᾶσι (ἐν), 184.
πεπληρωμένοι καρπὸν δικαιοσύνης, 19.
πεποιθώς, 10.
περιπατεῖν, 152.
περισσεύειν, 184.
περιτομὴ ὀκταήμερος, 124.
πίστει (ἐπὶ τῇ), 132.
πίστει (τῇ), 49.
πλείονας τῶν ἀδελφῶν (τοὺς), 24.
πλήν, 149.
πληρώσατέ μου τὴν χαράν, 58.
πόθος, 162.
πολιτεύεσθε, 48.
πολίτευμα, 156.
πολλῷ μᾶλλον κρεῖσσον, 43.
πολυπραγμοσύνη, 65.
προκοπή, 21.
πρόφασις, 29.
προσευχή, 7, 174.
προσφιλῆ, 178.
πτυρόμενοι, 50.

σαρκί (ἐν τῇ), 36.
σεμνά, 178.
σκοπεῖτε, 151.
σκοπόν (κατὰ), 145.
σκύβαλον, 129.
σοφία, 18.
σπένδομαι, 101.
σπλάγχνα, 15, 57.
σπουδαιοτέρως, 113.
στήκετε, 163.
στοιχεῖν, 152.
συγκοινωνήσαντες, 187.
συγκοινωνοί, 14.
σύζυγε γνήσιε, 165.
συλλαμβάνου, 166, 167.
συμμιμηταί, 151.
συμμορφούμενος, 134.
συμπάθεια, 113.
σύμψυχοι, 59.

INDEX OF GREEK WORDS AND PHRASES. 231

συναθλοῦντες, 49.
συνεπισκόποις, 3.
σύν ἐπισκόποις καὶ διακόνοις, 5.
συνεργός, 110, 168.
συνεχόμαι ἐκ τῶν δύο, 41.
συνήθλησάν μοι, 166, 167.
συνομοίως, 202.
συντομή, 203.
συστρατιώτης, 110.
σχῆμα, 77.
σώματι (ἐν τῷ), 36.
σωτηρία, 89.
σωτηρίαν (εἰς), 32.

ταπεινοῦσθαι, 184.
τὰ περὶ ἐμέ, 109.
τέλειοι, 146.
τελείωσις, 137.
τετελείωμαι, 136.
τὴν ἐπιθυμίαν ἔχων, 41.
τί γάρ, 28.
τὸ αὐτὸ φρονῆτε, 58.
τὸ ἓν φρονοῦντες, 58.
τὸ σῶμα τῆς ταπεινώσεως ἡμῶν, 159.
τύπος, 152.

ὑπάρχει, 156.
ὑπάρχων, 69.
ὑπερύψωσεν, 80.
ὑστέρημα, 115.
ὑστέρησιν (κατὰ), 183.

φαίνεσθε, 97.
φθάνειν, 149.
φιλαυτία, 64.
φόβου καὶ τρόμου (μετὰ), 90.
φρονεῖν, 12, 155.
φρουρήσει, 177.
φύσις, 67, 68.
φωστῆρες, 97—99.

χαίρετε, 116.
χαίρετε (ἐν Κυρίῳ), 117.
χαρά, 162.
χάρις, 14.
χρεία, 111.
Χριστῷ (ἐν), 22.

ψυχῇ (μιᾷ), 49.

ὥστε, 161.

PRINTED BY MESSRS. PARKER, CORNMARKET, OXFORD.

A List of Books

RECENTLY PUBLISHED BY

JOHN HENRY AND JAMES PARKER,

OXFORD, AND 377, STRAND, LONDON.

NEW THEOLOGICAL WORKS.

REV. DR. MOBERLY.

SERMONS ON THE BEATITUDES, with others mostly preached before the University of Oxford; to which is added a Preface relating to the recent volume of "Essays and Reviews." By the Rev. GEORGE MOBERLY, D.C.L., Head Master of Winchester College. 8vo., price 10s. 6d.

ARCHDEACON CHURTON.

A MEMOIR OF THE LATE JOSHUA WATSON, Esq. By the Venerable Archdeacon CHURTON. 2 vols., post 8vo., *nearly ready.*

THE LATE REV. H. NEWLAND.

A NEW CATENA ON ST. PAUL'S EPISTLES.—A PRACTICAL AND EXEGETICAL COMMENTARY ON THE EPISTLES OF ST. PAUL: in which are exhibited the Results of the most learned Theological Criticisms, from the Age of the Early Fathers down to the Present Time. Edited by the late Rev. HENRY NEWLAND, M.A., Vicar of St. Mary Church, Devon, and Chaplain to the Bishop of Exeter. Vol. I., containing THE EPISTLE TO THE EPHESIANS. 8vo., 10s. 6d.

——————— Vol. II., containing THE EPISTLE TO THE PHILIPPIANS. *Just ready.*

REV. WILLIAM BRIGHT.

A HISTORY OF THE CHURCH, from the EDICT of MILAN, A.D. 313, to the COUNCIL of CHALCEDON, A.D. 451. By WILLIAM BRIGHT, M.A., Fellow of University College, Oxford; late Professor of Ecclesiastical History in the Scottish Church. Post 8vo., price 10s. 6d.

THE LORD BISHOP OF OXFORD.

A CHARGE delivered at the Triennial Visitation of the Diocese, November, 1860. By SAMUEL, LORD BISHOP OF OXFORD, Lord High Almoner to Her Majesty the Queen, and Chancellor of the Order of the Garter. Published by request. *Just ready.*

THE ORDINATION SERVICE. ADDRESSES ON THE QUESTIONS TO THE CANDIDATES FOR ORDINATION. By the Right Rev. the LORD BISHOP OF OXFORD. *Second Edition, containing an additional Address.* Crown 8vo., cl., 6s.

MONTAGU BURROWS, M.A.

PASS AND CLASS. An Oxford Guide-Book through the Courses of *Literæ Humaniores*, Mathematics, Natural Science, and Law and Modern History. By MONTAGU BURROWS, M.A. Fcap. 8vo. *A New Edition in the press.*

1260—1500.

REV. R. W. MORGAN.

ST. PAUL IN BRITAIN; or, THE ORIGIN OF BRITISH AS OPPOSED TO PAPAL CHRISTIANITY. By the Rev. R. W. MORGAN, Perpetual Curate of Tregynon, Montgomeryshire, Author of " Verities of the Church," " The Churches of England and Rome," "Christianity and Infidelity intellectually contrasted," &c. Crown 8vo. [*Just ready.*

OXFORD LENTEN SERMONS.

A SERIES OF SERMONS preached in Oxford during the Season of Lent, 1859. Fcap. 8vo., 5s.

REV. T. LATHBURY, M.A.

A HISTORY OF THE BOOK OF COMMON PRAYER, AND OTHER AUTHORIZED BOOKS, from the Reformation; and an Attempt to ascertain how the Rubrics, Canons, and Customs of the Church have been understood and observed from the same time: with an Account of the State of Religion in England from 1640 to 1660. By the Rev. THOMAS LATHBURY, M.A., Author of "A History of the Convocation," "The Nonjurors," &c. *Second Edition, with an Index.* 8vo., 10s. 6d.

REV. E. B. PUSEY, D.D.

THE COUNCILS OF THE CHURCH, from the Council of Jerusalem, A.D. 51, to the Council of Constantinople, A.D. 381; chiefly as to their Constitution, but also as to their Objects and History. By the Rev. E. B. PUSEY, D.D., Regius Professor of Hebrew; Canon of Christ Church; late Fellow of Oriel College. 8vo., 10s. 6d.

NINE SERMONS preached before the University of Oxford, and printed chiefly A.D. 1843—1855, now collected into one volume. By the Rev. E. B. PUSEY, D.D. 8vo., 9s.

REV. H. DOWNING.

SHORT NOTES ON THE ACTS OF THE APOSTLES, intended for the use of Teachers in Parish Schools, and other Readers of the English Version. By HENRY DOWNING, M.A., Incumbent of St. Mary's, Kingswinford. Fcap. 8vo., cloth, 2s.

THE DEAN OF FERNS.

THE LIFE AND CONTEMPORANEOUS CHURCH HISTORY OF ANTONIO DE DOMINIS, Archbishop of Spala'ro, which included the Kingdoms of Dalmatia and Croatia; afterwards Dean of Windsor, Master of the Savoy, and Rector of West Ilsley in the Church of England, in the reign of James I. By HENRY NEWLAND, D.D., Dean of Ferns. 8vo., cloth lettered, 7s.

THE LATE REV. C. MARRIOTT.

LECTURES ON THE EPISTLE OF ST. PAUL TO THE ROMANS. By the late Rev. C. MARRIOTT, B.D., Fellow of Oriel College, Oxford; Vicar of St. Mary-the-Virgin in the City of Oxford; and sometime Principal of the Diocesan College, Chichester. Edited by his brother, the Rev. JOHN MARRIOTT, M.A., Curate of Bradfield, Berks. 12mo., cloth, 6s.

NEW ARCHITECTURAL WORKS.

EDITOR OF GLOSSARY.

SOME ACCOUNT OF DOMESTIC ARCHITECTURE IN ENGLAND, from Richard II. to Henry VIII. (or the Perpendicular style.) With Numerous Illustrations of Existing Remains from Original Drawings. By the EDITOR OF "THE GLOSSARY OF ARCHITECTURE." In 2 vols., 8vo., 1*l*. 10s.

Also,

VOL. I.—FROM WILLIAM I. TO EDWARD I. (or the Norman and Early English styles). 8vo., 21s.

VOL. II.—FROM EDWARD I. TO RICHARD II. (the Edwardian Period, or the Decorated Style). 8vo., 21s.

The work complete, with 400 *Engravings, and a General Index,*
4 vols. 8vo., price £3 12s.

PROFESSOR WILLIS.

FACSIMILE OF THE SKETCH-BOOK OF WILARS DE HONECORT, an Architect of the Thirteenth Century. With Commentaries and Descriptions by MM. LASSUS and QUICHERAT. Translated and Edited, with many additional Articles and Notes, by the Rev. ROBERT WILLIS, M.A., F.R.S., Jacksonian Professor at Cambridge, &c. With 64 Facsimiles, 10 Illustration Plates, and 43 Woodcuts. Royal 4to., cloth, 2*l*. 10s.

The English letterpress separate, for the purchasers of the French edition, 4to., 15s.

RAYMOND BORDEAUX.

SPECIMENS OF MEDIEVAL IRONWORK. Serrurerie du Moyen-Age, par RAYMOND BORDEAUX. Forty Lithographic Plates, by G. Bouet, and numerous Woodcuts. Small 4to., cloth, 20s.

JOHN HEWITT.

ANCIENT ARMOUR AND WEAPONS IN EUROPE. By JOHN HEWITT, Member of the Archæological Institute of Great Britain. Vols. II. and III., comprising the Period from the Fourteenth to the Seventeenth Century, completing the work, 1*l*. 12s. Also Vol. I., from the Iron Period of the Northern Nations to the end of the Thirteenth Century, 18s. The work complete, 3 vols., 8vo., 2*l*. 10s.

REV. HERBERT HAINES.

A MANUAL FOR THE STUDY OF MONUMENTAL BRASSES. With numerous Illustrations, and a List of those remaining in the British Isles. By the Rev. HERBERT HAINES, M.A. 2 vols., Medium 8vo., price £1 1s.

M. VIOLLET-LE-DUC.

THE MILITARY ARCHITECTURE OF THE MIDDLE AGES, Translated from the French of M. VIOLLET-LE-DUC. By M. MACDERMOTT, Esq., Architect. With the 151 original French Engravings. Medium 8vo., cloth, price £1 1s.

REV. C. H. HARTSHORNE.

AN HISTORICAL AND ARCHITECTURAL ACCOUNT OF ENGLISH CASTLES. By the Rev. C. H. HARTSHORNE, M.A. With numerous Engravings. Medium 8vo. [*In the press.*

OUR ENGLISH HOME: its Early History and Progress. With Notes on the Introduction of Domestic Inventions. Crown 8vo., 5s.

NEW THEOLOGICAL WORKS, (continued).

REV. J. E. BODE.

HYMNS FROM THE GOSPEL OF THE DAY, for each Sunday and the Festivals of our Lord. By the Rev. J. E. BODE, M.A., Rector of Westwell, Oxon.; Author of Ballads from Herodotus, Bampton Lectures, &c. 18mo., 1s.

PROFESSOR STANLEY.

THREE INTRODUCTORY LECTURES ON THE STUDY OF ECCLESIASTICAL HISTORY. By ARTHUR PENRHYN STANLEY, M.A., Regius Professor of Ecclesiastical History, and Canon of Christ Church. 8vo., sewed, 2s. 6d.

REV. L. P. MERCIER.

CONSIDERATIONS RESPECTING A FUTURE STATE. By the Rev. LEWIS P. MERCIER, M.A., University College, Oxford. Fcap. 8vo., 4s.

REV. J. M. NEALE.

A HISTORY OF THE SO-CALLED JANSENIST CHURCH OF HOLLAND; with a Sketch of its Earlier Annals, and some Account of the Brothers of the Common Life. By the Rev. J. M. NEALE, M.A., Warden of Sackville College. 8vo., cloth, 10s. 6d.

REV. E. HAWKINS, D.D.

A MANUAL FOR CHRISTIANS, designed for their use at any time after Confirmation. By EDWARD HAWKINS, D.D., Provost of Oriel College. *Seventh Edition*, 12mo., 6d., sewed.

REV. T. T. CARTER.

LIFE of JOHN ARMSTRONG, D.D., late Lord Bishop of Grahamstown. By the Rev. T. T. CARTER, M.A., Rector of Clewer. With an Introduction, by SAMUEL, LORD BISHOP OF OXFORD. *Third Edition*. Fcap. 8vo., with Portrait, cloth, 7s. 6d.

THE LATE BISHOP ARMSTRONG.

ESSAYS ON CHURCH PENITENTIARIES. Fcap. 8vo., cloth, price 2s. 6d.

THE PASTOR IN HIS CLOSET; or, A Help to the Devotions of the Clergy. By JOHN ARMSTRONG, D.D., late Lord Bishop of Grahamstown. Second Edition. Fcap. 8vo., cloth, 2s.

ST. AUGUSTINE.

ST. AUGUSTINE'S EXPOSITIONS ON THE BOOK OF PSALMS, translated with Notes and Indices. Complete in Six Volumes, 8vo., price in cloth, 2l. 16s. 6d.

ST. ANSELM.

MEDITATIONS AND SELECT PRAYERS, by ST. ANSELM, formerly Archbishop of Canterbury. Edited by E. B. PUSEY, D.D. Fcap. 8vo., 5s.

CUR DEUS HOMO, or WHY GOD WAS MADE MAN; by ST. ANSELM. Fcap. 8vo., 2s. 6d. *Second Edition in the press.*

NEW SERMONS.

PAROCHIAL SERMONS, by the Rev. HENRY W. BURROWS, B.D., Perpetual Curate of Christ Church, St. Pancras. Fcap. 8vo., cloth, 6s.

——————————— Second Series. Fcap. 8vo., cloth, 5s.

PARISH SERMONS. Second Series. By WILLIAM FRASER, B.C.L., Vicar of Alton, Staffordshire, and Domestic Chaplain to the Earl of Shrewsbury and Talbot. Fcap. 8vo., cloth, red edges, 3s.

THE WISDOM OF PIETY, AND OTHER SERMONS, addressed chiefly to Undergraduates. By the Rev. FREDERICK MEYRICK, M.A., Her Majesty's Inspector of Schools; Fellow of Trinity College; late Select Preacher before the University of Oxford, and Her Majesty's Preacher at Whitehall. Crown 8vo., 4s.

THE YEAR OF THE CHURCH. A Course of Sermons by the late Rev. RICHARD WEBSTER HUNTLEY, M.A., sometime Fellow of All Souls' College, Oxford; Rector of Boxwell-cum-Leighterton, Gloucestershire, and Vicar of Alberbury, Salop; and for eleven years Proctor in Convocation for the Clergy of the Diocese of Gloucester and Bristol: with a short Memoir by the Editor, the Rev. SIR GEORGE PREVOST, Bart., M.A. Fcap. 8vo., cloth lettered, 7s. 6d.

LEAMINGTON COLLEGE SERMONS. — School Life. — Sermons preached in the Chapel of Leamington College. By THOMAS BURBIDGE, LL.D., Master of the College. Fcap. 8vo., cloth, 5s.

ARMSTRONG'S PAROCHIAL SERMONS. Parochial Sermons, by JOHN ARMSTRONG, D.D., late Lord Bishop of Grahamstown. A New Edition, Fcap. 8vo., cloth, 5s

ARMSTRONG'S SERMONS FOR FASTS AND FESTIVALS. A new Edition. Fcap. 8vo, 5s.

PLAIN SERMONS ON THE BOOK OF COMMON PRAYER. By a Writer in the "Tracts for the Christian Seasons." Fcap. 8vo., cloth, 5s.

SHORT SERMONS FOR FAMILY READING. Ninety Short Sermons for Family Reading, following the course of the Christian Seasons. By the Author of "A Plain Commentary on the Gospels." 2 volumes, cloth, 8s.

SINGLE SERMONS.

Dr. Stanley.
FREEDOM AND LABOUR. Two Sermons preached before the University of Oxford. By ARTHUR PENRHYN STANLEY, D.D., Regius Professor of Ecclesiastical History, and Canon of Christ Church. *Second Edition.* 8vo., price 1s. 6d.

Rev. H. P. Liddon.
OUR LORD'S ASCENSION THE CHURCH'S GAIN. A Sermon preached before the University, in the Cathedral Church of Christ, at Oxford, on Ascension-day, 1860. By H. P. LIDDON, M.A., Student of Christ Church, and Vice-Principal of St. Edmund Hall. 8vo., price 1s.

Rev. H. E. Tweed.
THE APOSTLES AND THE OFFERTORY; or, The "Fellowship" of Acts ii. 42. A Sermon preached before the University of Oxford, by H. E. TWEED, M.A., Fellow of Oriel, and late Scholar of Trinity College. 8vo., price 1s.

Rev. H. J. Rose.
THE QUESTION, "WHY SHOULD WE PRAY FOR FAIR WEATHER?" ANSWERED. A Sermon preached at the Harvest-home Service at Market Harborough, October 24, 1860. By H. J. ROSE, B.D., Rector of Houghton Conquest, and late Fellow of St. John's College, Cambridge. Published by request. Fcap. 8vo., price 6d.

NEW THEOLOGICAL WORKS, (continued).

REV. P. FREEMAN.

THE HOLY EUCHARIST considered as a MYSTERY: being the Introduction to Part II. of THE PRINCIPLES OF DIVINE SERVICE. By the Rev. PHILIP FREEMAN, M.A. 8vo., cloth, 6s.

This treatise is complete in itself, and may be had separately. It is of about the compass of Bishop Bethell's work on Baptismal Regeneration, and is designed to serve as a similar manual on the doctrine of the Eucharist.

By the same Author.

THE PRINCIPLES OF DIVINE SERVICE. An Inquiry concerning the true manner of understanding and using the order for Morning and Evening Prayer, and for the Administration of the Holy Communion in the English Church. 8vo., cloth, 10s. 6d.

THE BOOK OF PSALMS.

A PLAIN COMMENTARY ON THE BOOK OF PSALMS, (Prayer-book Version,) chiefly grounded on the Fathers; *for the use of Families.* 2 vols. fcap. 8vo., cloth, 10s. 6d.

DAILY SERVICES.

DAILY SERVICES OF THE CHURCH OF ENGLAND. A new Edition, on thick paper and in clear type, with red Rubrics, in 2 vols., crown 8vo., morocco, 1l. 10s. Also on thin paper, in one volume crown 8vo., morocco, 16s.

Both editions of this work may be had in a variety of elegant bindings.

REV. J. DAVISON.

DISCOURSES ON PROPHECY, in which are considered its Structure, Use, and Inspiration: being the substance of Twelve Sermons preached in the Chapel of Lincoln's-Inn, by JOHN DAVISON, B.D. Sixth and cheaper Edition. 8vo., cloth, 9s.

REV. J. S. BARTLETT.

A BRIEF HISTORY OF THE CHRISTIAN CHURCH, from the First Century to the Reformation. By the Rev. J. S. BARTLETT. Fcap. 8vo., cloth, 2s. 6d.

MRS. HAMILTON GRAY.

THE EMPIRE AND THE CHURCH, from Constantine to Charlemagne. By Mrs. HAMILTON GRAY. Crown 8vo., cloth, 12s.

REV. C. E. KENNAWAY.

PERDITA AND ANGELINA; OR, THE LOST ONE FOUND. An Anglo-Roman Dialogue. By the Rev. C. E. KENNAWAY. Together with Romeward and Homeward. Fcap. 8vo., cloth, 3s. 6d. Pt. II., separately, 1s.

REV. A. WOODGATE.

ANOMALIES IN THE ENGLISH CHURCH no just grounds for Seceding; or, The Abnormal Condition of the Church considered with reference to the Analogy of Scripture and of History. By HENRY ARTHUR WOODGATE, B.D. Fcap. 8vo., cloth, 2s. 6d.

REV. E. MONRO.

PLAIN SERMONS ON THE BOOK OF COMMON PRAYER. By a Writer in the "Tracts for the Christian Seasons." Fcap. 8vo., cloth, 5s.

HISTORICAL AND PRACTICAL SERMONS ON THE SUFFERINGS AND RESURRECTION OF OUR LORD. By a Writer in the Tracts for the Christian Seasons. 2 vols., fcap. 8vo. cloth, 10s.

SERMONS ON NEW TESTAMENT CHARACTERS. By the Author of "Sermons on the Prayer-book," and "On the Sufferings and Resurrection of our Lord." Fcap. 8vo., 4s.

REV. G. ARDEN.

BREVIATES FROM HOLY SCRIPTURE, arranged for use by the Bed of Sickness. By the Rev. G. ARDEN, M.A., Rector of Winterborne-Came; Domestic Chaplain to the Right Hon. the Earl of Devon; Author of "A Manual of Catechetical Instruction." Fcap. 8vo. *Second Edition.* 2s.

THE CURE OF SOULS. By the Rev. G. ARDEN, M.A. Fcap. 8vo., 2s. 6d.

OXFORD SERIES OF DEVOTIONAL WORKS.

THE IMITATION OF CHRIST.
FOUR BOOKS. By Thomas A KEMPIS. A new Edition, revised, handsomely printed on tinted paper in fcap. 8vo., with Vignettes and red borders, cl., 5s.; antique calf, red edges, 10s. 6d.

LAUD'S DEVOTIONS.
THE PRIVATE DEVOTIONS of Dr. WILLIAM LAUD, Archbishop of Canterbury, and Martyr. A new and revised Edition, with Translations to the Latin Prayers, handsomely printed with Vignettes and red lines. Fcap. 8vo., antique cloth, 5s.

WILSON'S SACRA PRIVATA.
THE PRIVATE MEDITATIONS, DEVOTIONS, and PRAYERS of the Right Rev. T. WILSON, D.D., Lord Bishop of Sodor and Man. Now first printed entire. From the Original Manuscripts. Fcap. 8vo., 6s.

ANDREWES' DEVOTIONS.
DEVOTIONS. By the Right Rev. Father in God, LAUNCELOT ANDREWES, Translated from the Greek and Latin, and arranged anew. Fcap. 8vo., 5s.; morocco, 8s.; antique calf, red edges, 10s. 6d.

SPINCKES' DEVOTIONS.
TRUE CHURCH OF ENGLAND MAN'S COMPANION IN THE CLOSET; or, a complete Manual of Private Devotions, collected from the Writings of eminent Divines of the Church of England. Sixteenth Edition, corrected. Fcap. 8vo., floriated borders, cloth, antique, 4s.

The above set of 5 Volumes, in neat grained calf binding, £2 2s.

TAYLOR'S HOLY LIVING.
THE RULE AND EXERCISES OF HOLY LIVING. By BISHOP JEREMY TAYLOR. In which are described the means and instruments of obtaining every virtue, and the remedies against every vice. *In antique cloth binding,* 4s.

TAYLOR'S HOLY DYING.
THE RULE AND EXERCISES OF HOLY DYING. By BISHOP JEREMY TAYLOR. In which are described the means and instruments of preparing ourselves and others respectively for a blessed death, &c. *In antique cloth binding,* 4s.

NEW WORKS OF FICTION.

ALICE LISLE: A Tale of Puritan Times. Fcap. 8vo., cloth, 4s.

THE SCHOLAR AND THE TROOPER; OR, OXFORD DURING THE GREAT REBELLION. By the Rev. W. E. HEYGATE. *Second Edition.* Fcap. 8vo., cloth, 5s.

SOME YEARS AFTER: A Tale. Fcap. 8vo., cloth lettered, 7s.

ATHELINE; or, THE CASTLE BY THE SEA. A Tale. By LOUISA STEWART, Author of " Walks at Templecombe," " Floating away," &c. 2 vols., fcap. 8vo. 9s.

MIGNONETTE: A SKETCH. By the Author of "The Curate of Holy Cross." 2 vols., fcap., cloth, 10s.

STORM AND SUNSHINE; OR, THE BOYHOOD OF HERBERT FALCONER. A Tale. By W. E. DICKSON, M.A., Author of " Our Workshop," &c. With Frontispiece, cloth, 2s.

AMY GRANT; OR, THE ONE MOTIVE. A Tale designed principally for the Teachers of the Children of the Poor. *Second Edition.* Fcap. 8vo., cloth, 3s. 6d.

THE TWO HOMES. A Tale. By the Author of "Amy Grant." *Second Edition.* Fcap. 8vo., cloth, 2s. 6d.

DAWN AND TWILIGHT. A Tale. By the Author of "Amy Grant," "Two Homes," &c. 2 vols. fcap. 8vo., cloth, 7s.

KENNETH; OR, THE REAR-GUARD OF THE GRAND ARMY. By the Author of the "Heir of Redclyffe," "Heartsease," &c., &c. *Third Edition.* Fcap. 8vo., with Illustrations, 5s.

TALES FOR THE YOUNG MEN AND WOMEN OF ENGLAND. A Series of Tales adapted for Lending Libraries, Book Hawkers, &c. Fcap. 8vo., with Illustrations, strongly bound in coloured wrapper, 1s. each.

No. 1. Mother and Son.
No. 2. The Recruit. *A new Edition.*
No. 3. The Strike.
No. 4. James Bright, the Shopman.
No. 5. Jonas Clint.
No. 6. The Sisters.
No. 7. Caroline Elton; or, Vanity and Jealousy. } 1s.
No. 8. Servants' Influence.
No. 9. The Railway Accident.
No. 10. Wanted, a Wife.
No. 11. Irrevocable.
No. 12. The Tenants at Tinkers' End.
No. 13. Windycote Hall.
No. 14. False Honour.
No. 15. Old Jarvis's Will.
No. 16. The Two Cottages.
No. 17. Squitch.
No. 18. The Politician.
No. 19. Two to One.
No. 20. Hobson's Choice. 6d.
No. 21. Susan. 4d.
No. 22. Mary Thomas; or, Dissent at Evenly. } 4d.

" To make boys learn to read, and then to place no good books within their reach, is to give them an appetite, and leave nothing in the pantry save unwholesome and poisonous food which, depend upon it, they will eat rather than starve."—*Sir W. Scott.*

A NEW SERIES OF TALES.

HISTORICAL TALES, illustrating the chief events in Ecclesiastical History, British and Foreign, adapted for General Reading, Parochial Libraries, &c. Now publishing, in Monthly Volumes, with a Frontispiece, price 1s.

THE Series of Tales now announced will embrace the most important periods and transactions connected with the progress of the Church in ancient and modern times. They will be written by authors of acknowledged merit, in a popular style, upon sound Church principles, and with a single eye to the inculcation of a true estimate of the circumstances to which they relate, and the bearing of those circumstances upon the history of the Church. By this means it is hoped that many, who now regard Church history with indifference, will be led to the perusal of its singularly interesting and instructive episodes.

Each Tale, although forming a link of the entire Series, will be complete in itself, enabling persons to subscribe to portions only, or to purchase any single Tale separately.

Already published.

No. 1.—THE CAVE IN THE HILLS; or, Cæcilius Viriāthus.

No 2. THE EXILES OF THE CEBENNA: a Journal written during the Decian Persecution, by Aurelius Gratianus, Priest of the Church of Arles; and now done into English.

No. 3.—THE CHIEF'S DAUGHTER; or, The Settlers in Virginia.

No. 4.—THE LILY OF TIFLIS: a Sketch from Georgian Church History.

No. 5.—WILD SCENES AMONGST THE CELTS.

No 6.—THE LAZAR-HOUSE OF LEROS: a Tale of the Eastern Church in the Seventeenth Century.

No. 7.—THE RIVALS: a Tale of the Anglo-Saxon Church.

No. 8.—THE CONVERT OF MASSACHUSETTS.

No. 9.—THE QUAY OF THE DIOSCURI: a Tale of Nicene Times.

No. 10.—THE BLACK DANES.

No. 11.—THE CONVERSION OF ST. VLADIMIR; or, The Martyrs of Kief. A Tale of the Early Russian Church.

No. 12.—THE SEA-TIGERS: a Tale of Mediæval Nestorianism.

No. 13.—THE CROSS IN SWEDEN; or, The Days of King Ingi the Good.

No. 14.—THE ALLELUIA BATTLE; or, Pelagianism in Britain.

No. 15.—THE BRIDE OF RAMCUTTAH: A Tale of the Jesuit Missions to the East Indies in the Sixteenth Century.

No. 16.—ALICE OF FOBBING; or, The Times of Jack Straw and Wat Tyler.

No. 17.—THE NORTHERN LIGHT: a Tale of Iceland and Greenland in the Eleventh Century.

No. 18.—AUBREY DE L'ORNE; or, The Times of St. Anselm.

No. 19.—LUCIA'S MARRIAGE; or, The Lions of Wady-Araba.

No. 20.—WOLFINGHAM; or, The Convict-Settler of Jervis Bay: a Tale of the Church in Australia.

No. 21.—THE FORSAKEN; or, The Times of St. Dunstan.

No. 22.—THE DOVE OF TABENNA; and THE RESCUE, a Tale of the Moorish Conquest of Spain.

THE AUTHOR OF "THE CHRISTIAN YEAR."

THE CHRISTIAN YEAR. Thoughts in verse for the Sundays and Holydays throughout the Year. *Imperial Octavo*, with Illuminated Titles,—Cloth, 1l. 5s.; morocco, 1l. 11s. 6d.; best morocco, 2l. 2s. *Octavo Edition*,—Large type, cloth, 10s. 6d.; morocco by Hayday, 21s.; antique calf, 18s. *Foolscap Octavo Edition*,—Cloth, 7s. 6d.; morocco, 10s. 6d.; morocco by Hayday, 15s.; antique calf, 12s. *32mo. Edition*,—Cloth, 3s. 6d.; morocco, plain, 5s.; morocco by Hayday, 7s. *Cheap Edition*,—Cloth, 1s. 6d.; bound, 2s.

LYRA INNOCENTIUM. Thoughts in Verse for Christian Children. *Foolscap Octavo Edition*,—Cloth, 7s. 6d.; morocco, plain, 10s. 6d.; morocco by Hayday, 15s.; antique calf, 12s. *18mo. Edition*,—Cloth, 6s.; morocco, 8s. 6d. *32mo. Edition*,—Cloth, 3s. 6d.; morocco, plain, 5s.; morocco by Hayday, 7s. *Cheap Edition*,—Cloth, 1s. 6d.; bound, 2s.

THE AUTHOR OF "THE CATHEDRAL."

THE CATHEDRAL. Foolscap 8vo., cloth, 7s. 6d.; 32mo., with Engravings, 4s. 6d.

THOUGHTS IN PAST YEARS. The Sixth Edition, with several new Poems, 32mo., cloth, 4s. 6d.

THE BAPTISTERY; or, The Way of Eternal Life. 32mo., cloth, 3s. 6d.

The above Three Volumes uniform, 32mo., neatly bound in morocco, 18s.

THE CHRISTIAN SCHOLAR. Foolscap 8vo., 10s. 6d.; 32mo., cloth, 4s. 6d.

THE SEVEN DAYS; or, The Old and New Creation. Second Edition, foolscap 8vo., 7s. 6d.

MORNING THOUGHTS. By a CLERGYMAN. Suggested by the Second Lessons for the Daily Morning Service throughout the year. 2 vols. foolscap 8vo., cloth, 5s. each.

THE CHILD'S CHRISTIAN YEAR. Hymns for every Sunday and Holyday throughout the year. Cheap Edition, 18mo., cloth, 1s.

COXE'S CHRISTIAN BALLADS. Foolscap 8vo., cloth, 3s. Also selected Poems in a packet, sewed, 1s.

FLORUM SACRA. By the Rev. G. HUNT SMYTTAN. Second Edition, 16mo., 1s.

CATECHETICAL WORKS, Designed to aid the Clergy in Public Catechising. Uniform in size and type with the "Parochial Tracts."

Already published in this Series.

I. CATECHETICAL LESSONS on the Creed. 6d.
II. CATECHETICAL LESSONS on the Lord's Prayer. 6d.
III. CATECHETICAL LESSONS on the Ten Commandments. 6d.
IV. CATECHETICAL LESSONS on the Sacraments. 6d.
V. CATECHETICAL LESSONS on the Parables of the New Testament. Part I. Parables I.—XXI. 1s.
VI. PART II. PARABLES XXII.—XXXVII. 1s.
VII. CATECHETICAL NOTES on the Thirty-Nine Articles. 1s. 6d.
VIII. CATECHETICAL LESSONS on the Order for Morning and Evening Prayer, and the Litany. 1s.
IX. CATECHETICAL LESSONS on the Miracles of our Lord. Part I. Miracles I—XVII. 1s.
X. PART II. MIRACLES XVIII.—XXXVII. 1s.
XI. CATECHETICAL NOTES on the Saints' Days. 1s.
QUESTIONS ON THE COLLECTS, EPISTLES, AND GOSPELS, throughout the Year; edited by the Rev. T. L. CLAUGHTON, Vicar of Kidderminster. For the use of Teachers in Sunday-Schools. Two Parts, 18mo., cloth, each 2s. 6d.

COTTAGE PICTURES. Cottage Pictures from the Old Testament. Twenty-eight large Illustrations, coloured by hand. The set, folio, 7s. 6d.

COTTAGE PICTURES from the New Testament, (uniform with above). The set of 28, 7s. 6d.

SCRIPTURE PRINTS FOR PAROCHIAL USE. Printed in Sepia, with Ornamental Borders. Price One Penny each; or the set in an ornamental envelope, One Shilling.

1. The Nativity.
2. St. John Preaching.
3. The Baptism of Christ.
4. Jacob's Dream.
5. The Transfiguration.
6. The Good Shepherd.
7. The Tribute-Money.
8. The Preparation for the Cross.
9. The Crucifixion.
10. Leading to Crucifixion.
11. Healing the Sick.
12. The Return of the Prodigal.

Ninety thousand have already been sold of these prints. They are also kept mounted and varnished, 3d. each.

PARKER'S CHURCH CALENDAR AND GENERAL ALMANACK, published Annually, contains, besides the usual information of an Almanack, much that is contained in no other, particularly with regard to the state and progress of the Church in America and the Colonies. 12mo. 6d.

THE CHURCH, with information regarding the several Dioceses of England, Scotland, and Ireland, the Colonies and America.

THE UNIVERSITIES, with other Educational Institutions, Theological Colleges, Schools, &c.

THE STATE. The Members of the Royal Family, Houses of Parliament, &c., &c.

MISCELLANEOUS. The Kings and Queens of England, Statistics of the Population, Post Office, &c., &c.

ANNALS OF ENGLAND. An Epitome of English History. From Cotemporary Writers, the Rolls of Parliament, and other Public Records. 3 vols. fcap. 8vo., with Illustrations, cloth, 15s. *Recommended by the Examiners in the School of Modern History at Oxford.*

Vol. I. From the Roman Era to the deposition of Richard II. Cloth, 5s.
Vol. II. From the Accession of the House of Lancaster to Charles I. Cloth, 5s.
Vol. III. From the Commonwealth to the Death of Queen Anne. Cloth, 5s.

Each Volume is sold separately.

" The book strikes us as being most useful as a Handbook for teachers. It is just the sort of help for a tutor to have lying by him as a guide to his lecture. The main facts he will find marshalled in strict chronological order, and he will be assisted by references to the statute-book and the old chronicles. The 'ANNALS' will, in short, supply the dry bones of an historical lecture, which each teacher must clothe for himself with life and spirit. But the work will also be highly useful to students, especially for the purpose of refreshing the memory and getting details into order, after the perusal of more regular narratives. We trust to see it extensively employed in the Universities. At Oxford it may be especially serviceable. A reliable guide to the original authorities, and one which gives its proper prominence to the early history, may, if it falls into the hands of either students or teachers, do something to dispel the illusion that English history can be profitably studied by beginning at the momentary overthrow of English nationality, and that, after all the labours of Turner, Lingard, Palgrave, Kemble, Lappenberg, and Pauli, David Hume still remains the one correct, orthodox, and unapproachable text-book for its study."—*Saturday Review.*

THE ETHICS OF ARISTOTLE. With Notes by the Rev. W. E. JELF, B.D., Author of "A Greek Grammar," &c. 8vo., cloth, 12s.

The Text separately, 5s. The Notes separately, 7s. 6d.

SOPHOCLIS TRAGŒDIÆ, with Notes, adapted to the use of Schools and Universities. By THOMAS MITCHELL, M.A. 2 vols. 8vo., £1 8s.

The Plays may also be had separately, at 5s. each.

ŒDIPUS TYRANNUS.   AJAX.
ŒDIPUS COLONEUS.   TRACHINIÆ.
ELECTRA.   ANTIGONE.
           PHILOCTETES.

THUCYDIDES, with Notes, chiefly Historical and Geographical. By the late T. ARNOLD, D.D. With Indices by the Rev. R. P. G. TIDDEMAN. 8vo. *Complete, 3 volumes, 8vo., cloth lettered, £1 16s.*

MADVIG'S LATIN GRAMMAR. A Latin Grammar for the Use of Schools. By Professor MADVIG, with additions by the Author. Translated by the Rev. G. F. WOODS, M.A. Uniform with JELF's "Greek Grammar." *Fourth Edition, with an Index of Authors,* 8vo., cloth, 12s.

Competent authorities pronounce this work to be the very best Latin Grammar yet published in England. This new Edition contains an Index to the Authors quoted.

JELF'S GREEK GRAMMAR.—A Grammar of the Greek Language, chiefly from the text of Raphael Kühner. By WM. EDW. JELF, M.A., Student of Ch. Ch. 2 vols. 8vo. *Second Edition.* 1l. 10s.

This Grammar is now in general use at Oxford, Cambridge, Dublin, and Durham; at Eton, King's College, London, and other public schools.

A MANUAL OF GREEK AND LATIN PROSE COMPOSITION, specially designed to illustrate the differences of Idiom between those Languages and the English. By E. R. HUMPHREYS, LL.D., late Head Master of Cheltenham Grammar-school. Crown 8vo., cloth, 3s. 6d.

LAWS OF THE GREEK ACCENTS. By JOHN GRIFFITHS, M.A. 16mo. *Fifth Edition. Price Sixpence.*

THE OXFORD POCKET CLASSICS. 13

A NEW SERIES of the Greek and Latin Classics for the use of Schools.

"Mr. Parker is supplying a want long felt, in issuing a series of good classical texts, well edited, and in a cheap form. The expensiveness of our school-books is a crying evil, which cannot be too soon abated. It is absurd extravagance to put costly books into the hands of schoolboys, to be thumbed and torn to pieces, when cheaper ones would answer every useful purpose just as well. In this respect our neighbours on the Continent are far more rational than we are. We look with satisfaction upon Mr. Parker's efforts to bring about an amendment. Though we think it would have been better to announce the editor's name, we willingly bear testimony to the ability with which he has executed his task, and have much pleasure in recommending the Texts as suitable for school purposes."—*Athenæum*.

GREEK POETS.

	Paper.		Bound.	
	s.	d.	s.	d.
Æschylus	2	6	3	0
Aristophanes. 2 vols.	5	0	6	0
Euripides. 3 vols.	5	0	6	6
Or the 6 *Plays only*	3	0	3	6
Sophocles	2	6	3	0
Homeri Ilias	3	0	3	6
——— Odyssea	2	6	3	0

GREEK PROSE WRITERS.

Aristotelis Ethica	1	6	2	0
Demosthenes de Corona, et Æschines in Ctesiphontem	1	6	2	0
Herodotus. 2 vols.	5	0	6	0
Thucydides. 2 vols.	4	0	5	0
Xenophontis Memorabilia	1	0	1	4
——— Anabasis	1	6	2	0

LATIN POETS.

Horatius	1	6	2	0
Juvenalis et Persius	1	0	1	6
Lucanus	2	0	2	6
Lucretius	1	6	2	0
Phædrus	1	0	1	4
Virgilius	2	0	2	6

LATIN PROSE WRITERS.

Cæsar	2	0	2	6
Cicero De Officiis, de Senectute, et de Amicitia	1	6	2	0
Ciceronis Tusculanarum Disputationum Libri V.	1	6	2	0
Cornelius Nepos	1	0	1	4
Livius. 4 vols.	5	0	6	0
Sallustius	1	6	2	0
Tacitus. 2 vols.	4	0	5	0

NEW SERIES OF ENGLISH NOTES.

THE PLAYS OF SOPHOCLES, with English Notes by Members of the University of Oxford. Complete in 2 vols., cloth, 6s., or separately—

	s. d.		s. d.
Ajax (Text with Notes)	1 0	Antigone	1 0
Electra	1 0	Philoctetes	1 0
Œdipus Rex	1 0	Trachiniæ	1 0
Œdipus Coloneus	1 0		

THE PLAYS OF ÆSCHYLUS, with English Notes by Members of the University of Oxford. Complete in 2 vols., cloth, 7s. 6d.

Prometheus Vinctus (Text with Notes)	1 0	Agamemnon	1 0
		Choephoræ	1 0
Septem Contra Thebas	1 0	Eumenides	1 0
Persæ	1 0	Supplices	1 0

THE PLAYS OF EURIPIDES, with English Notes by Members of the University of Oxford. Complete in 2 vols., cloth, 6s. 6d.

Hecuba (Text with Notes)	1 0	Hippolytus	1 0
Medea	1 0	Phœnissæ	1 0
Orestes	1 0	Alcestis	1 0

"The notes contain sufficient information, without affording the pupil so much assistance as to supersede all exertion on his part."— *Athenæum,* Jan. 27, 1855.
"Be all this as it may, it is a real benefit to public schoolboys to be able to purchase any Greek Play they want for One Shilling. When we were introduced to Greek Plays, about forty years ago, we had put into our hands a portly 8vo. volume, containing Porson's four Plays, without one word of English in the shape of notes; and we have no doubt the book cost nearer twenty than ten shillings, and after all was nothing near so useful as these neat little copies at One Shilling each." — *Educational Times.*

The Text of SOPHOCLES separately. One vol., cloth, 3s.—The Notes, ditto, 3s.
The Text of ÆSCHYLUS separately. One vol., cloth, 3s.—The Notes, ditto, 3s. 6d.
The Text of EURIPIDES separately. One vol., cloth, 3s. 6d.—The Notes, ditto, 3s.

Pocket Editions of the following have also been published with Short Notes.

DEMOSTHENES.
DE CORONA . . . . 2 0 | ÆSCHINES IN CTESIPHONTEM . 2 0

VIRGIL.
The BUCOLICS . . . . 1 0 | The GEORGICS . . . 2 0
The First Three Books of the ÆNEID, 1s.

HORACE.
ODES and EPODES . . . 2 0 | SATIRES 1 0
EPISTLES and ARS POETICA, 1s.

SALLUST.
JUGURTHA . . . . 1 6 | CATILINE 1 0

CORNELIUS NEPOS—LIVES (with Short Notes) . . . 1 6
PHÆDRUS—FABLES (with Short Notes) 1 0
HOMER—FIRST SIX BOOKS OF ILIAD (with Short Notes) . 2 0
LIVY.—BOOKS XXI.—XXIV. 4 6

In the Press.
Short Notes to CICERO, and CÆSAR.

THE LITERARY CHURCHMAN. A Journal devoted to the interest and advancement of Religious Literature.

THE LITERARY CHURCHMAN was established in order to extend to RELIGIOUS LITERATURE the advantages which General Literature already possessed in the *Athenæum, Literary Gazette, Critic,* and other similar journals. Previously, Religious Literature had been dependent for publicity on a few scattered notices in Newspapers or Religious Magazines; while the weekly issue of some twenty or thirty works, bearing more or less on Religious subjects, proved an importance sufficient to demand a journal distinctly set apart for the interests of that class of publications.

It is intended by this Journal to place the Subscriber entirely *au courant* with what is being published, by reviewing and noticing all religious works, of whatever class or kind, as they are issued from the press. To many, whose duties render it almost necessary for them to be acquainted with the Books or Tracts which are constantly issued, calculated to assist them in their labours, and who, residing perhaps at a distance from any town, or without access to any good Bookseller's shop, see at most but one Church Periodical, this Journal supplies a great desideratum.

The usual contents of the Journal are as follows:—

A SUMMARY OF CHURCH EVENTS, and short Articles on the Religious Topics of the day.

REVIEWS AND NOTICES of all the new Religious Publications,—as far as possible explaining their nature and object, with criticism, &c., when needed.

FOREIGN BOOKS, with lists of all new Religious Works as published in France, Germany, and America.

A SUMMARY of the GENERAL LITERATURE of the fortnight, with Notices of the important Books suitable for Reading Clubs, &c., arranged according to subjects, with size, price, &c.

Index, with prices of Books noticed,--Literary Notes and Queries, &c., &c.

SUBSCRIPTIONS.

For the Year	8s. 0d.
Ditto Free by post	10s. 0d.
For Six Months	4s. 0d.
Ditto Free by post	5s. 0d.

Orders will be received by most Booksellers and Newsmen throughout the Country, or at the Office, 377, Strand.

THE PENNY POST. A Church of England Illustrated Magazine, issued Monthly. Price One Penny.

That this Magazine is wanted, a circulation of 22,000 copies of each number testifies. It is *the only Penny Magazine* upholding sound Church principles. That it does good, and is appreciated, testimony whence it would be least expected, abundantly proves. But at the same time it must be borne in mind, that this is a small circulation for a Penny religious periodical. Those who differ depend much upon their periodicals for inculcating doctrine hostile to the Church, and circulate thousands, where the Church of England, unfortunately, circulates only hundreds.

MONTHLY.—ONE PENNY.

Subscribers' names received by all Booksellers and Newsmen.

Vols. I., II., III., and IV. of the Old Series, crown 8vo., cloth, may be obtained price 1s. 6d. each.

Vols. I., II., III., IV., V., and VI. of the New Series of the "Penny Post," 8vo., in handsome wrapper, 1s.; or in cloth, 1s. 8d. each.

WITH the year of our Lord 1859, *Sylvanus Urban* closed his 207th volume, and the 128th year of his literary existence. This is a length of days that, so far as he knows, has never before been attained by a Journalist; but he ventures to affirm, with thankfulness as well as some degree of self-complacency, that he is still in a green old age, and that to his thinking the time is yet very distant when, to borrow the words of one of his earliest and most valued friends, it may be said of him— "Superfluous lags the veteran on the stage."

The times, it is readily allowed, have greatly changed since *Sylvanus Urban* first solicited public attention, but it may be fairly doubted whether the tastes and habits of thought of the educated classes, to whom he addresses himself, have changed in a like degree. Hence he does not fear that History and Antiquities, in their widest sense, can ever become unpalatable to them, but, on the contrary, he is glad to mark an increased avidity in pursuing such studies. This is a state of things that he thinks he may claim a considerable share in bringing about, and the steady progress of which he is desirous of forwarding by all available means. He alludes to the growing appreciation of the Past, as the key to the understanding of the Present, and (in a sense) of the Future, as testified by the formation of Archæological and Literary Societies, which have already achieved much good, and may do still more; and as a means to that end, he devotes a portion of his pages every month, under the title of "ANTIQUARIAN AND LITERARY INTELLIGENCER," to a record of their progress.

Sylvanus Urban therefore ventures to suggest to the Councils of such Societies, that if brief reports of their proceedings and publications are systematically supplied to the GENTLEMAN'S MAGAZINE, where they will be always highly acceptable, an interchange of knowledge and good offices may thus be established between learned bodies in the most distant parts of the Empire—an interchange that does not now exist, but the want of which few will be found to deny.

It has ever been the desire of *Sylvanus Urban* to see his CORRESPONDENCE a leading feature in his pages, and he has had the gratification of reckoning many of the most erudite men of the time as his fellow-workers, who have, through him, conveyed an invaluable amount of knowledge to the world. He invites those of the present day to imitate them. Another important feature has been, and will be, the OBITUARY, to the completeness of which he requests friends or relatives to contribute by communicating fitting notices of eminent persons daily removed by the hand of death from among us. He believes that he shall not be disappointed in the extent of this friendly co-operation, but that, on the contrary, the increasing number of his contributors will render the motto that he has so long borne more than ever applicable:—"*E pluribus Unum.*"

All Communications to be addressed to MR. URBAN, 377, STRAND, W.C.

www.ingramcontent.com/pod-product-compliance
Lightning Source LLC
Chambersburg PA
CBHW021348230426
43666CB00006B/450